WIRED UP WRONG

For my mum

First edition published in 2017 by Rachael Smith

This edition published in the UK and the USA in 2022
by Icon Books Ltd,
Omnibus Business Centre,
39–41 North Road, London N7 9DP
email: info@iconbooks.com • www.iconbooks.com

Sold in the UK, Europe and Asia
by Faber & Faber Ltd,
Bloomsbury House,
74–77 Great Russell Street,
London WC1B 3DA or their agents

Distributed in the UK, Europe and Asia
by Grantham Book Services,
Trent Road, Grantham NG31 7XQ

Distributed in the USA
by Publishers Group West,
1700 Fourth Street, Berkeley, CA 94710

Distributed in Australia and New Zealand
by Allen & Unwin Pty Ltd,
PO Box 8500, 83 Alexander Street,
Crows Nest, NSW 2065

Distributed in South Africa
by Jonathan Ball,
Office B4, The District,
41 Sir Lowry Road, Woodstock 7925

Distributed in India
by Penguin Books India,
7th Floor, Infinity Tower – C, DLF Cyber City,
Gurgaon 122002, Haryana

Distributed in Canada
by Publishers Group Canada,
76 Stafford Street, Unit 300
Toronto, Ontario M6J 2S1

ISBN: 978-178578-837-6

Typeset in Gotham by Marie Doherty

MIX
Paper from
responsible sources
FSC® C018072

Printed and bound in Italy, by Elcograf S.p.A.

WIRED UP WRONG

RACHAEL SMITH

ICON

MAIN CAST...

RACHAEL

OUR... HERO? 31 YEARS OLD.
CARTOONIST. ANXIOUS.
CONFUSED BY MOST THINGS,
ESPECIALLY HER OWN
BRAIN.

ADAM

RACHAEL'S BOYFRIEND. 34
YEARS OLD. ALSO A CARTOONIST.
IS AMAZING. AND LOVING.
AND PATIENT

RUFUS

RACHAEL'S CAT. 6 YEARS OLD. WEARS A RED BANDANA. IS QUITE SQUEAKY.

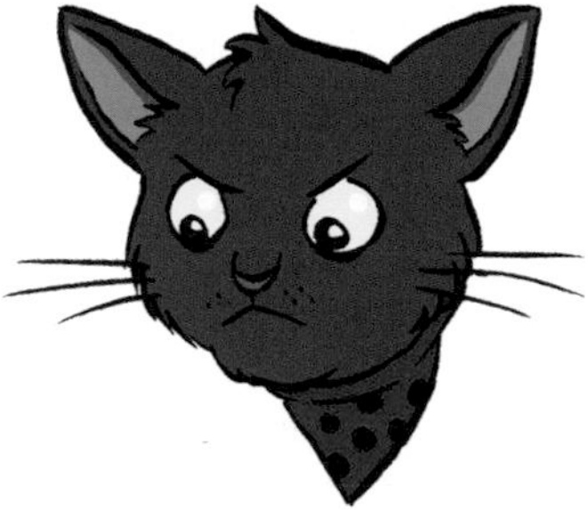

BARKY

A BIG BLACK DOG. RACHAEL'S VISUALISATION OF HER MENTAL HEALTH PROBLEMS.

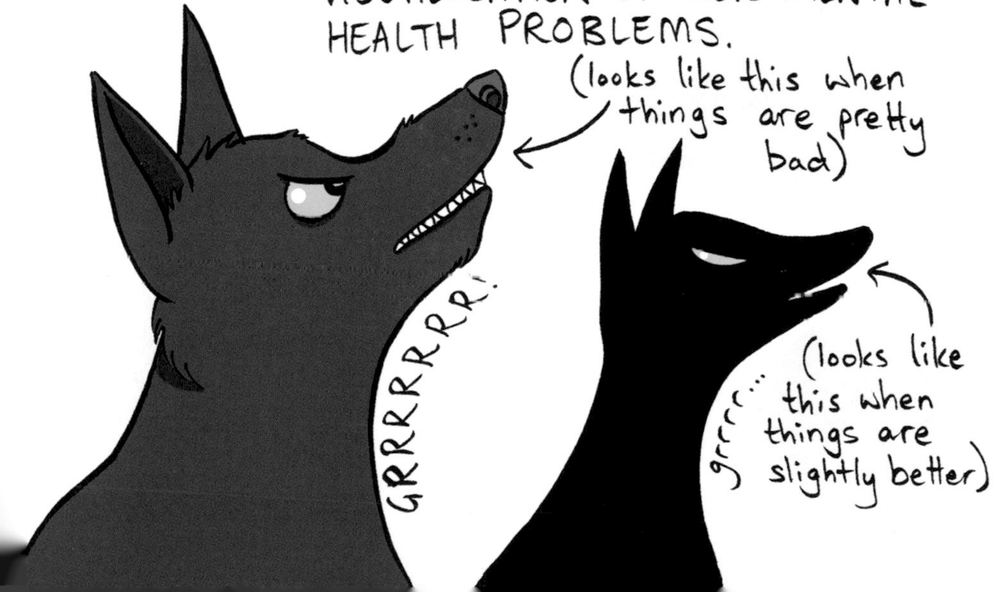
(looks like this when things are pretty bad)
GRRRRRRRRR!
grrrr...
(looks like this when things are slightly better)

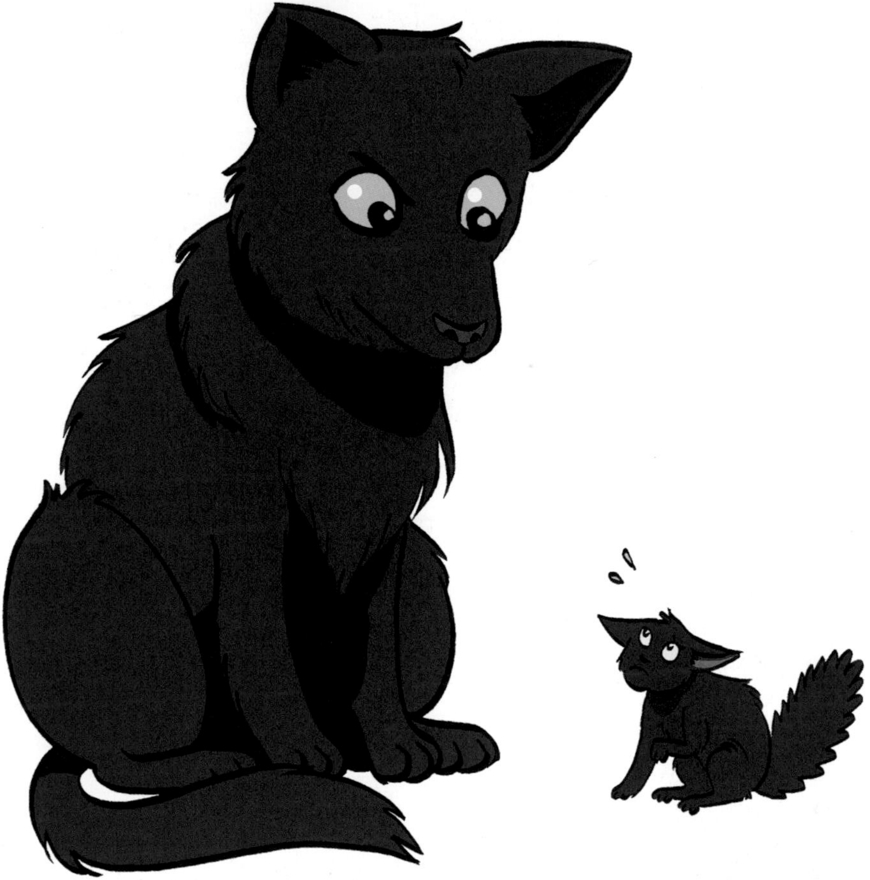

A NOTE BEFORE WE GET STARTED...

THIS BOOK IS A PERSONAL RECORD OF LIVING WITH DEPRESSION, AND WHILE SOME MAY FIND IT HELPFUL, IT IS NOT A "SELF HELP" BOOK. I AM NOT A DOCTOR, AND PEOPLE ARE ALL DIFFERENT. IF YOU'RE THINKING OF BUYING THIS BOOK *INSTEAD* OF SEEKING MEDICAL CARE, THEN PLEASE PUT THIS BOOK DOWN AND CALL YOUR DOCTOR. I MEAN, I'D LOVE FOR YOU TO DO *BOTH*, BUT IF YOU'RE CHOOSING BETWEEN THE TWO, GO SEE YOUR DOCTOR. EVERYTHING IS GOING TO BE OK. I BELIEVE IN YOU. YOU ARE NOT ALONE. OK? OK. ♥

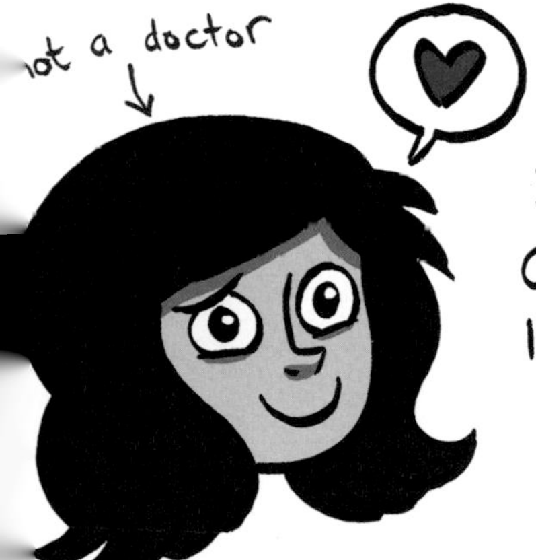
ot a doctor

LOVE Rachael xxx

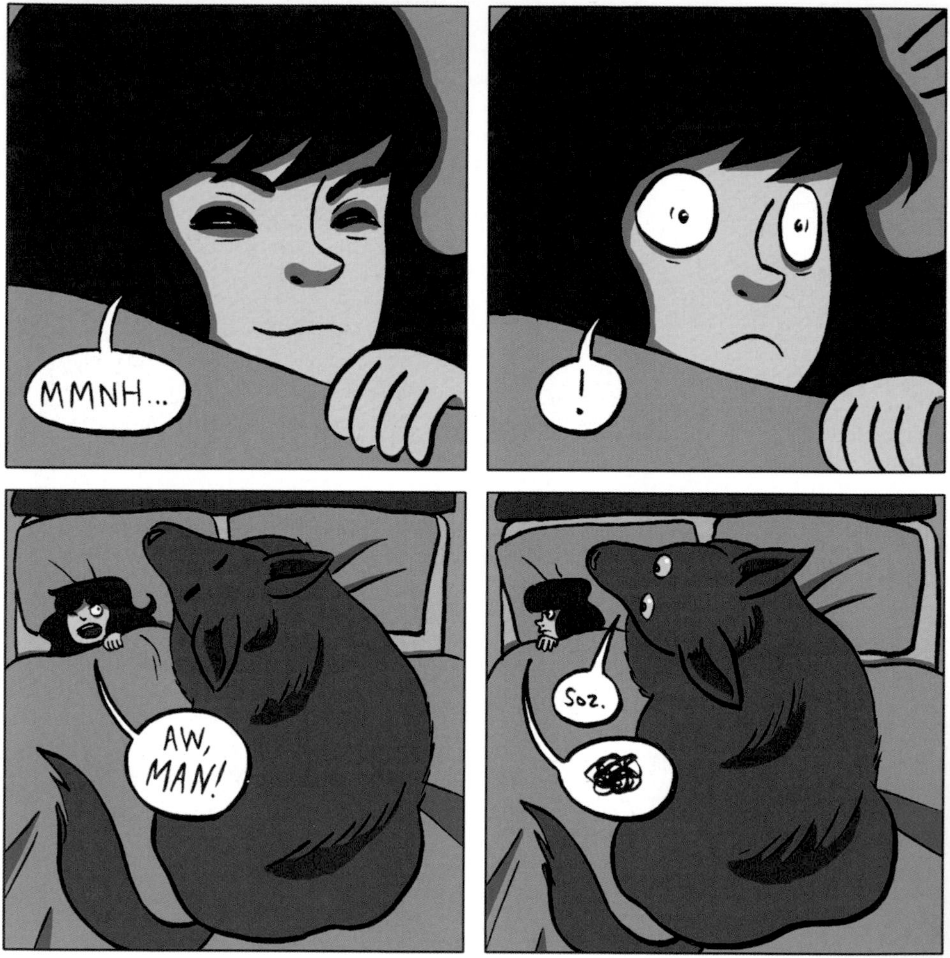
MMNH...
!
AW, MAN!
Soz.

Barky makes his entrance.

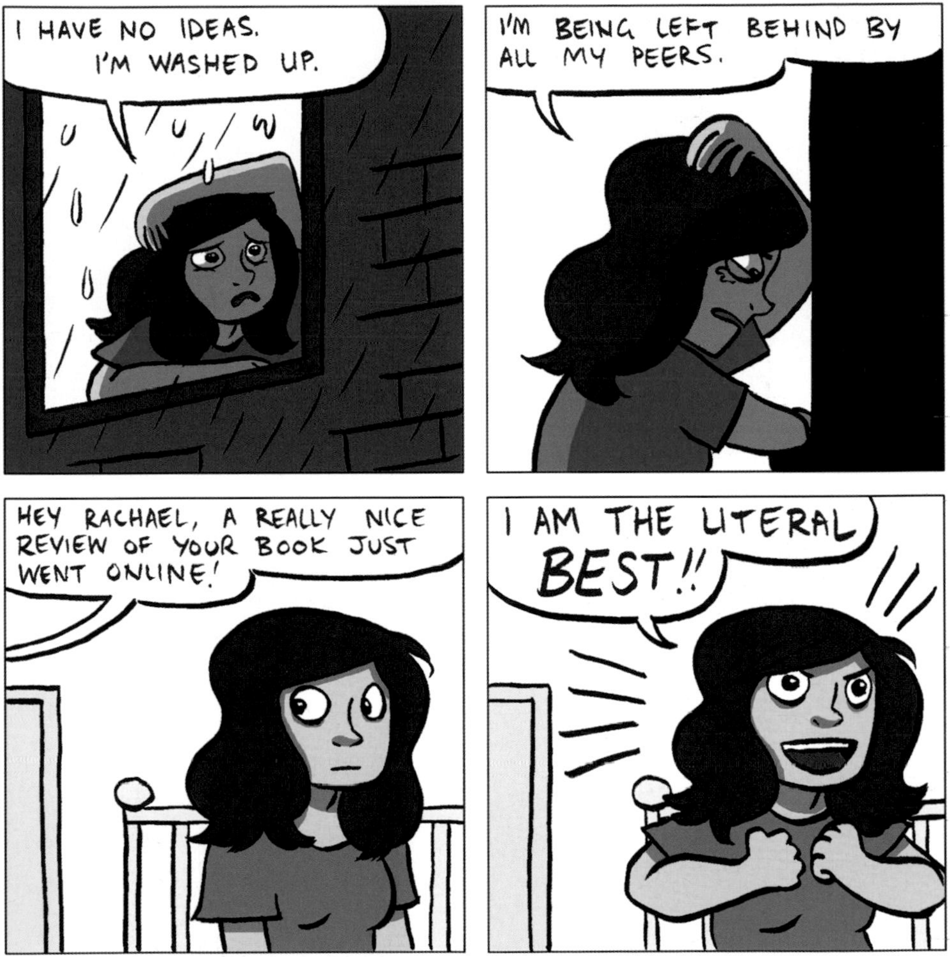
I HAVE NO IDEAS. I'M WASHED UP.
I'M BEING LEFT BEHIND BY ALL MY PEERS.
HEY RACHAEL, A REALLY NICE REVIEW OF YOUR BOOK JUST WENT ONLINE!
I AM THE LITERAL BEST!!

Hi I'm Rachael and I'm a self-confidence yoyo.

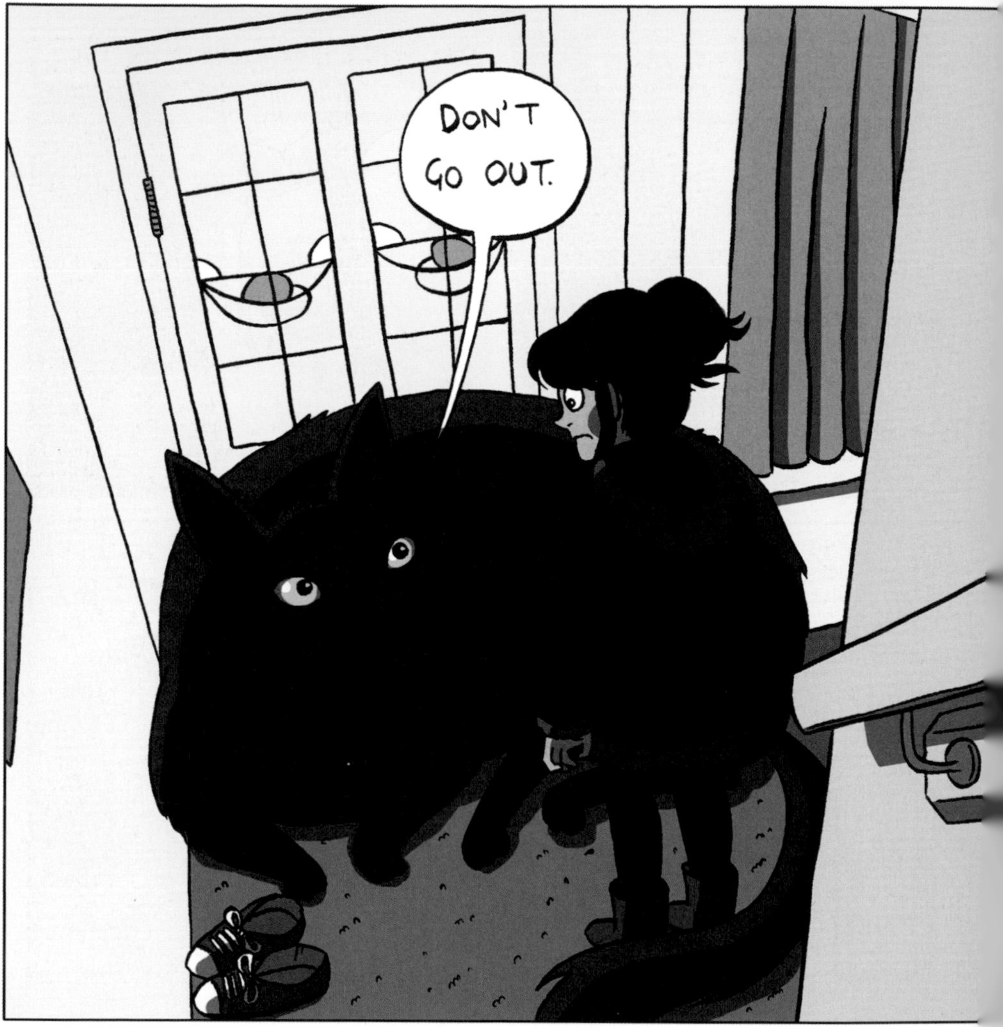
DON'T GO OUT.

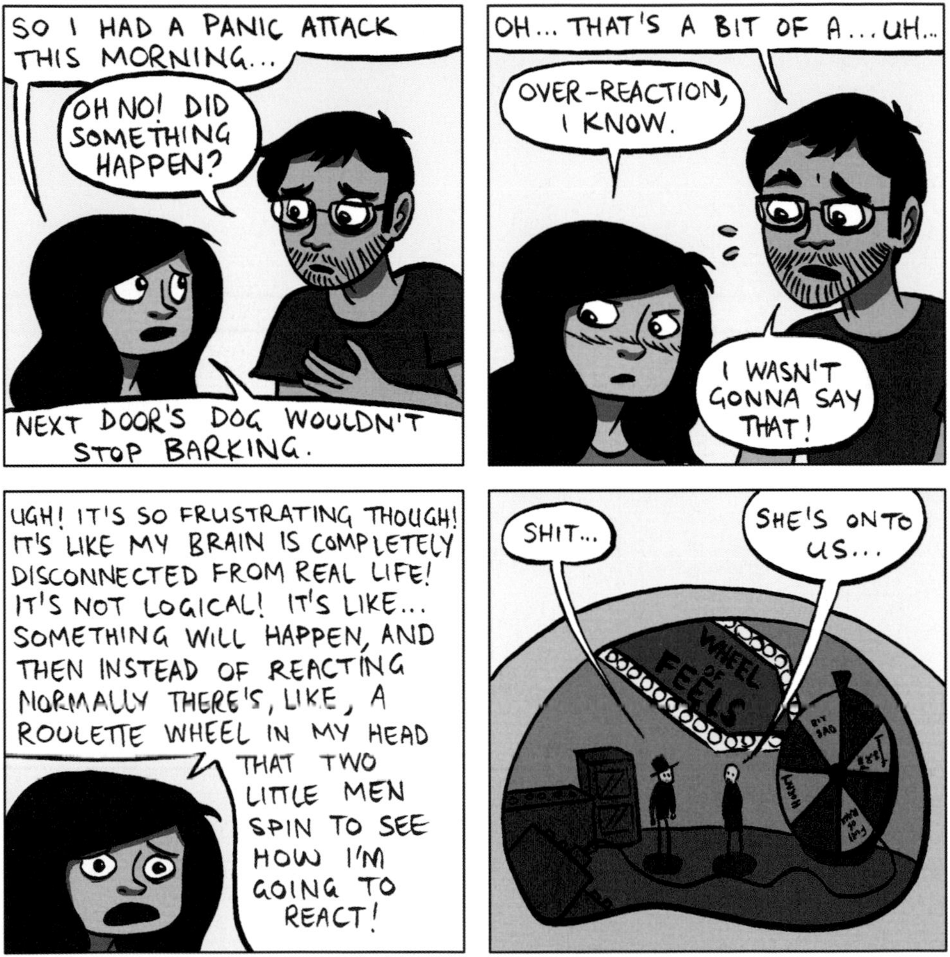
SO I HAD A PANIC ATTACK THIS MORNING...
OH NO! DID SOMETHING HAPPEN?
NEXT DOOR'S DOG WOULDN'T STOP BARKING.
OH... THAT'S A BIT OF A... UH...
OVER-REACTION, I KNOW.
I WASN'T GONNA SAY THAT!
UGH! IT'S SO FRUSTRATING THOUGH! IT'S LIKE MY BRAIN IS COMPLETELY DISCONNECTED FROM REAL LIFE! IT'S NOT LOGICAL! IT'S LIKE... SOMETHING WILL HAPPEN, AND THEN INSTEAD OF REACTING NORMALLY THERE'S, LIKE, A ROULETTE WHEEL IN MY HEAD
THAT TWO LITTLE MEN SPIN TO SEE HOW I'M GOING TO REACT!
SHIT...
SHE'S ONTO US...
WHEEL OF FEELS

In my defence, next door's dog is a real dick. I can say that 'cause he's probably not gonna read this.

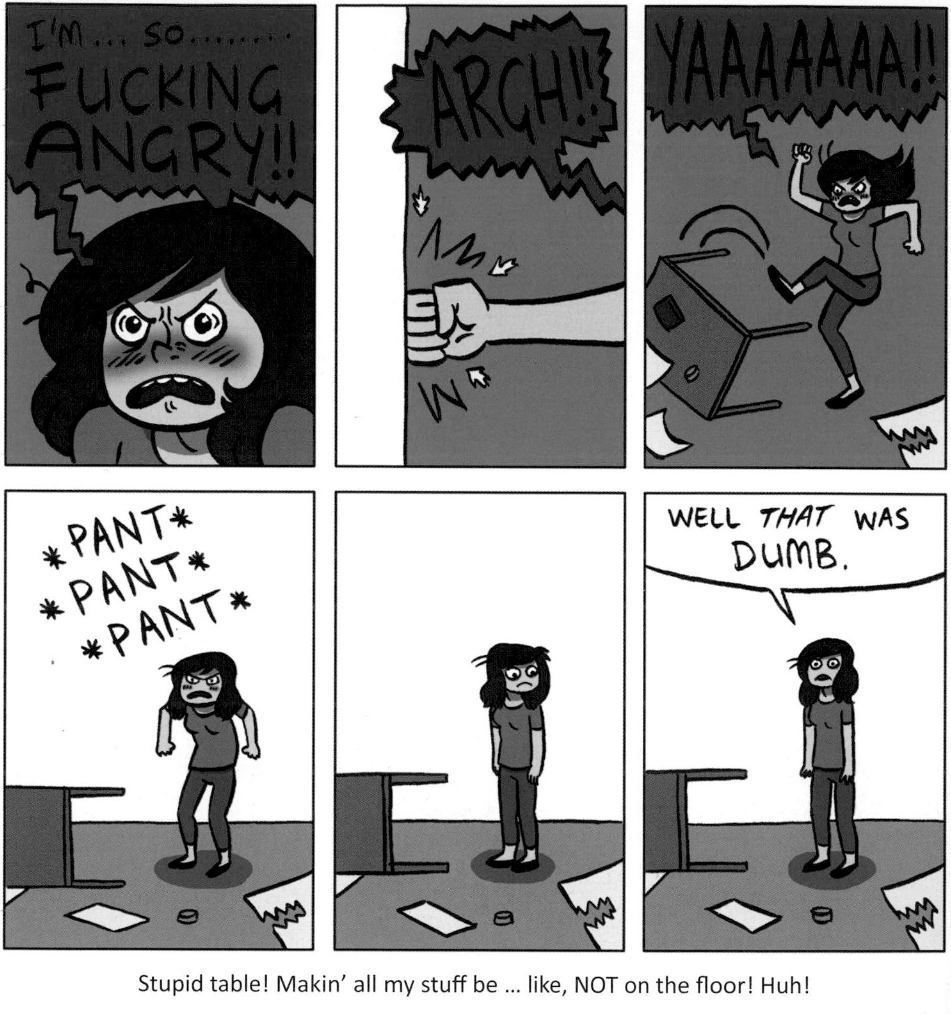
I'M ... SO.........
FUCKING ANGRY!!
ARCH!!
YAAAAAAA!!
PANT
PANT
PANT
WELL THAT WAS DUMB.

Stupid table! Makin' all my stuff be ... like, NOT on the floor! Huh!

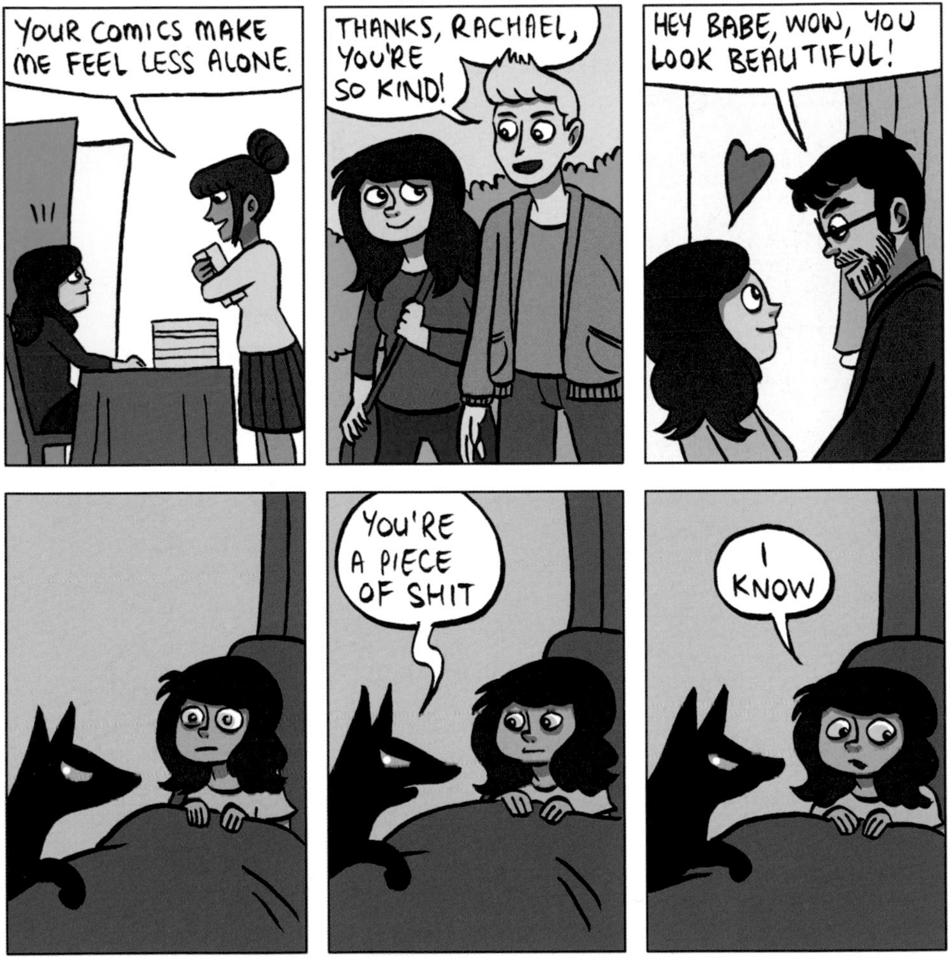
YOUR COMICS MAKE ME FEEL LESS ALONE.
THANKS, RACHAEL, YOU'RE SO KIND!
HEY BABE, WOW, YOU LOOK BEAUTIFUL!
YOU'RE A PIECE OF SHIT
I KNOW

Hashtag humblebrag.

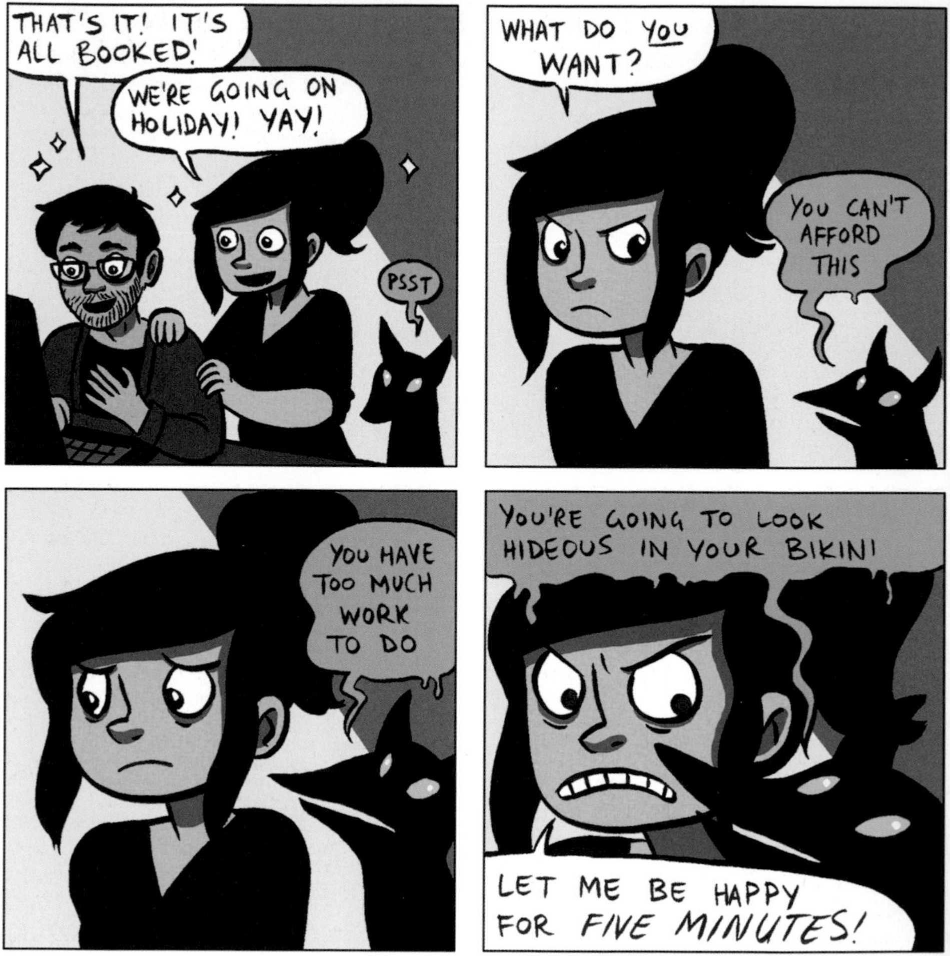
THAT'S IT! IT'S ALL BOOKED!
WE'RE GOING ON HOLIDAY! YAY!
PSST
WHAT DO YOU WANT?
YOU CAN'T AFFORD THIS
YOU HAVE TOO MUCH WORK TO DO
YOU'RE GOING TO LOOK HIDEOUS IN YOUR BIKINI
LET ME BE HAPPY FOR FIVE MINUTES!

Barky was right on the first two counts, but my bikini was badass.

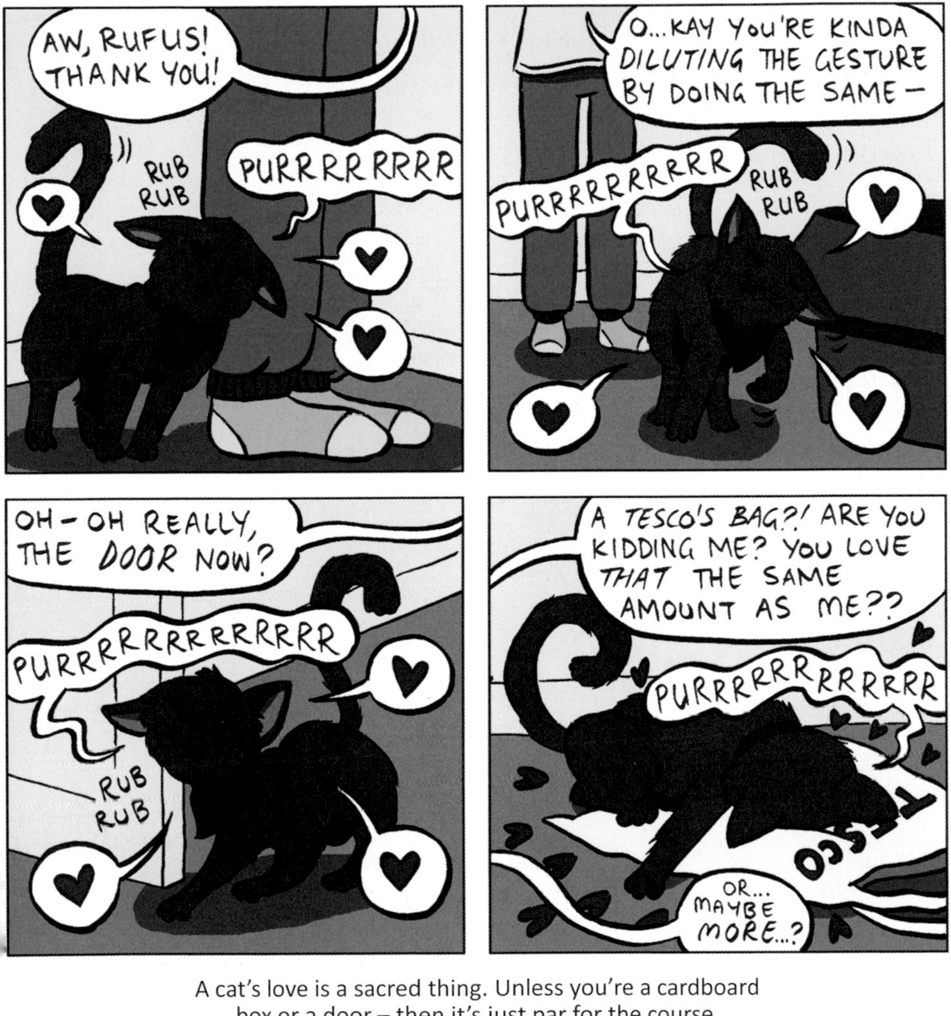
AW, RUFUS! THANK YOU!
RUB RUB
PURRRRRRRR
O...KAY YOU'RE KINDA *DILUTING* THE GESTURE BY DOING THE SAME –
PURRRRRRRRRR
RUB RUB
OH – OH REALLY, THE *DOOR* NOW?
PURRRRRRRRRRRR
RUB RUB
A *TESCO'S BAG?!* ARE YOU KIDDING ME? YOU LOVE *THAT* THE SAME AMOUNT AS ME??
PURRRRRRRRRRRR
TESCO
OR... MAYBE *MORE*...?

A cat's love is a sacred thing. Unless you're a cardboard box or a door – then it's just par for the course.

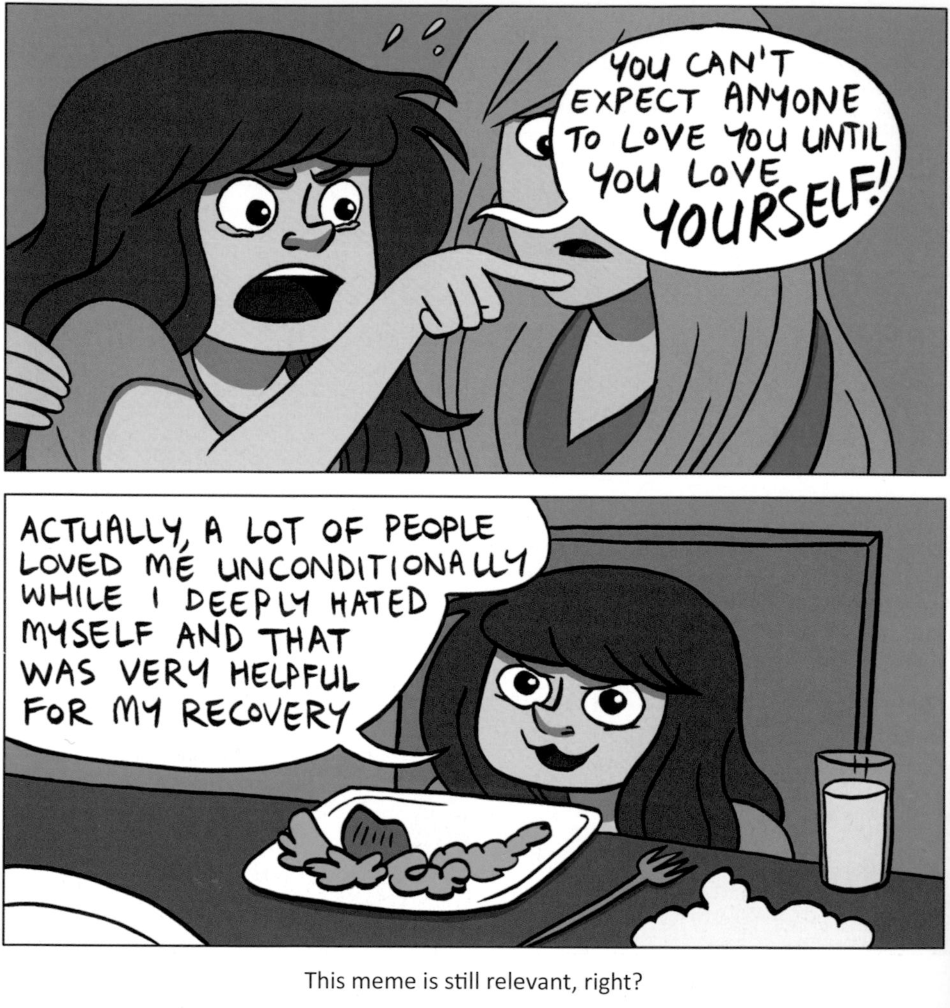
YOU CAN'T EXPECT ANYONE TO LOVE YOU UNTIL YOU LOVE YOURSELF!
ACTUALLY, A LOT OF PEOPLE LOVED ME UNCONDITIONALLY WHILE I DEEPLY HATED MYSELF AND THAT WAS VERY HELPFUL FOR MY RECOVERY

This meme is still relevant, right?

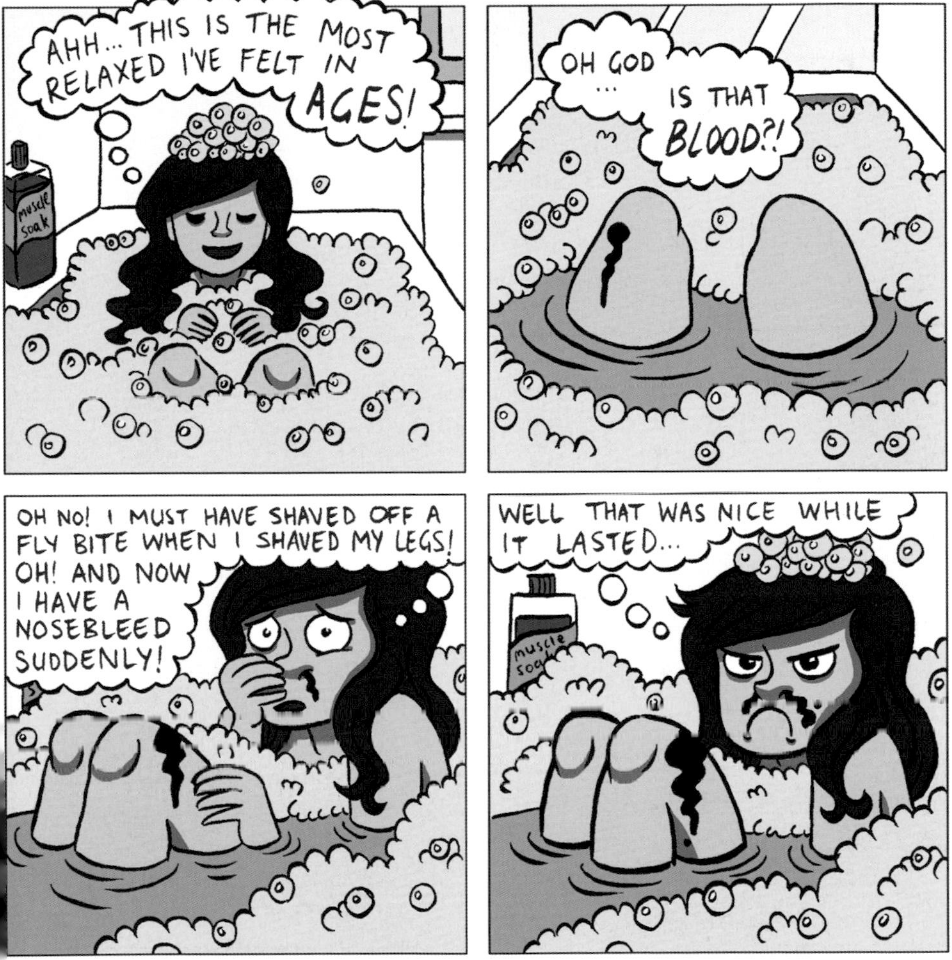
AHH... THIS IS THE MOST RELAXED I'VE FELT IN AGES!
muscle soak
OH GOD ...
IS THAT BLOOD?!
OH NO! I MUST HAVE SHAVED OFF A FLY BITE WHEN I SHAVED MY LEGS! OH! AND NOW I HAVE A NOSEBLEED SUDDENLY!
WELL THAT WAS NICE WHILE IT LASTED...
muscle soak

Who screws up having a bath? I am the worst.

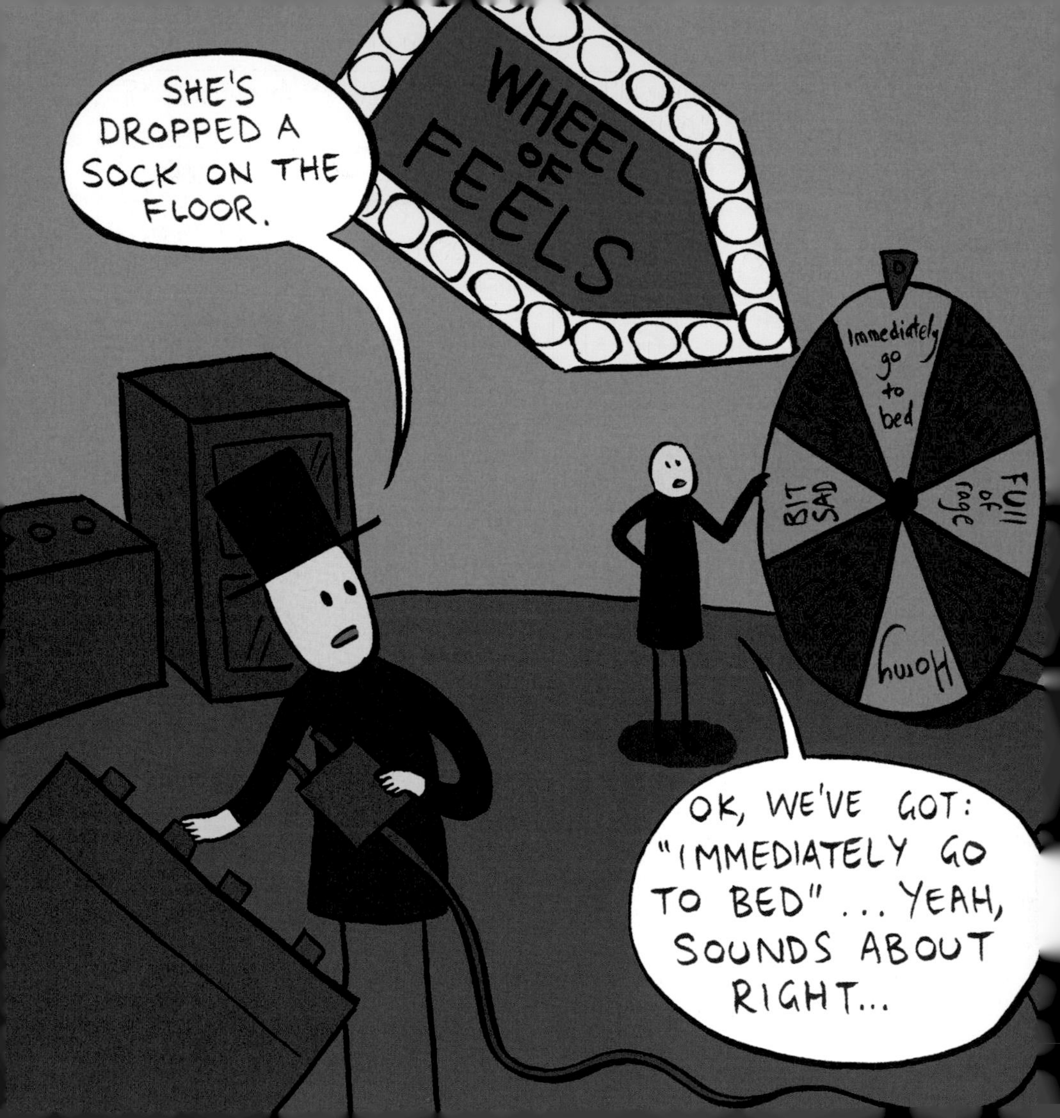
SHE'S DROPPED A SOCK ON THE FLOOR.
WHEEL OF FEELS
Immediately go to bed
FULL of rage
Horny
BIT SAD
OK, WE'VE GOT: "IMMEDIATELY GO TO BED" ... YEAH, SOUNDS ABOUT RIGHT...

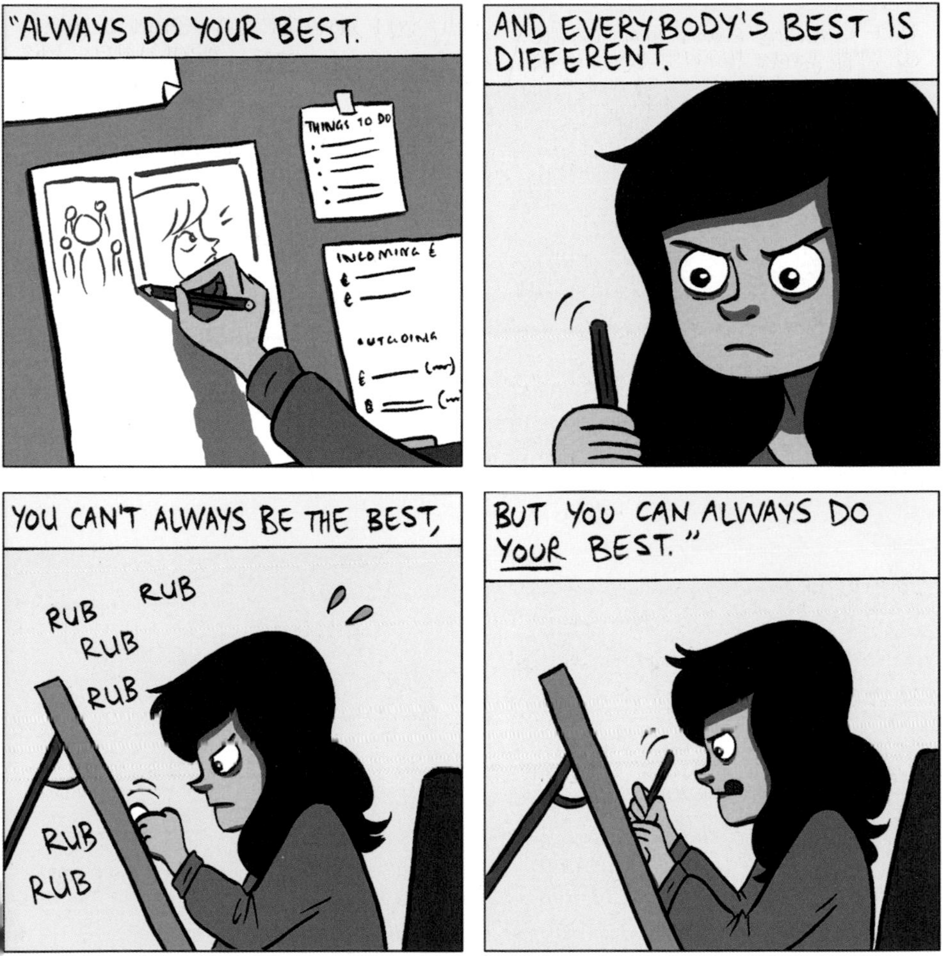
"ALWAYS DO YOUR BEST.
THINGS TO DO
INCOMING £
OUTGOING
AND EVERYBODY'S BEST IS DIFFERENT.
YOU CAN'T ALWAYS BE THE BEST,
RUB RUB RUB RUB RUB RUB
BUT YOU CAN ALWAYS DO YOUR BEST."

– Janet, *The Great British Bake Off*

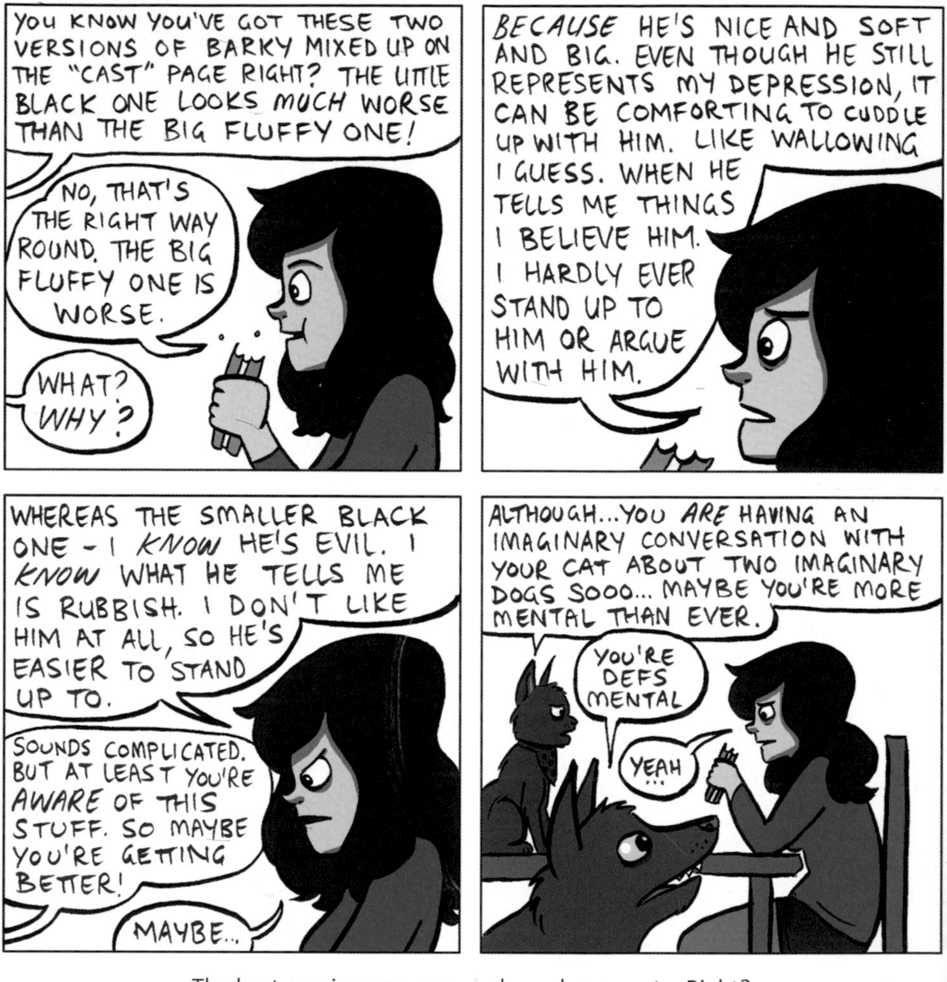
YOU KNOW YOU'VE GOT THESE TWO VERSIONS OF BARKY MIXED UP ON THE "CAST" PAGE RIGHT? THE LITTLE BLACK ONE LOOKS *MUCH* WORSE THAN THE BIG FLUFFY ONE!
NO, THAT'S THE RIGHT WAY ROUND. THE BIG FLUFFY ONE IS WORSE.
WHAT? *WHY?*
BECAUSE HE'S NICE AND SOFT AND BIG. EVEN THOUGH HE STILL REPRESENTS MY DEPRESSION, IT CAN BE COMFORTING TO CUDDLE UP WITH HIM. LIKE WALLOWING I GUESS. WHEN HE TELLS ME THINGS I BELIEVE HIM. I HARDLY EVER STAND UP TO HIM OR ARGUE WITH HIM.
WHEREAS THE SMALLER BLACK ONE - I *KNOW* HE'S EVIL. I *KNOW* WHAT HE TELLS ME IS RUBBISH. I DON'T LIKE HIM AT ALL, SO HE'S EASIER TO STAND UP TO.
SOUNDS COMPLICATED. BUT AT LEAST YOU'RE *AWARE* OF THIS STUFF. SO MAYBE YOU'RE GETTING BETTER!
MAYBE...
ALTHOUGH...YOU *ARE* HAVING AN IMAGINARY CONVERSATION WITH YOUR CAT ABOUT TWO IMAGINARY DOGS SOOO... MAYBE YOU'RE MORE MENTAL THAN EVER.
YOU'RE DEFS MENTAL
YEAH ...

The best comics are very wordy, and very meta. Right?

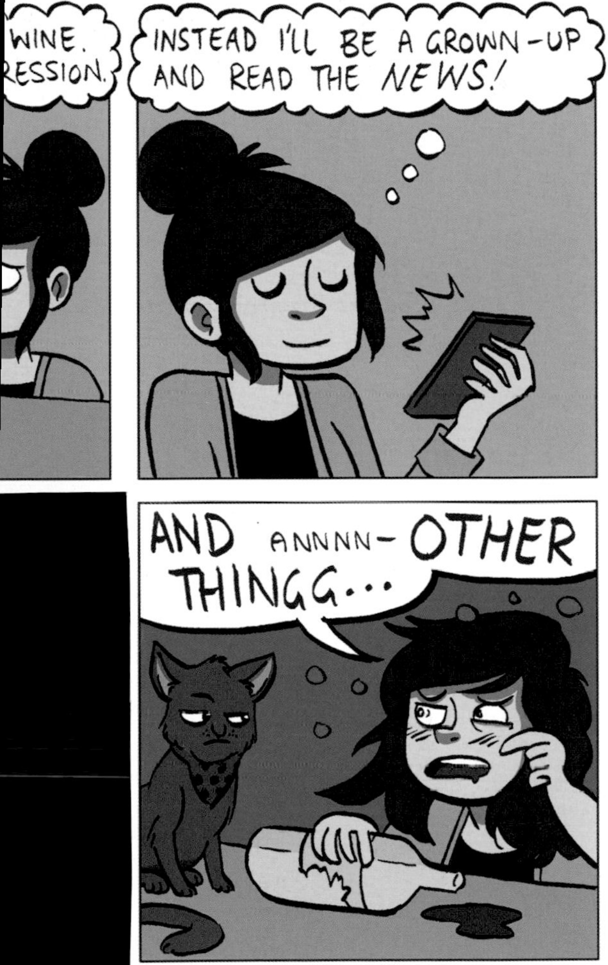
WINE.
INSTEAD I'LL BE A GROWN-UP AND READ THE *NEWS!*
AND ANNNN-OTHER THINGG...

[redacted] me as I am with news.

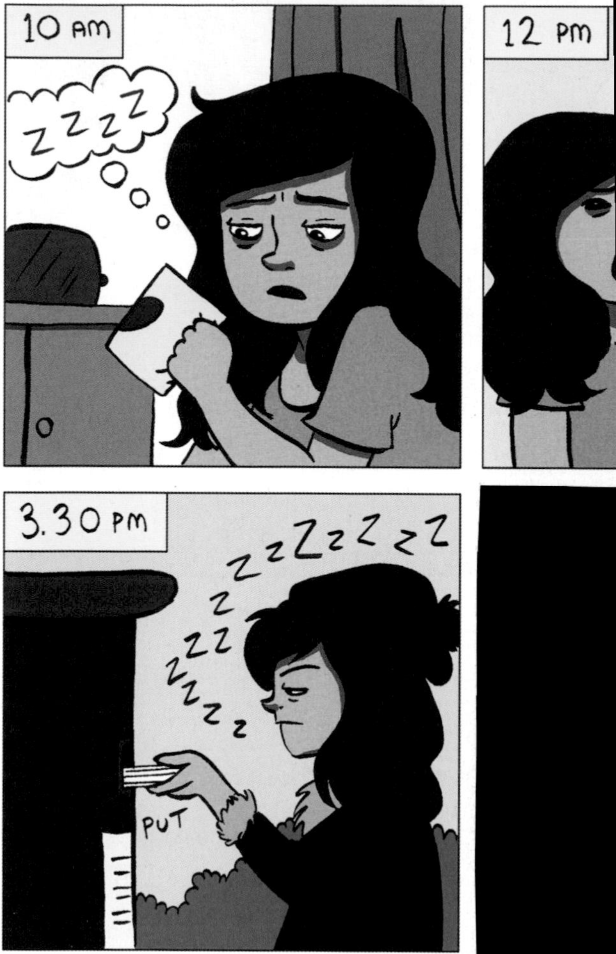
10 AM
ZZZZZ
12 PM
3.30 PM
ZZZZZZZZZ
ZZZZZZZ
PUT

I'm too sleepy to come [redacted]

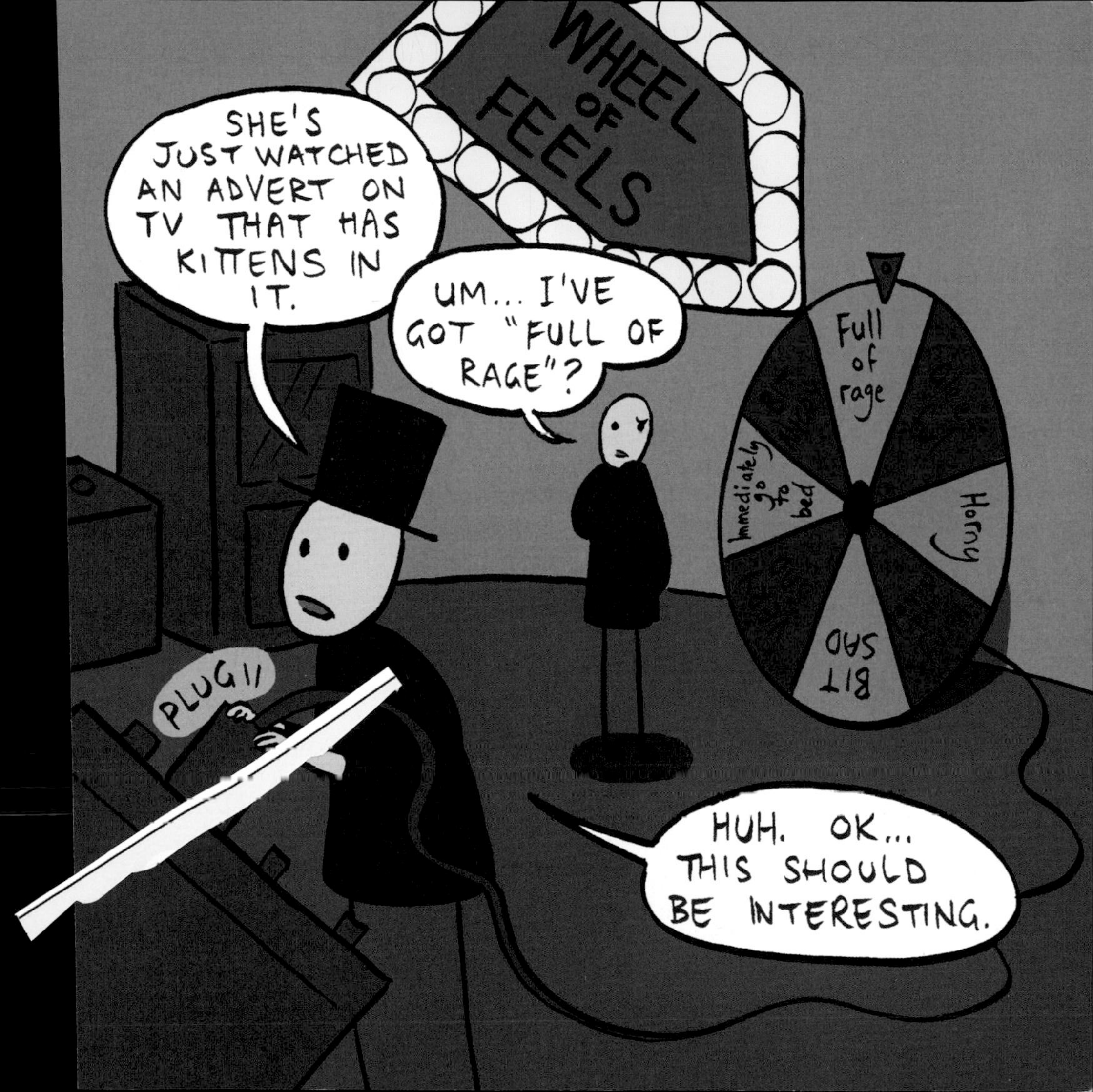
WHEEL OF FEELS
SHE'S JUST WATCHED AN ADVERT ON TV THAT HAS KITTENS IN IT.
UM... I'VE GOT "FULL OF RAGE"?
Full of rage
Horny
BIT SAD
Immediately go to bed
PLUG!!
HUH. OK... THIS SHOULD BE INTERESTING.

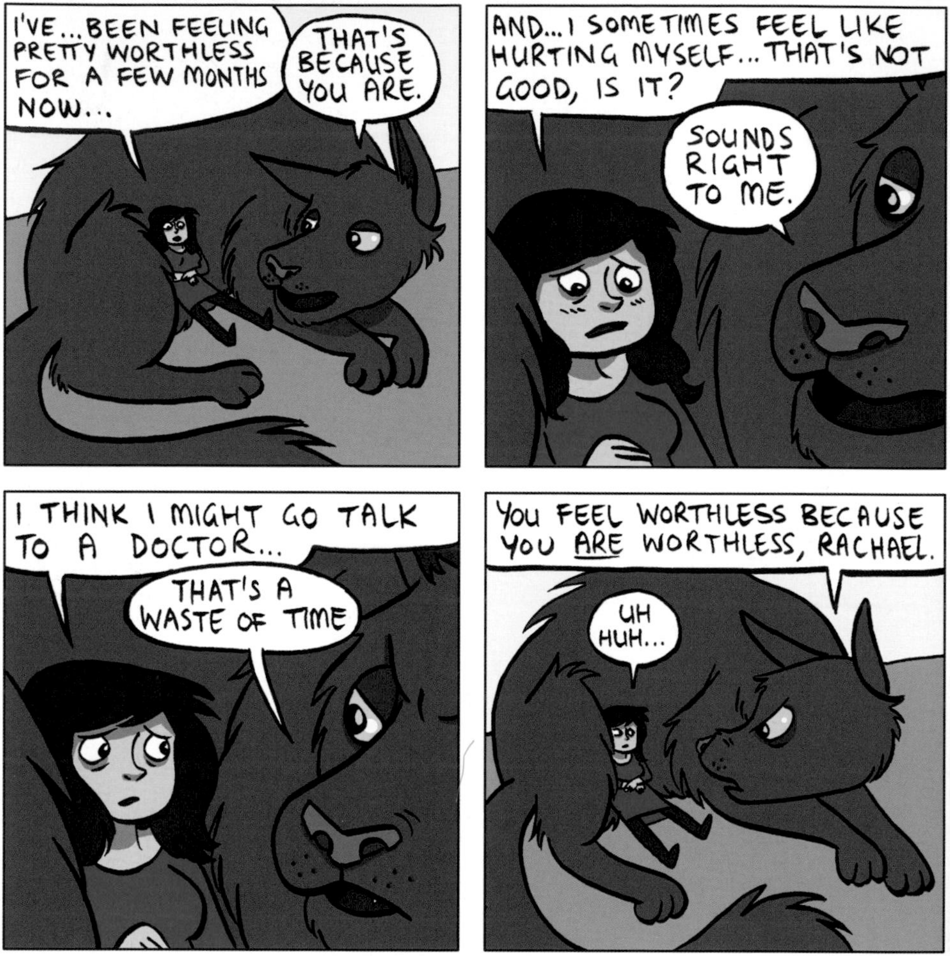
I'VE... BEEN FEELING PRETTY WORTHLESS FOR A FEW MONTHS NOW...
THAT'S BECAUSE YOU ARE.
AND... I SOMETIMES FEEL LIKE HURTING MYSELF... THAT'S NOT GOOD, IS IT?
SOUNDS RIGHT TO ME.
I THINK I MIGHT GO TALK TO A DOCTOR...
THAT'S A WASTE OF TIME
YOU FEEL WORTHLESS BECAUSE YOU ARE WORTHLESS, RACHAEL.
UH HUH...

Gosh darn it Barky, I know you're talking shit but you're just SO comfy ...

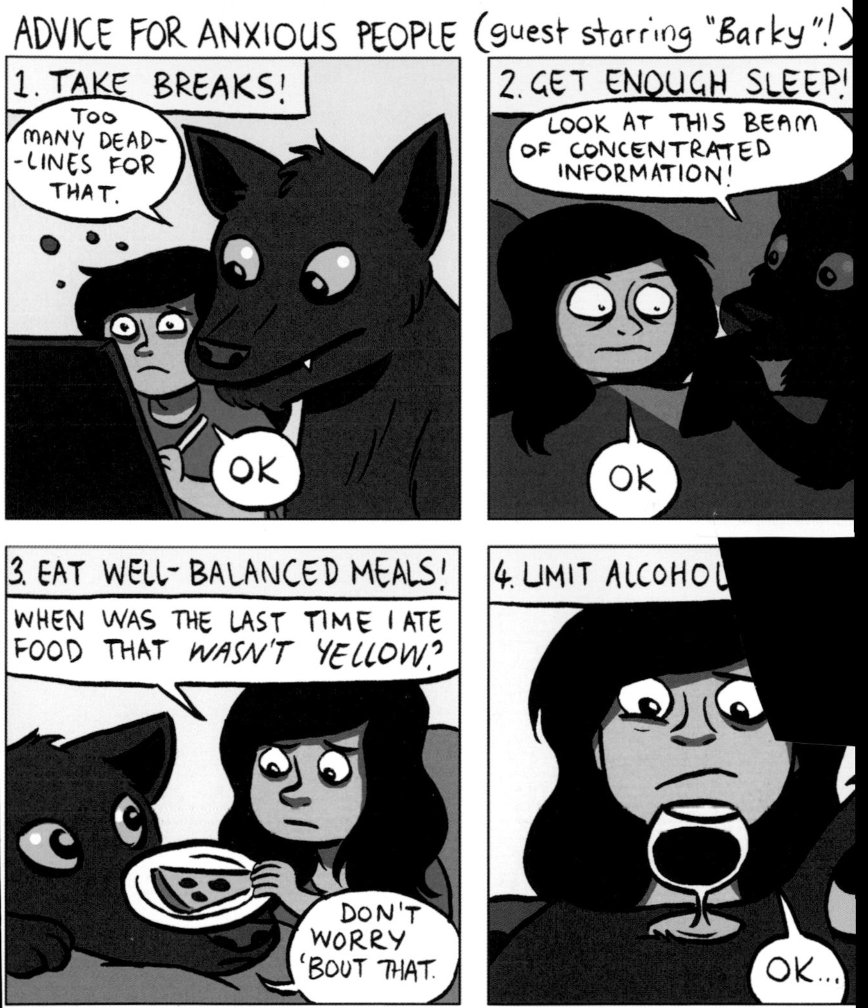
ADVICE FOR ANXIOUS PEOPLE (guest starring "Barky"!)
1. TAKE BREAKS!
TOO MANY DEAD-LINES FOR THAT.
OK
2. GET ENOUGH SLEEP!
LOOK AT THIS BEAM OF CONCENTRATED INFORMATION!
OK
3. EAT WELL-BALANCED MEALS!
WHEN WAS THE LAST TIME I ATE FOOD THAT *WASN'T YELLOW*?
DON'T WORRY 'BOUT THAT.
4. LIMIT ALCOHO[redacted]
OK...

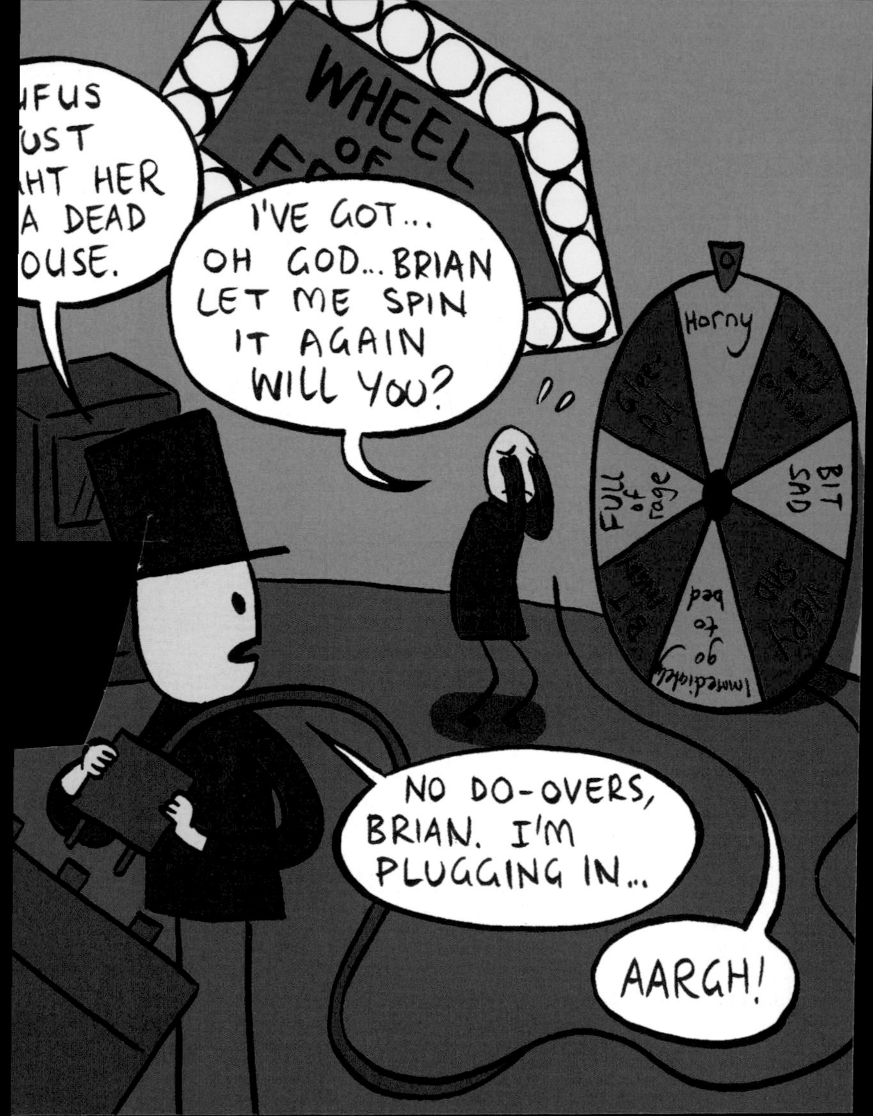
FUS UST HT HER A DEAD OUSE.
WHEEL OF
I'VE GOT... OH GOD... BRIAN LET ME SPIN IT AGAIN WILL YOU?
Horny
BIT SAD
FULL of rage
Immediately go to bed
NO DO-OVERS, BRIAN. I'M PLUGGING IN...
AARGH!

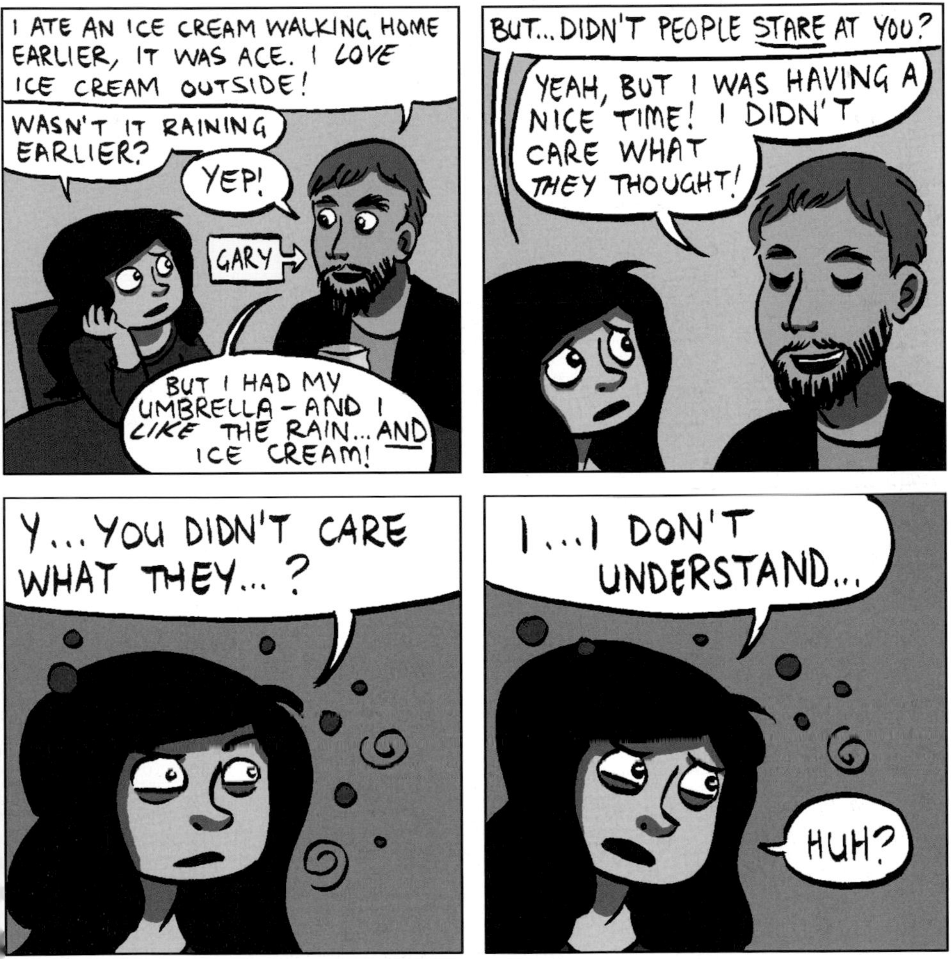
I ATE AN ICE CREAM WALKING HOME EARLIER, IT WAS ACE. I LOVE ICE CREAM OUTSIDE!
WASN'T IT RAINING EARLIER?
YEP!
GARY
BUT I HAD MY UMBRELLA - AND I LIKE THE RAIN... AND ICE CREAM!
BUT... DIDN'T PEOPLE STARE AT YOU?
YEAH, BUT I WAS HAVING A NICE TIME! I DIDN'T CARE WHAT THEY THOUGHT!
Y... YOU DIDN'T CARE WHAT THEY... ?
I... I DON'T UNDERSTAND...
HUH?

I will never possess this superpower.

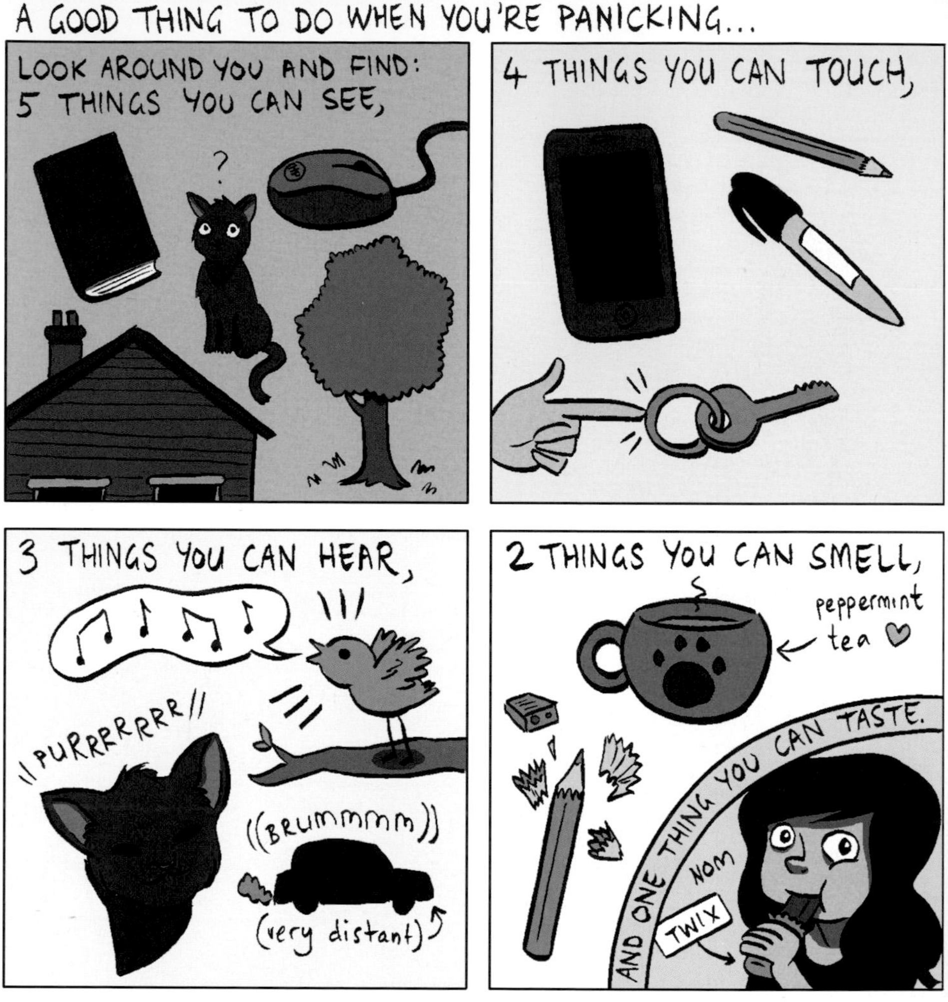
A GOOD THING TO DO WHEN YOU'RE PANICKING...
LOOK AROUND YOU AND FIND:
5 THINGS YOU CAN SEE,
?
4 THINGS YOU CAN TOUCH,
3 THINGS YOU CAN HEAR,
PURRRRRRR
((BRUMMMM))
(very distant)
2 THINGS YOU CAN SMELL,
peppermint tea ♡
AND ONE THING YOU CAN TASTE.
NOM
TWIX

You don't HAVE to eat the one thing you can taste – but if it happens to be a Twix then I can recommend doing so.

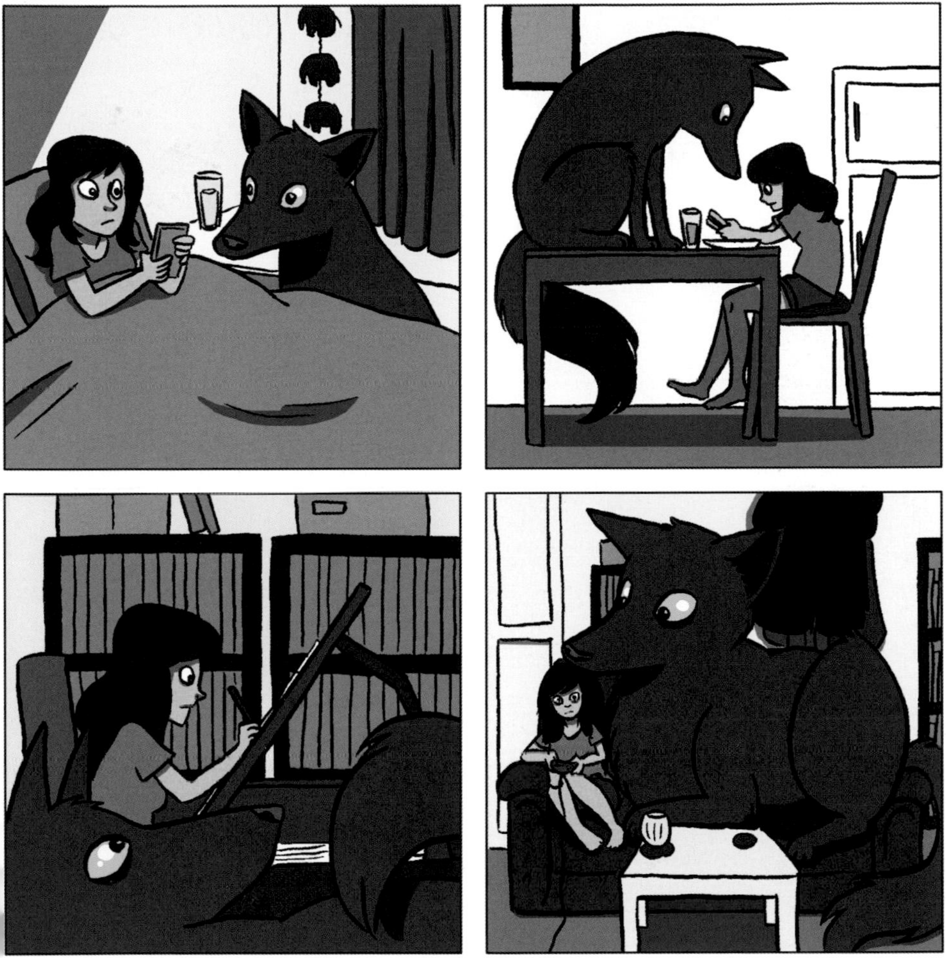

Never alone.

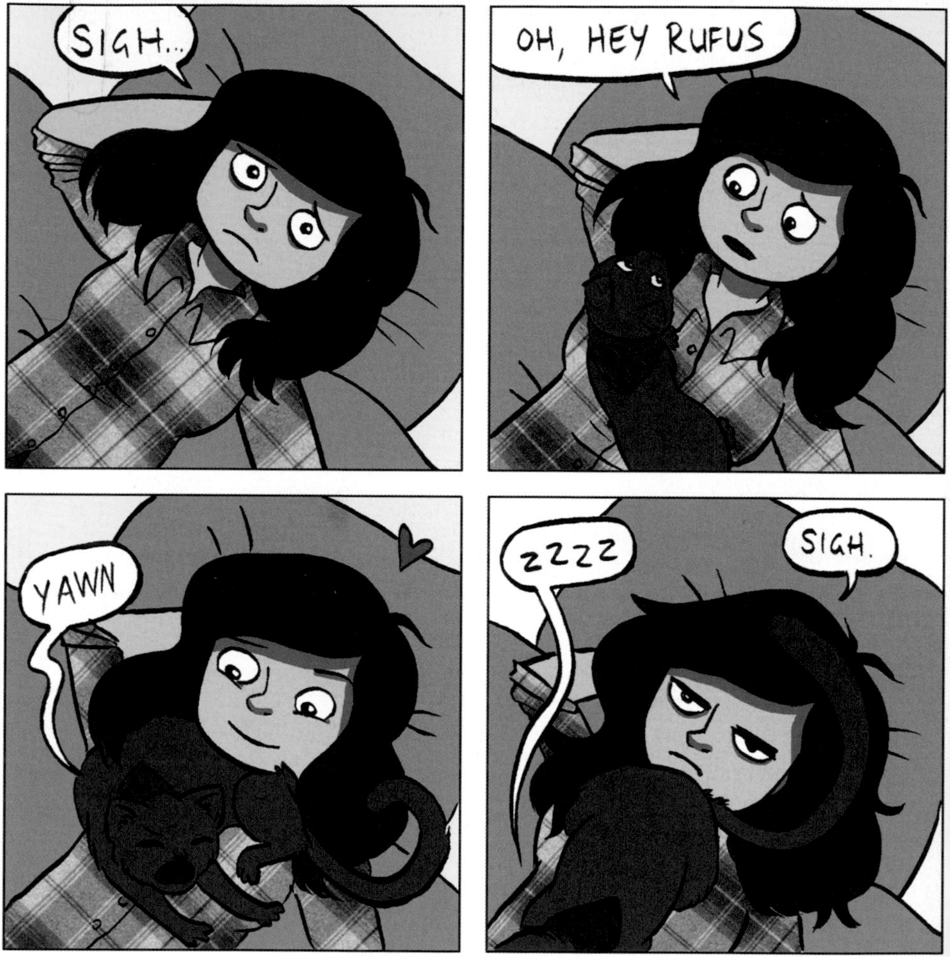
SIGH...
OH, HEY RUFUS
YAWN
ZZZZ
SIGH.

An almost daily occurrence.

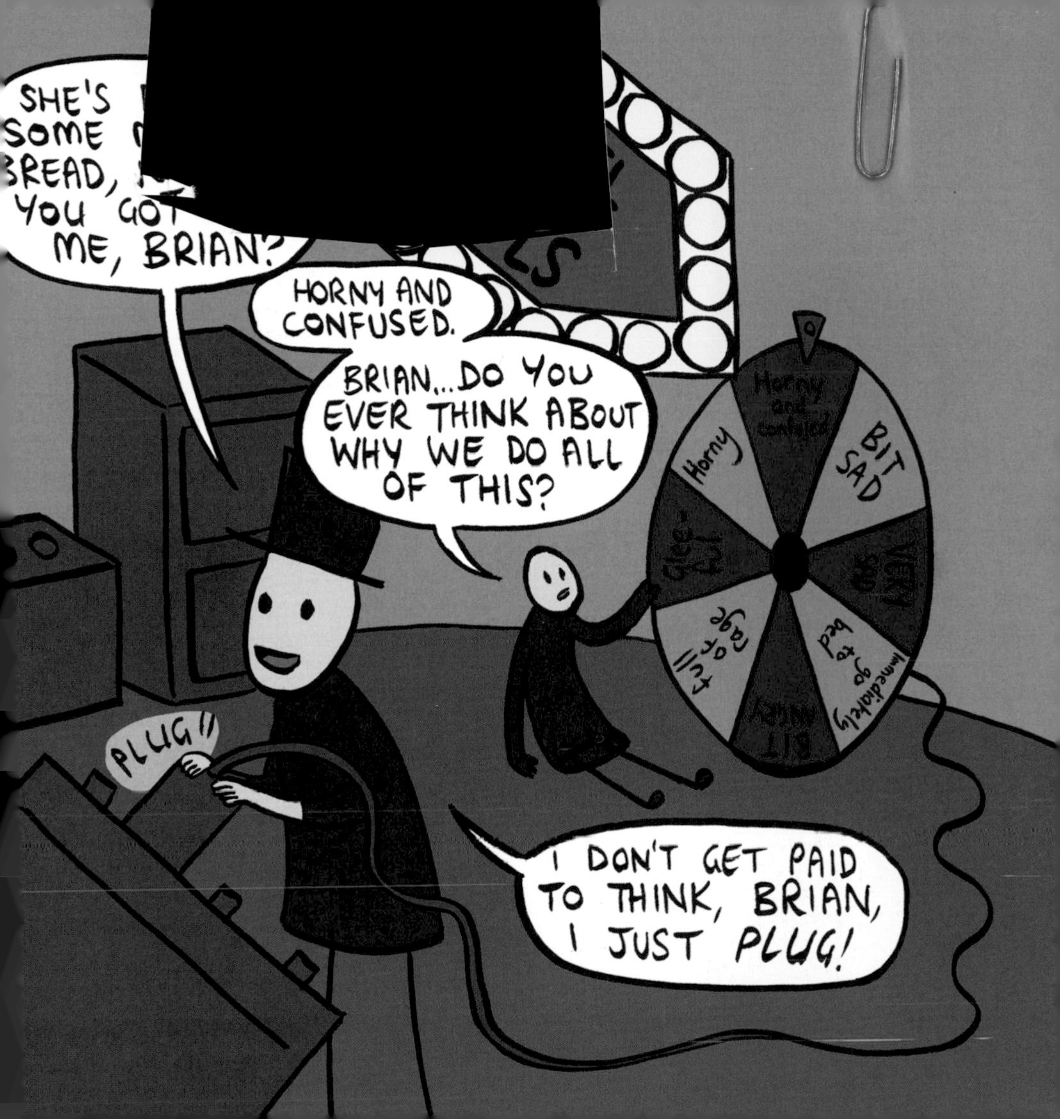
SHE'S [redacted] SOME [redacted] BREAD, [redacted] YOU GOT [redacted] ME, BRIAN?
HORNY AND CONFUSED.
BRIAN... DO YOU EVER THINK ABOUT WHY WE DO ALL OF THIS?
Horny and confused
BIT SAD
VERY SAD
immediately go to bed
BIT HORNY
full of rage
Horny
PLUG!!
I DON'T GET PAID TO THINK, BRIAN, I JUST *PLUG!*

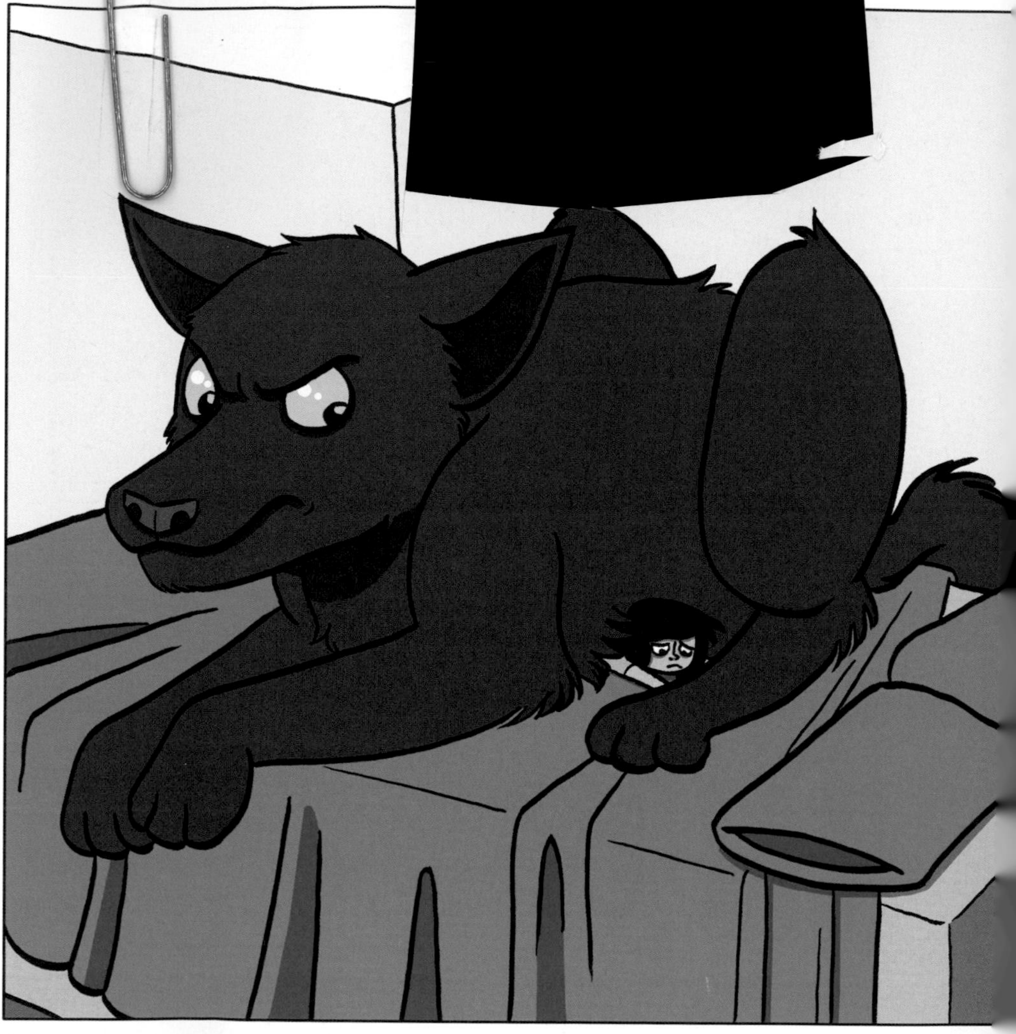
[redacted]

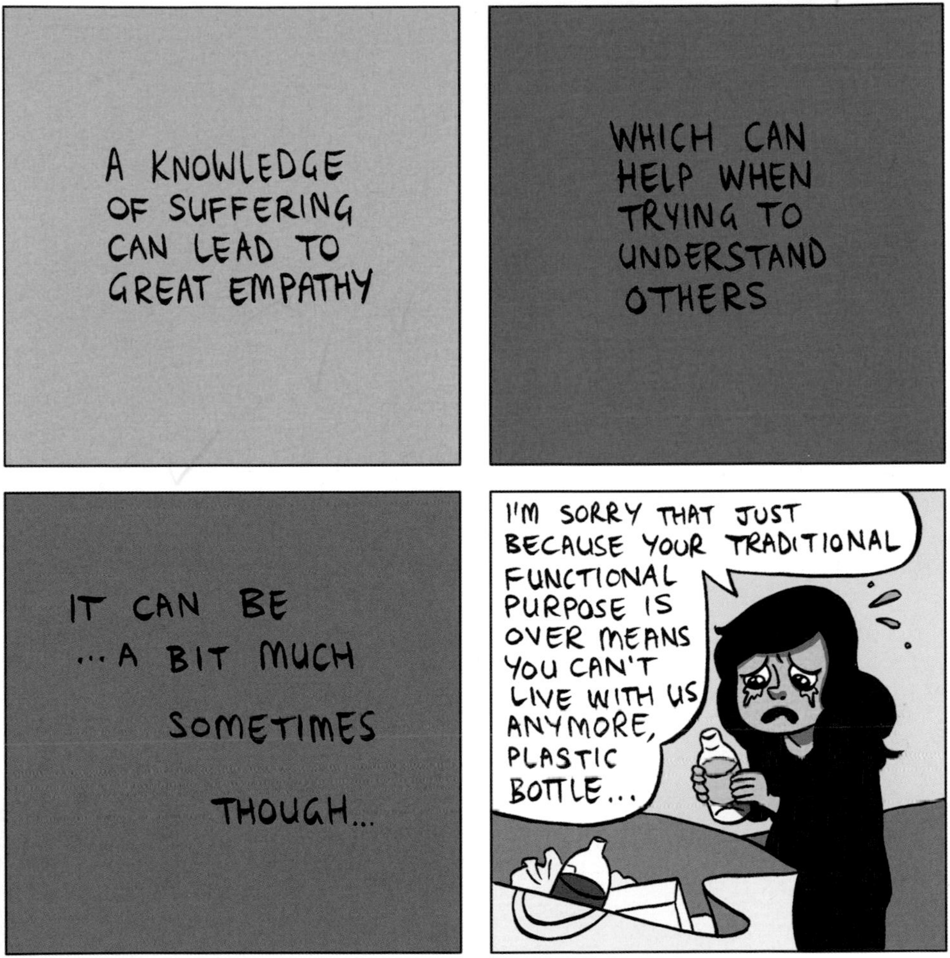
A KNOWLEDGE OF SUFFERING CAN LEAD TO GREAT EMPATHY
WHICH CAN HELP WHEN TRYING TO UNDERSTAND OTHERS
IT CAN BE ...A BIT MUCH
SOMETIMES
THOUGH...
I'M SORRY THAT JUST BECAUSE YOUR TRADITIONAL FUNCTIONAL PURPOSE IS OVER MEANS YOU CAN'T LIVE WITH US ANYMORE, PLASTIC BOTTLE...

Here, meet your new family ... this is Jeremy the box, Sheila the packaging, Eric the cling film ...

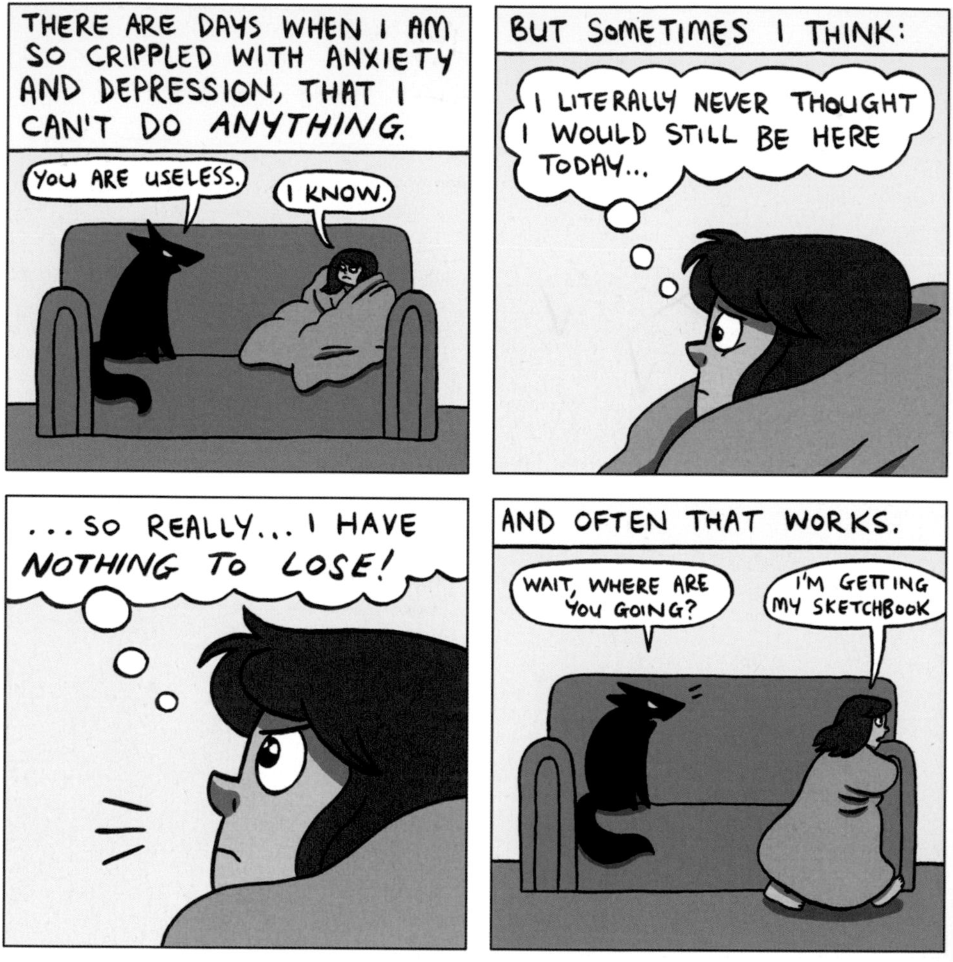
THERE ARE DAYS WHEN I AM SO CRIPPLED WITH ANXIETY AND DEPRESSION, THAT I CAN'T DO ANYTHING.
YOU ARE USELESS.
I KNOW.
BUT SOMETIMES I THINK:
I LITERALLY NEVER THOUGHT I WOULD STILL BE HERE TODAY...
...SO REALLY... I HAVE NOTHING TO LOSE!
AND OFTEN THAT WORKS.
WAIT, WHERE ARE YOU GOING?
I'M GETTING MY SKETCHBOOK

Anything is better than not being here at all.

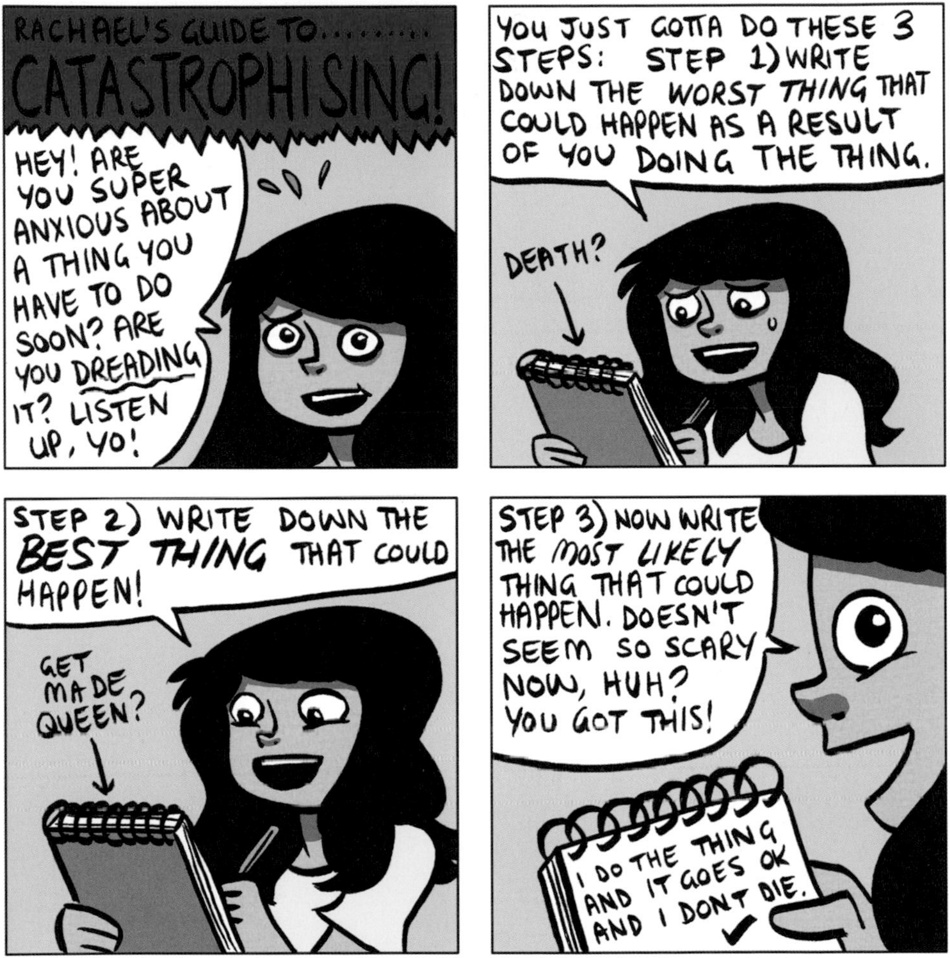
RACHAEL'S GUIDE TO.........
CATASTROPHISING!
HEY! ARE YOU SUPER ANXIOUS ABOUT A THING YOU HAVE TO DO SOON? ARE YOU DREADING IT? LISTEN UP, YO!
YOU JUST GOTTA DO THESE 3 STEPS: STEP 1) WRITE DOWN THE WORST THING THAT COULD HAPPEN AS A RESULT OF YOU DOING THE THING.
DEATH?
STEP 2) WRITE DOWN THE BEST THING THAT COULD HAPPEN!
GET MADE QUEEN?
STEP 3) NOW WRITE THE MOST LIKELY THING THAT COULD HAPPEN. DOESN'T SEEM SO SCARY NOW, HUH? YOU GOT THIS!
I DO THE THING AND IT GOES OK AND I DONT DIE.

I don't know what kind of event would involve the possibility of death and/or being crowned but I'd *totally* go.

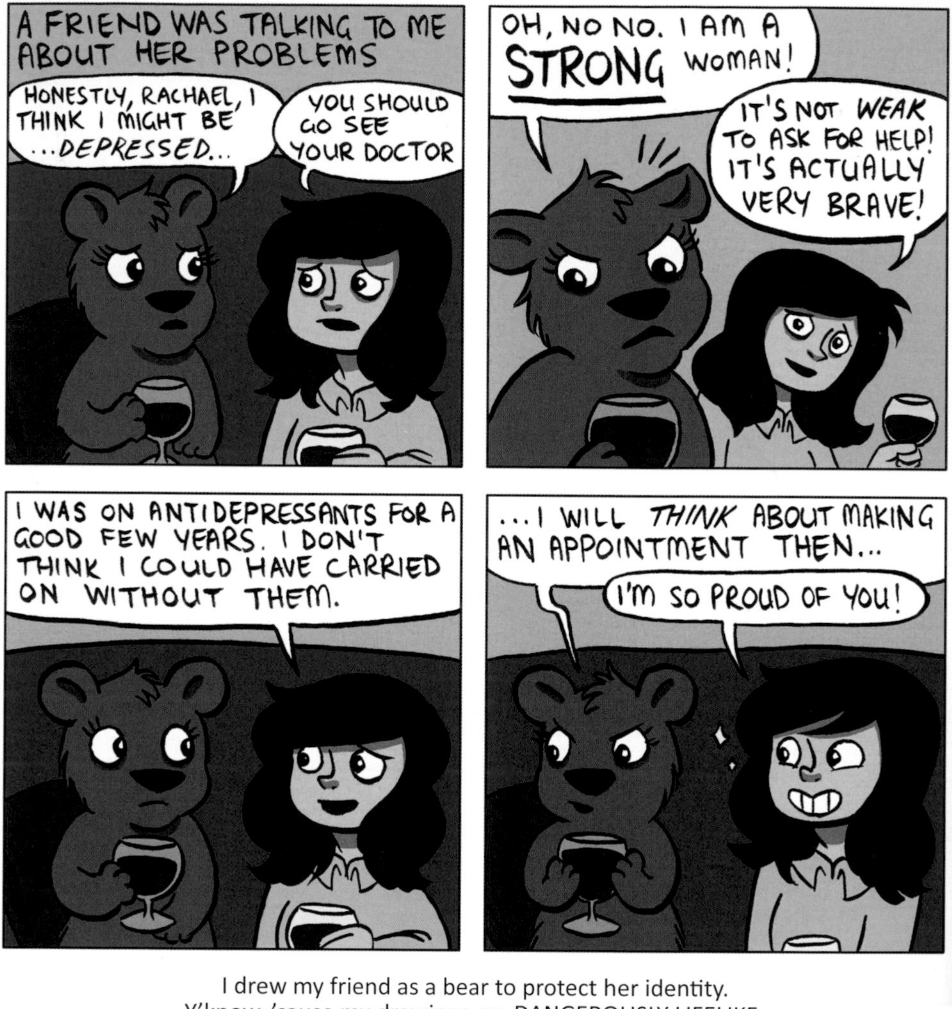
A FRIEND WAS TALKING TO ME ABOUT HER PROBLEMS
HONESTLY, RACHAEL, I THINK I MIGHT BE ...DEPRESSED...
YOU SHOULD GO SEE YOUR DOCTOR
OH, NO NO. I AM A STRONG WOMAN!
IT'S NOT WEAK TO ASK FOR HELP! IT'S ACTUALLY VERY BRAVE!
I WAS ON ANTIDEPRESSANTS FOR A GOOD FEW YEARS. I DON'T THINK I COULD HAVE CARRIED ON WITHOUT THEM.
...I WILL THINK ABOUT MAKING AN APPOINTMENT THEN...
I'M SO PROUD OF YOU!

I drew my friend as a bear to protect her identity.
Y'know, 'cause my drawings are DANGEROUSLY LIFELIKE.

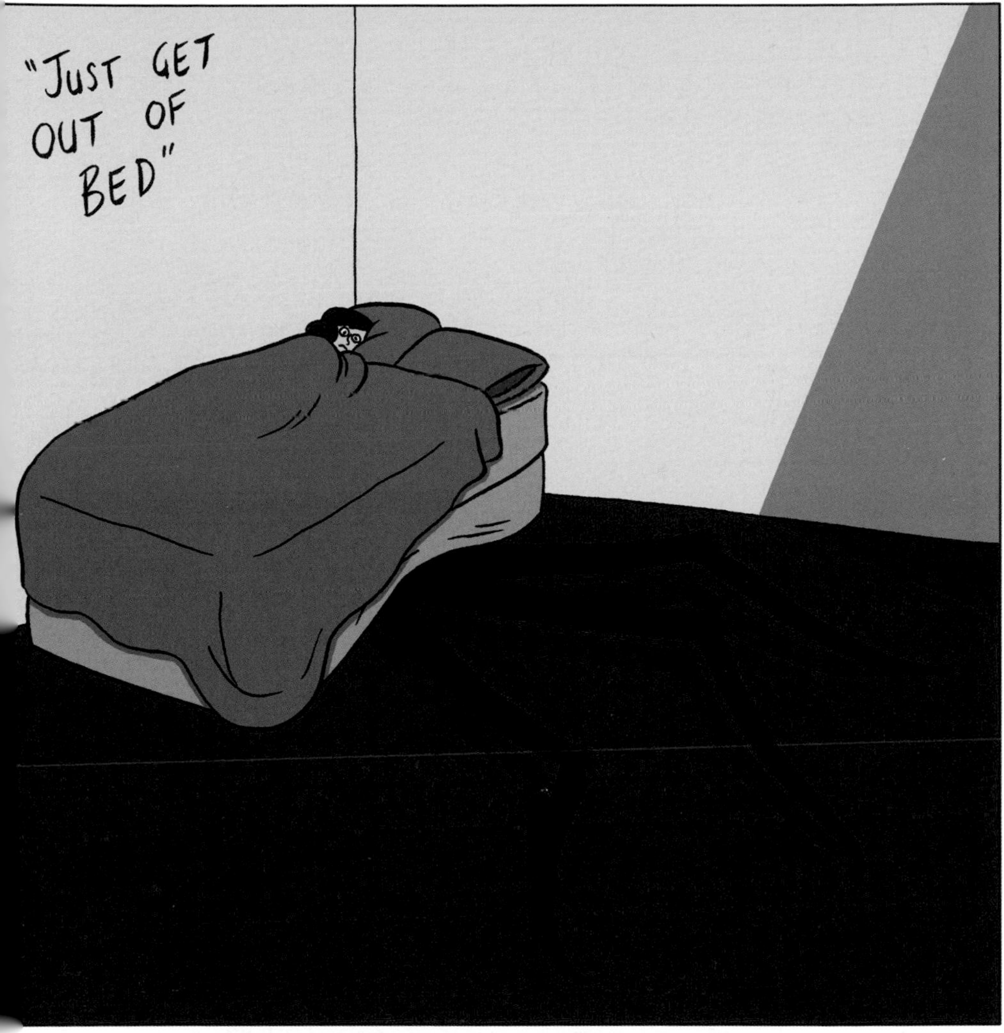
"JUST GET OUT OF BED"

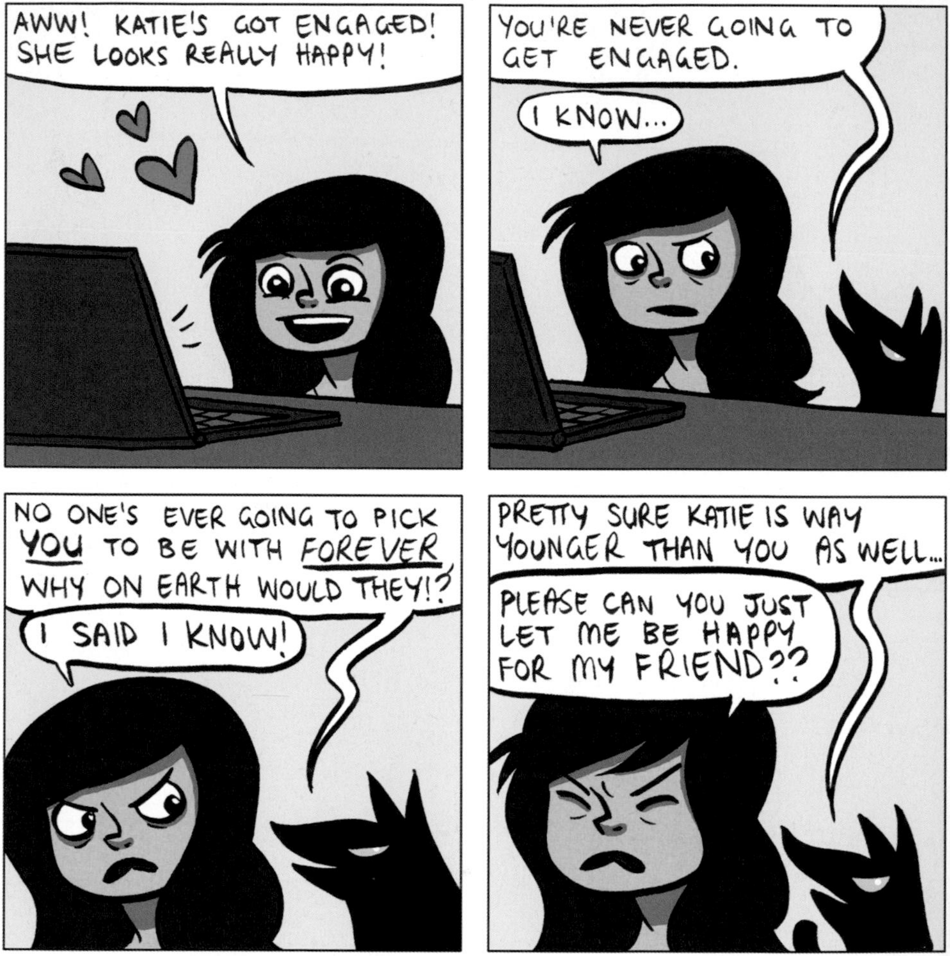
AWW! KATIE'S GOT ENGAGED! SHE LOOKS REALLY HAPPY!
YOU'RE NEVER GOING TO GET ENGAGED.
I KNOW...
NO ONE'S EVER GOING TO PICK YOU TO BE WITH FOREVER WHY ON EARTH WOULD THEY!?
I SAID I KNOW!
PRETTY SURE KATIE IS WAY YOUNGER THAN YOU AS WELL...
PLEASE CAN YOU JUST LET ME BE HAPPY FOR MY FRIEND??

Barky is always a dick about engagements.
Maybe he was left at the altar?

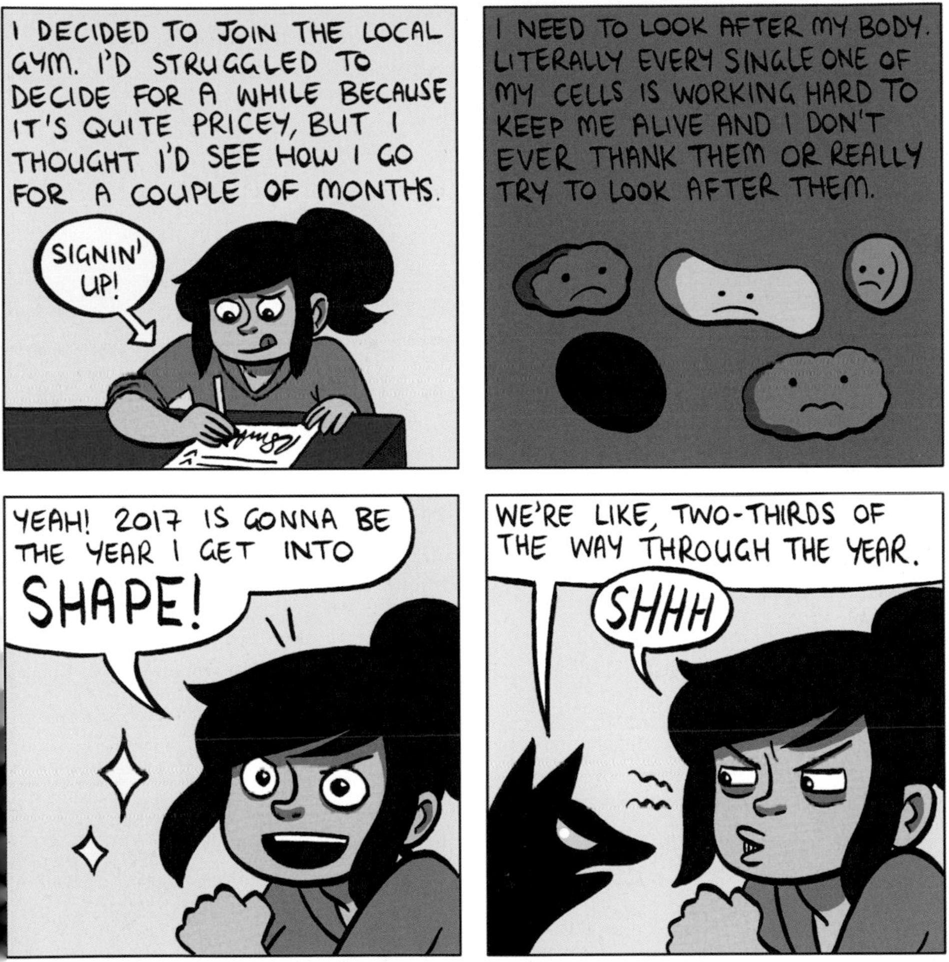
I DECIDED TO JOIN THE LOCAL GYM. I'D STRUGGLED TO DECIDE FOR A WHILE BECAUSE IT'S QUITE PRICEY, BUT I THOUGHT I'D SEE HOW I GO FOR A COUPLE OF MONTHS.
SIGNIN' UP!
I NEED TO LOOK AFTER MY BODY. LITERALLY EVERY SINGLE ONE OF MY CELLS IS WORKING HARD TO KEEP ME ALIVE AND I DON'T EVER THANK THEM OR REALLY TRY TO LOOK AFTER THEM.
YEAH! 2017 IS GONNA BE THE YEAR I GET INTO SHAPE!
WE'RE LIKE, TWO-THIRDS OF THE WAY THROUGH THE YEAR.
SHHH

What do you mean I don't know what my cells look like?
I just know they're all very unhappy with me, OK?

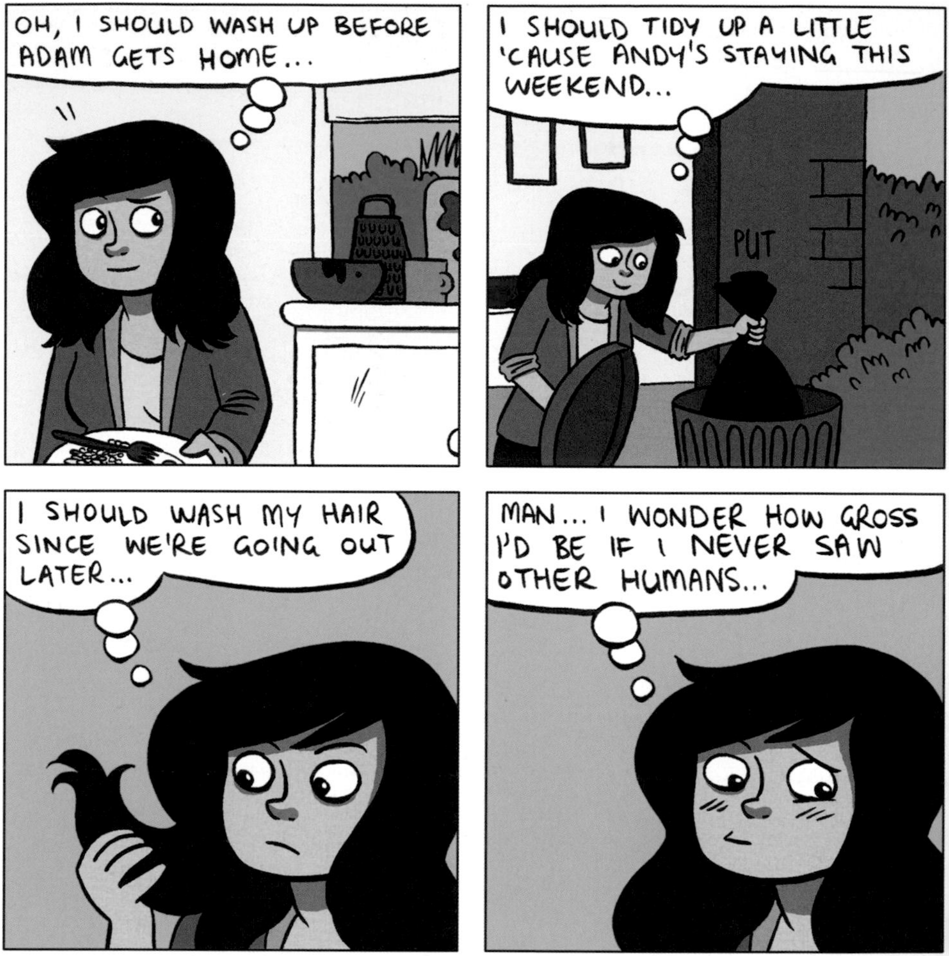
OH, I SHOULD WASH UP BEFORE ADAM GETS HOME...
I SHOULD TIDY UP A LITTLE 'CAUSE ANDY'S STAYING THIS WEEKEND...
PUT
I SHOULD WASH MY HAIR SINCE WE'RE GOING OUT LATER...
MAN... I WONDER HOW GROSS I'D BE IF I NEVER SAW OTHER HUMANS...

I mean, can grossness *really* exist when there are no other humans around to witness it? Oh, you're nodding? I mean ... yeah of course it can, I totally thought that too.

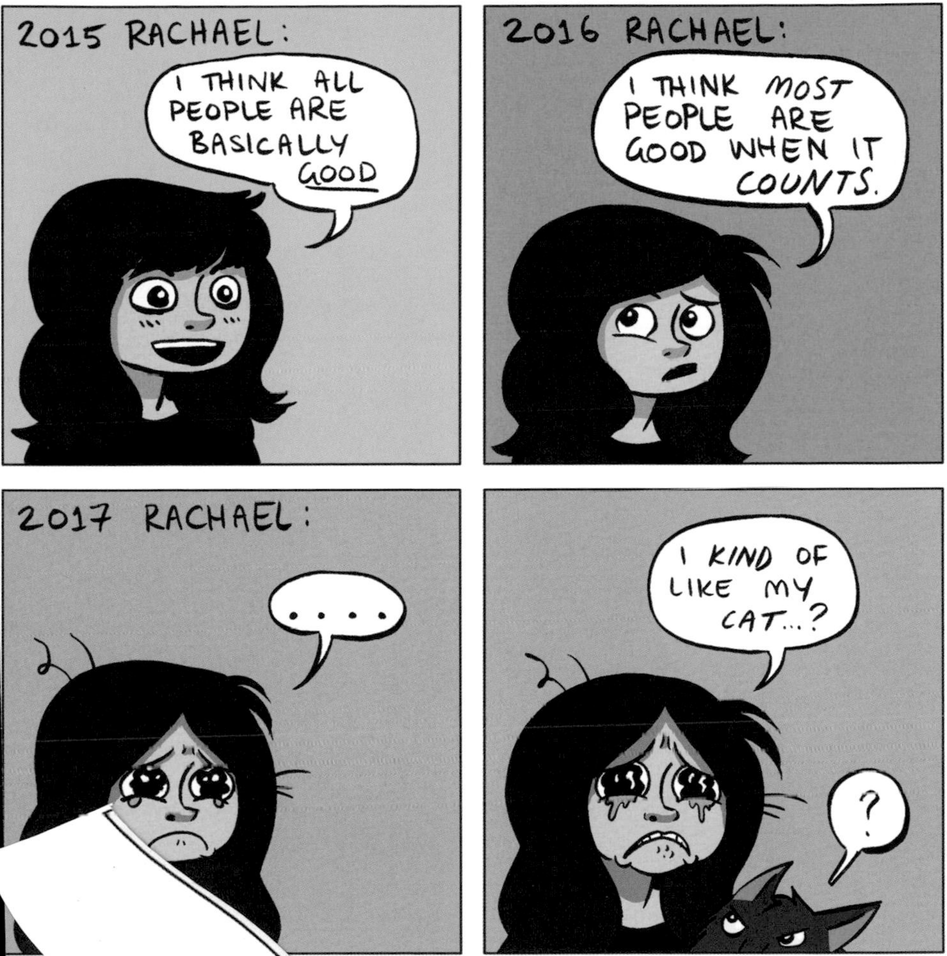
2015 RACHAEL:
I THINK ALL PEOPLE ARE BASICALLY GOOD
2016 RACHAEL:
I THINK MOST PEOPLE ARE GOOD WHEN IT COUNTS.
2017 RACHAEL:
. . . .
I KIND OF LIKE MY CAT...?
?

I ... arlier in the year, which is why my hair is a little different.
I was go... paragraphs so they matched better ... but the expressions ... perfect not to share with you guys!

Rufus is as done with

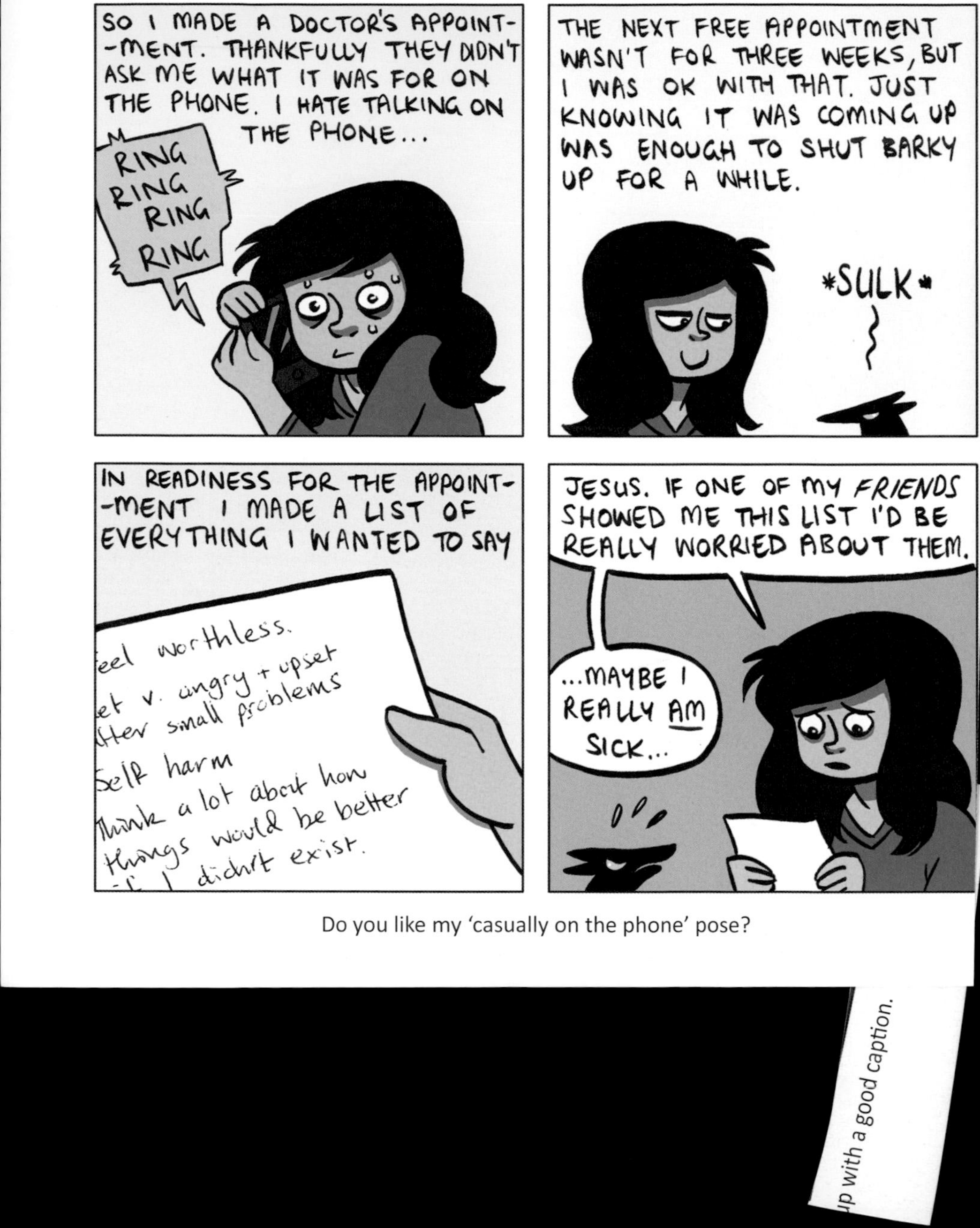
SO I MADE A DOCTOR'S APPOINT- -MENT. THANKFULLY THEY DIDN'T ASK ME WHAT IT WAS FOR ON THE PHONE. I HATE TALKING ON THE PHONE...
RING RING RING RING
THE NEXT FREE APPOINTMENT WASN'T FOR THREE WEEKS, BUT I WAS OK WITH THAT. JUST KNOWING IT WAS COMING UP WAS ENOUGH TO SHUT BARKY UP FOR A WHILE.
SULK
IN READINESS FOR THE APPOINT- -MENT I MADE A LIST OF EVERYTHING I WANTED TO SAY
eel worthless.
et v. angry + upset
fter small problems
Self harm
Think a lot about how
things would be better
didn't exist.
JESUS. IF ONE OF MY *FRIENDS* SHOWED ME THIS LIST I'D BE REALLY WORRIED ABOUT THEM.
...MAYBE I REALLY AM SICK...

Do you like my 'casually on the phone' pose?

up with a good caption.

THE DOCTOR'S APPOINTMENT

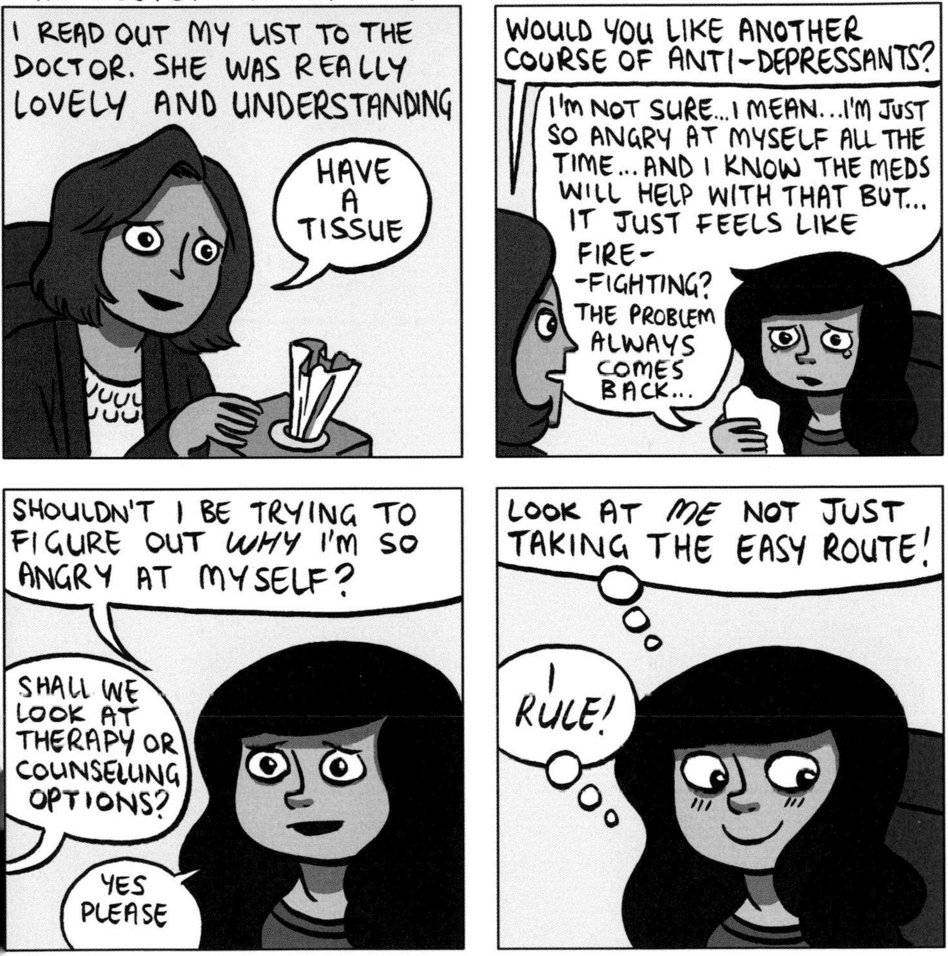
I READ OUT MY LIST TO THE DOCTOR. SHE WAS REALLY LOVELY AND UNDERSTANDING
HAVE A TISSUE
WOULD YOU LIKE ANOTHER COURSE OF ANTI-DEPRESSANTS?
I'M NOT SURE...I MEAN...I'M JUST SO ANGRY AT MYSELF ALL THE TIME...AND I KNOW THE MEDS WILL HELP WITH THAT BUT... IT JUST FEELS LIKE FIRE- -FIGHTING? THE PROBLEM ALWAYS COMES BACK...
SHOULDN'T I BE TRYING TO FIGURE OUT *WHY* I'M SO ANGRY AT MYSELF?
SHALL WE LOOK AT THERAPY OR COUNSELLING OPTIONS?
YES PLEASE
LOOK AT *ME* NOT JUST TAKING THE EASY ROUTE!
I RULE!

Full disclosure: I did make another appointment with her just in case I changed my mind, but decided to give therapy a go first.

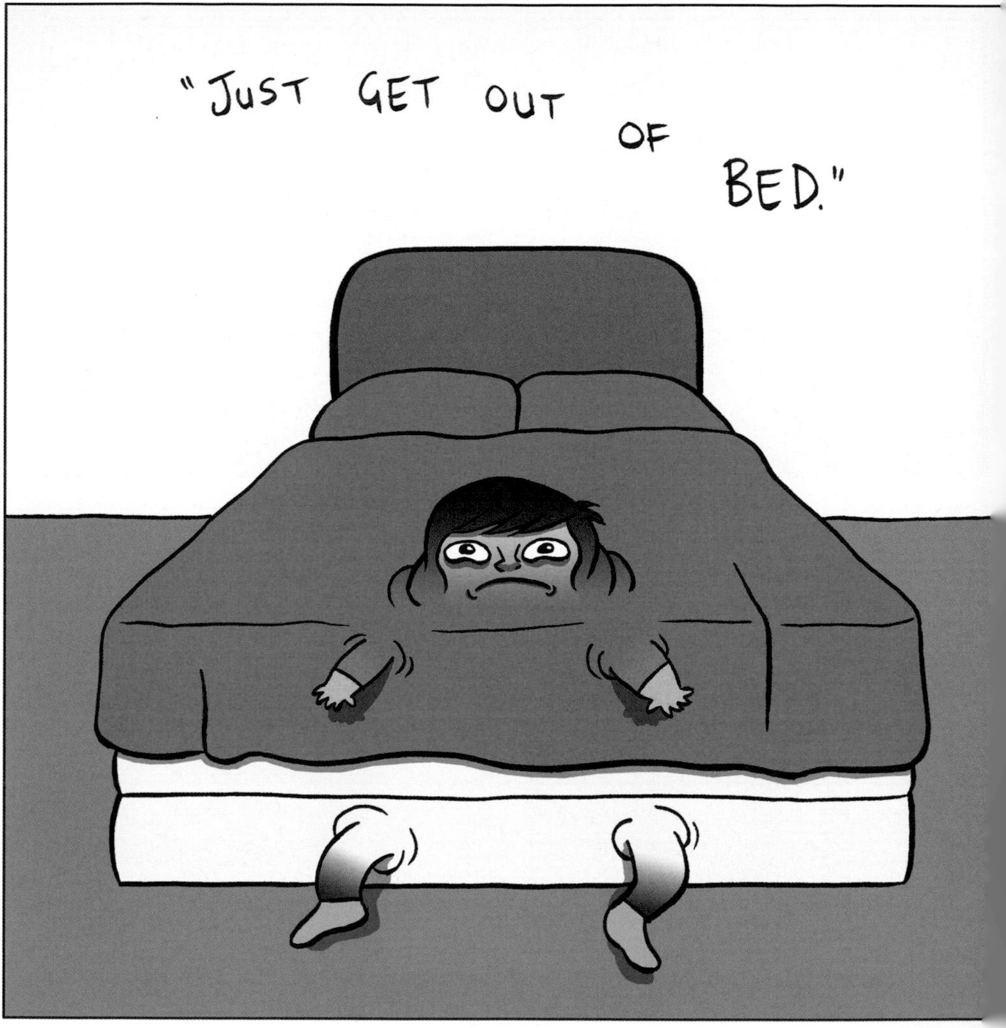
"JUST GET OUT OF BED."

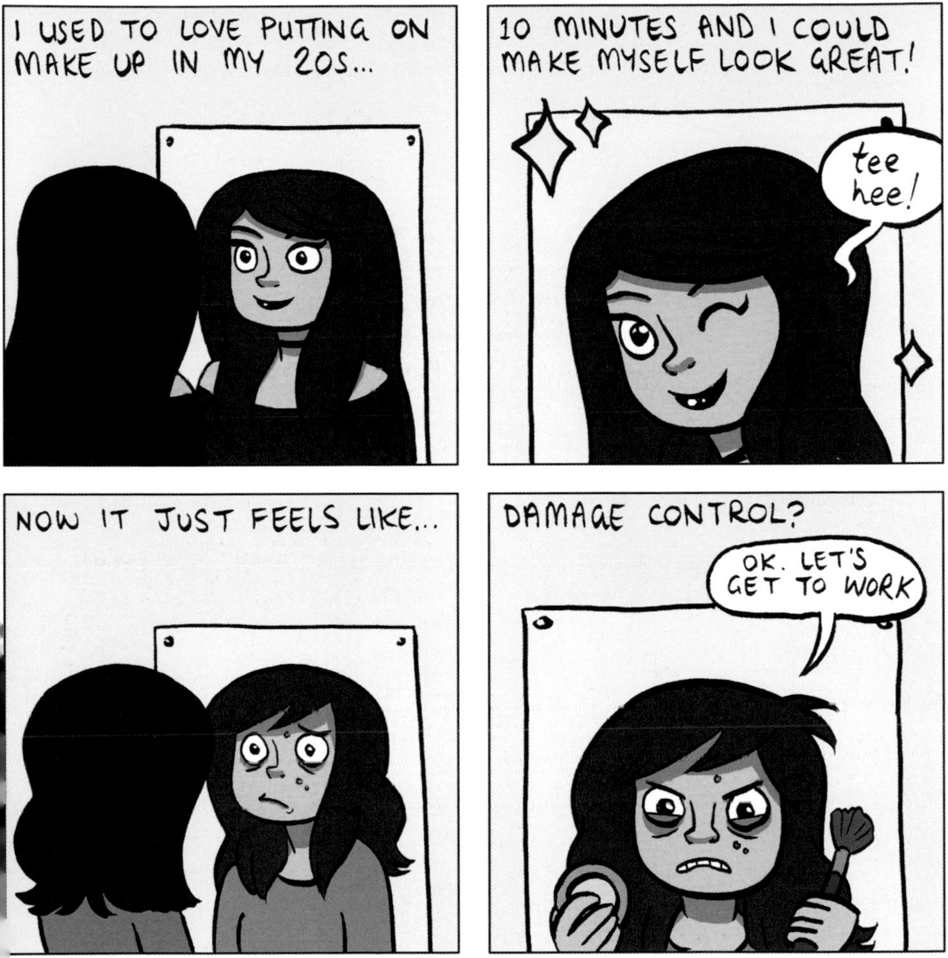
I USED TO LOVE PUTTING ON MAKE UP IN MY 20S...
10 MINUTES AND I COULD MAKE MYSELF LOOK GREAT!
tee hee!
NOW IT JUST FEELS LIKE...
DAMAGE CONTROL?
OK. LET'S GET TO WORK

Give me 45 minutes and an industrial sander
and I could probably pass for ... 30?

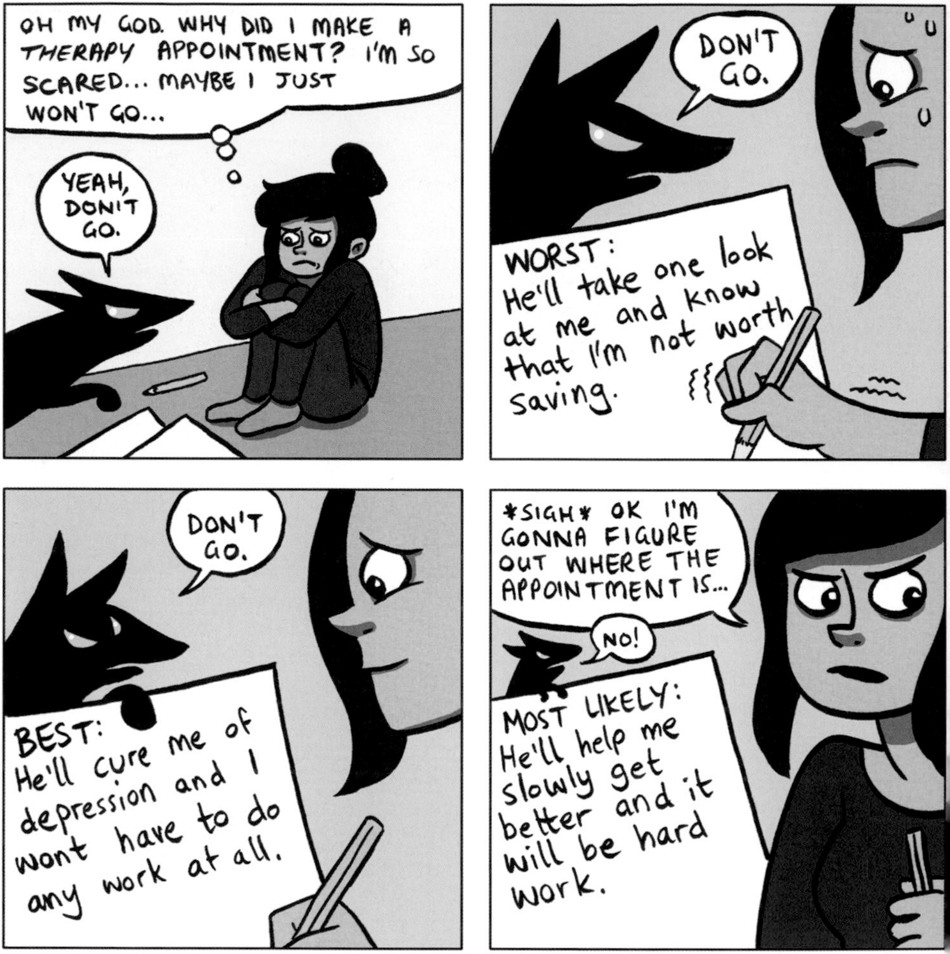
OH MY GOD. WHY DID I MAKE A THERAPY APPOINTMENT? I'M SO SCARED... MAYBE I JUST WON'T GO...
YEAH, DON'T GO.
DON'T GO.
WORST: He'll take one look at me and know that I'm not worth saving.
DON'T GO.
BEST: He'll cure me of depression and I wont have to do any work at all.
SIGH OK I'M GONNA FIGURE OUT WHERE THE APPOINTMENT IS...
NO!
MOST LIKELY: He'll help me slowly get better and it will be hard work.

I'll take hard work over not being saved any day. Well, most days.
It's probably like, 60/40.

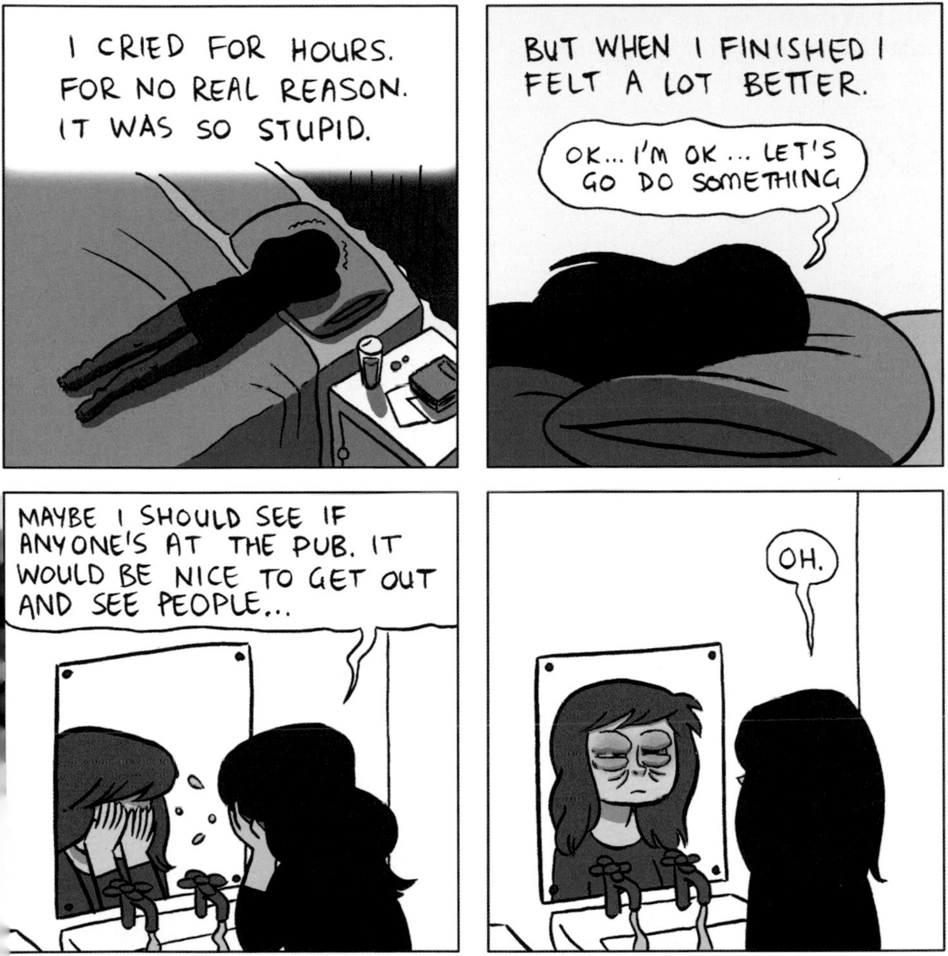
I CRIED FOR HOURS. FOR NO REAL REASON. IT WAS SO STUPID.
BUT WHEN I FINISHED I FELT A LOT BETTER.
OK... I'M OK ... LET'S GO DO SOMETHING
MAYBE I SHOULD SEE IF ANYONE'S AT THE PUB. IT WOULD BE NICE TO GET OUT AND SEE PEOPLE...
OH.

I was blessed with a tender heart and equally tender eyes.
Whoever blessed me was a bit of a dick.

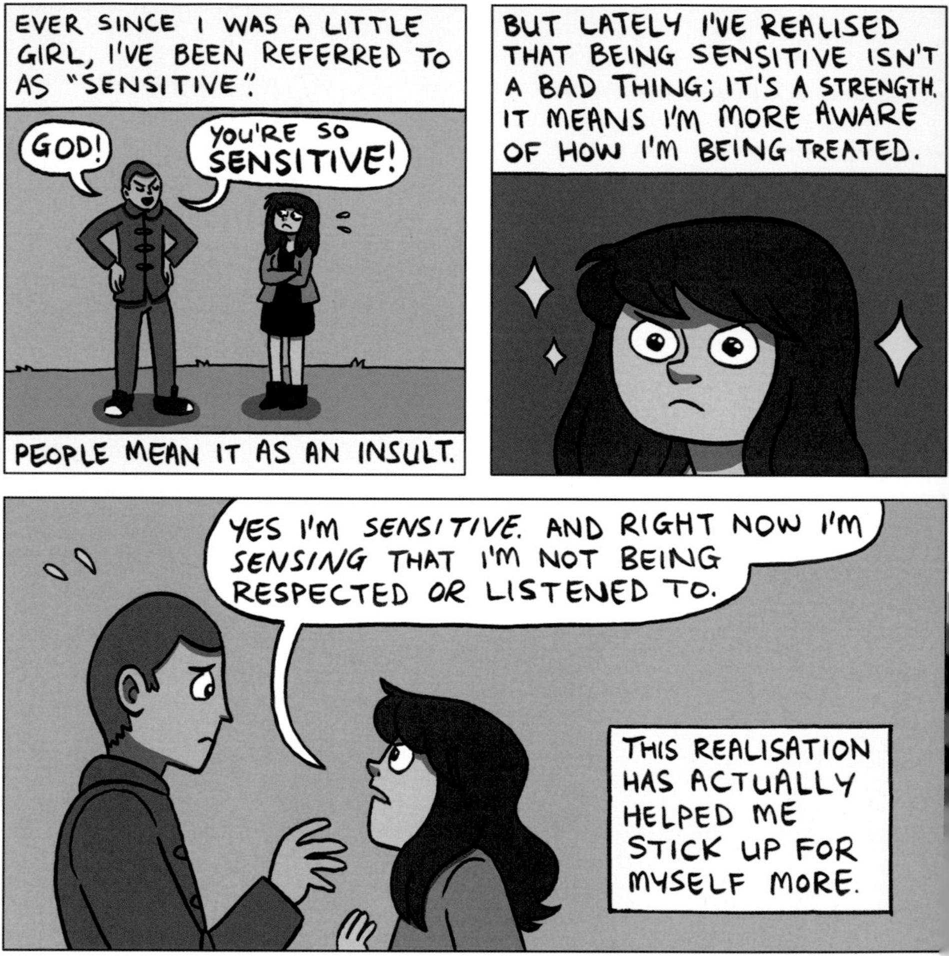
EVER SINCE I WAS A LITTLE GIRL, I'VE BEEN REFERRED TO AS "SENSITIVE".
GOD!
YOU'RE SO SENSITIVE!
PEOPLE MEAN IT AS AN INSULT.
BUT LATELY I'VE REALISED THAT BEING SENSITIVE ISN'T A BAD THING; IT'S A STRENGTH. IT MEANS I'M MORE AWARE OF HOW I'M BEING TREATED.
YES I'M SENSITIVE. AND RIGHT NOW I'M SENSING THAT I'M NOT BEING RESPECTED OR LISTENED TO.
THIS REALISATION HAS ACTUALLY HELPED ME STICK UP FOR MYSELF MORE.

My Superhero name would be Sensitive Soul. Or something.

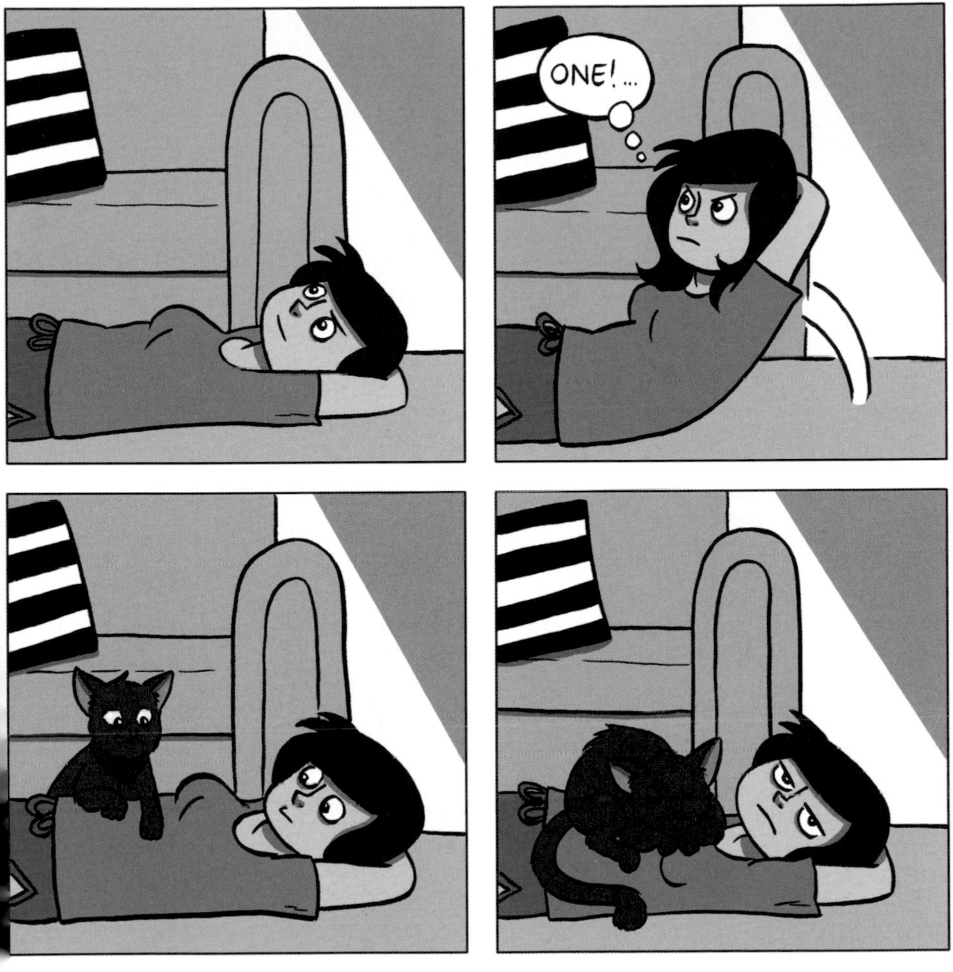
ONE! ...

One.

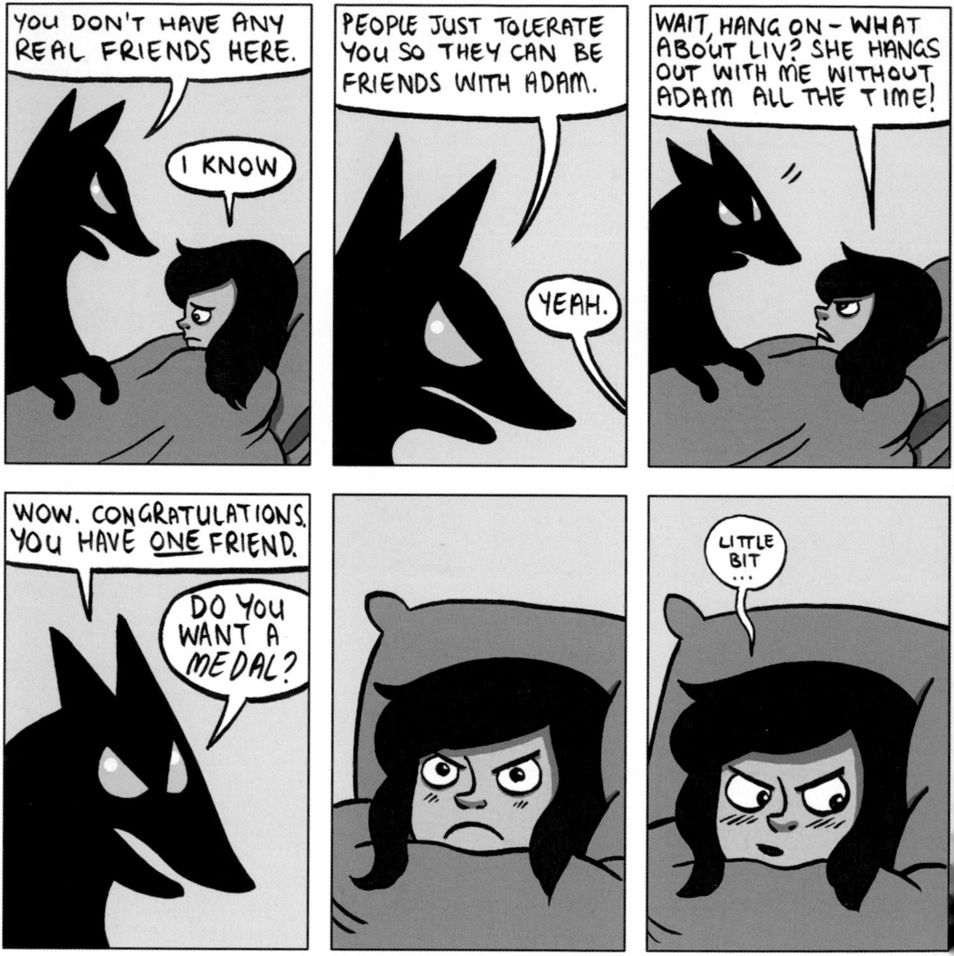
YOU DON'T HAVE ANY REAL FRIENDS HERE.
I KNOW
PEOPLE JUST TOLERATE YOU SO THEY CAN BE FRIENDS WITH ADAM.
YEAH.
WAIT, HANG ON - WHAT ABOUT LIV? SHE HANGS OUT WITH ME WITHOUT ADAM ALL THE TIME!
WOW. CONGRATULATIONS. YOU HAVE ONE FRIEND.
DO YOU WANT A MEDAL?
LITTLE BIT ...

Can't believe my imaginary dog offered me a medal
which he DIDN'T EVEN HAVE. omg. fml. smh.

ANTI-DEPRESSANTS!

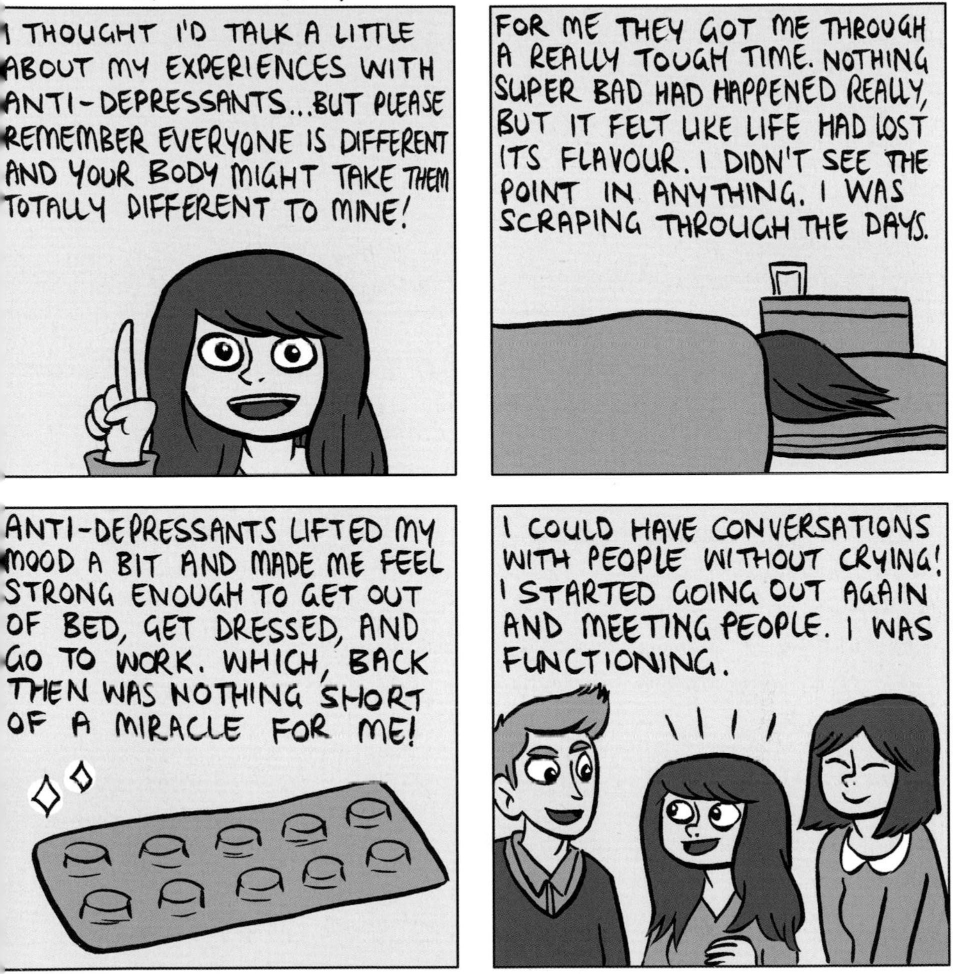
I THOUGHT I'D TALK A LITTLE ABOUT MY EXPERIENCES WITH ANTI-DEPRESSANTS...BUT PLEASE REMEMBER EVERYONE IS DIFFERENT AND YOUR BODY MIGHT TAKE THEM TOTALLY DIFFERENT TO MINE!
FOR ME THEY GOT ME THROUGH A REALLY TOUGH TIME. NOTHING SUPER BAD HAD HAPPENED REALLY, BUT IT FELT LIKE LIFE HAD LOST ITS FLAVOUR. I DIDN'T SEE THE POINT IN ANYTHING. I WAS SCRAPING THROUGH THE DAYS.
ANTI-DEPRESSANTS LIFTED MY MOOD A BIT AND MADE ME FEEL STRONG ENOUGH TO GET OUT OF BED, GET DRESSED, AND GO TO WORK. WHICH, BACK THEN WAS NOTHING SHORT OF A MIRACLE FOR ME!
I COULD HAVE CONVERSATIONS WITH PEOPLE WITHOUT CRYING! I STARTED GOING OUT AGAIN AND MEETING PEOPLE. I WAS FUNCTIONING.

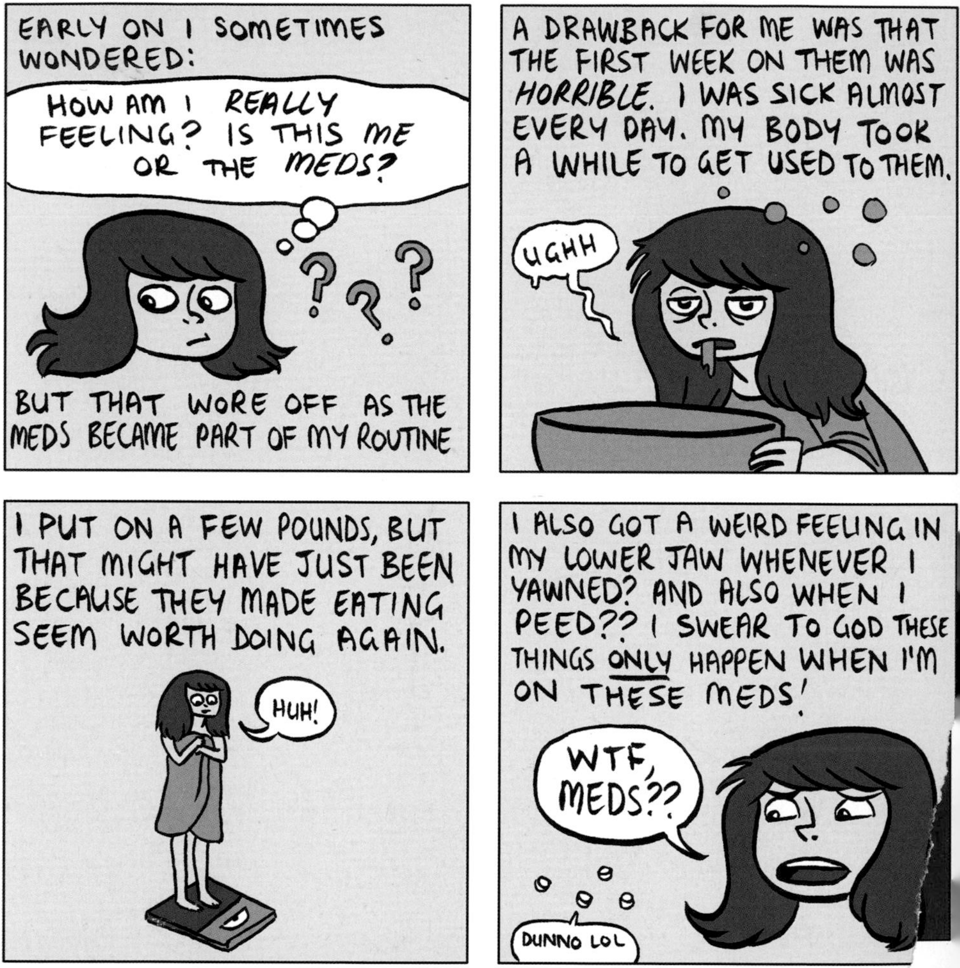
EARLY ON I SOMETIMES WONDERED:
HOW AM I REALLY FEELING? IS THIS ME OR THE MEDS?
BUT THAT WORE OFF AS THE MEDS BECAME PART OF MY ROUTINE
A DRAWBACK FOR ME WAS THAT THE FIRST WEEK ON THEM WAS HORRIBLE. I WAS SICK ALMOST EVERY DAY. MY BODY TOOK A WHILE TO GET USED TO THEM.
UGHH
I PUT ON A FEW POUNDS, BUT THAT MIGHT HAVE JUST BEEN BECAUSE THEY MADE EATING SEEM WORTH DOING AGAIN.
HUH!
I ALSO GOT A WEIRD FEELING IN MY LOWER JAW WHENEVER I YAWNED? AND ALSO WHEN I PEED?? I SWEAR TO GOD THESE THINGS ONLY HAPPEN WHEN I'M ON THESE MEDS!
WTF, MEDS??
DUNNO LOL

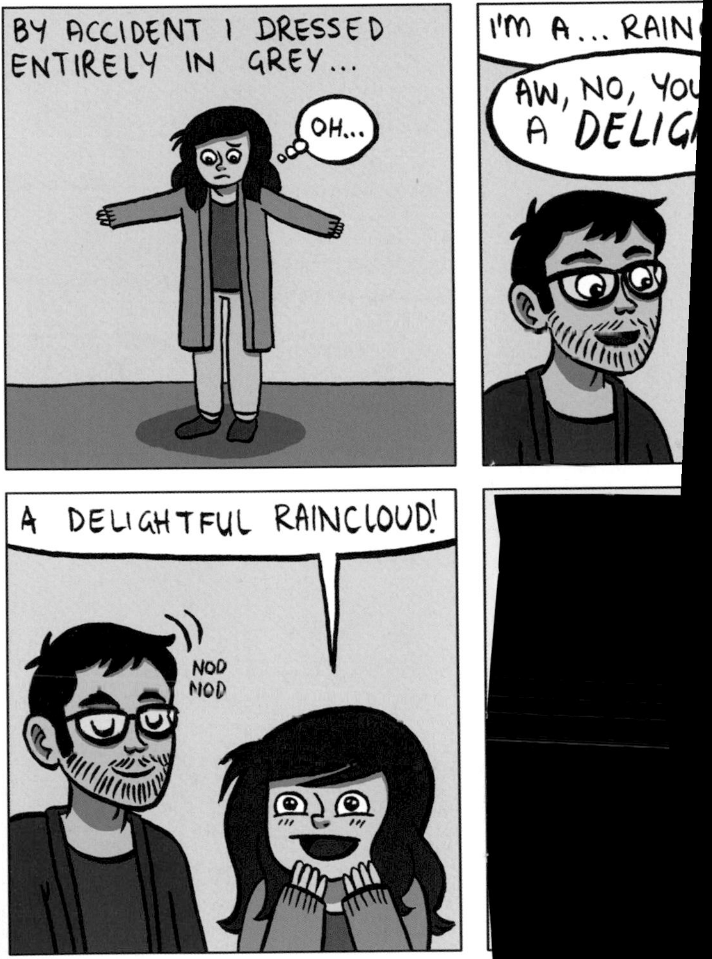
BY ACCIDENT I DRESSED ENTIRELY IN GREY...
OH...
I'M A... RAIN
AW, NO, YO
A DELIG
A DELIGHTFUL RAINCLOUD!
NOD NOD

Raincloud Rachael looked a lot le
At least she looks like she

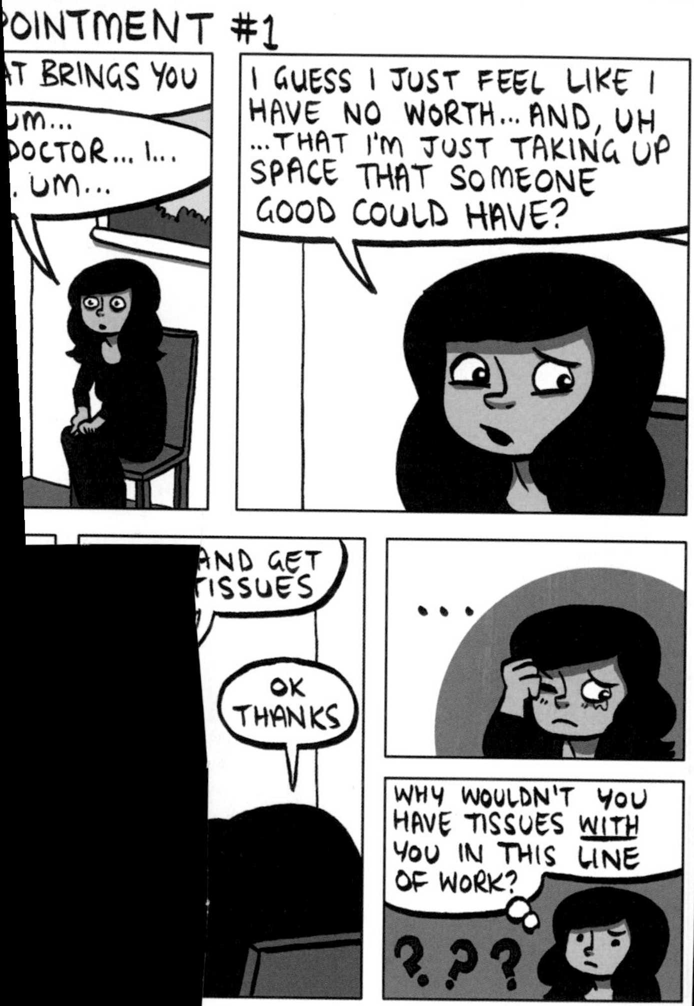
POINTMENT #1
AT BRINGS YOU
UM... DOCTOR... I... . UM...
I GUESS I JUST FEEL LIKE I HAVE NO WORTH... AND, UH ...THAT I'M JUST TAKING UP SPACE THAT SOMEONE GOOD COULD HAVE?
[redacted] AND GET [redacted] TISSUES
OK THANKS
...
WHY WOULDN'T YOU HAVE TISSUES WITH YOU IN THIS LINE OF WORK?
???

[redacted] anel 1 is indicative of how
[redacted] TABLE I am with this situation.

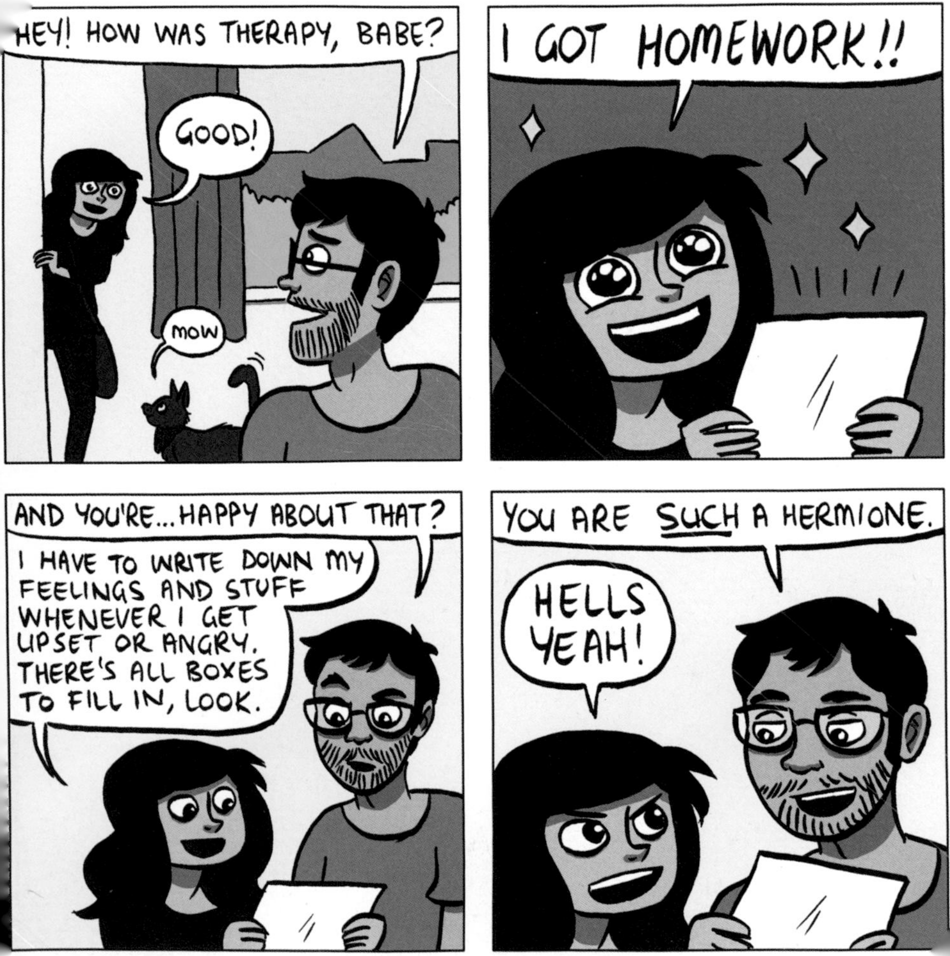
HEY! HOW WAS THERAPY, BABE?
GOOD!
MOW
I GOT HOMEWORK!!
AND YOU'RE... HAPPY ABOUT THAT?
I HAVE TO WRITE DOWN MY FEELINGS AND STUFF WHENEVER I GET UPSET OR ANGRY. THERE'S ALL BOXES TO FILL IN, LOOK.
YOU ARE SUCH A HERMIONE.
HELLS YEAH!

"I hope something upsets me this afternoon so I can do my *homework* yaaay!"

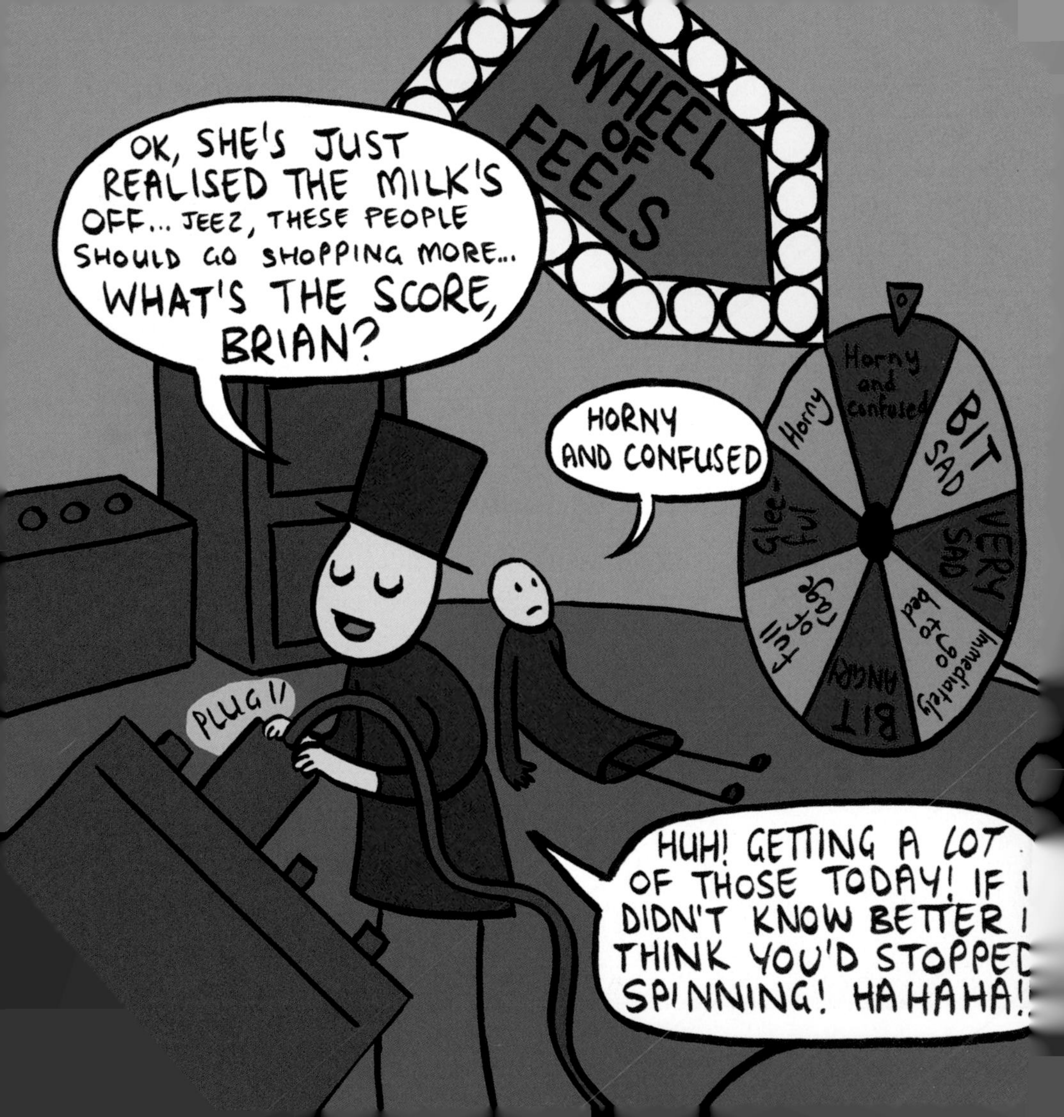
WHEEL OF FEELS
OK, SHE'S JUST REALISED THE MILK'S OFF... JEEZ, THESE PEOPLE SHOULD GO SHOPPING MORE... WHAT'S THE SCORE, BRIAN?
HORNY AND CONFUSED
Horny
Horny and confused
BIT SAD
VERY SAD
Immediately go to bed
BIT ANGRY
full of rage
Glee-ful
PLUG!!
HUH! GETTING A LOT OF THOSE TODAY! IF I DIDN'T KNOW BETTER I THINK YOU'D STOPPED SPINNING! HAHAHA!

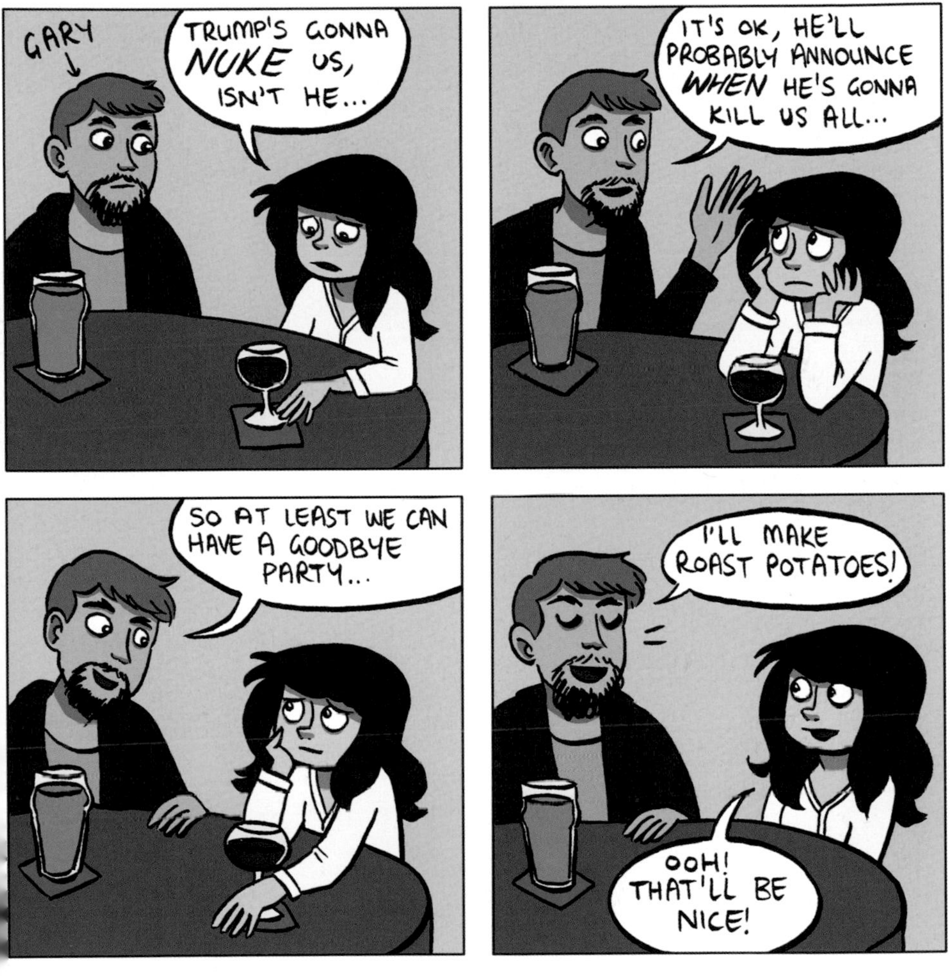
GARY
TRUMP'S GONNA *NUKE* US, ISN'T HE...
IT'S OK, HE'LL PROBABLY ANNOUNCE *WHEN* HE'S GONNA KILL US ALL...
SO AT LEAST WE CAN HAVE A GOODBYE PARTY...
I'LL MAKE ROAST POTATOES!
OOH! THAT'LL BE NICE!

When you're worried about the nuclear apocalypse and your friend manages to make you happy about potatoes ... hold onto that friend.

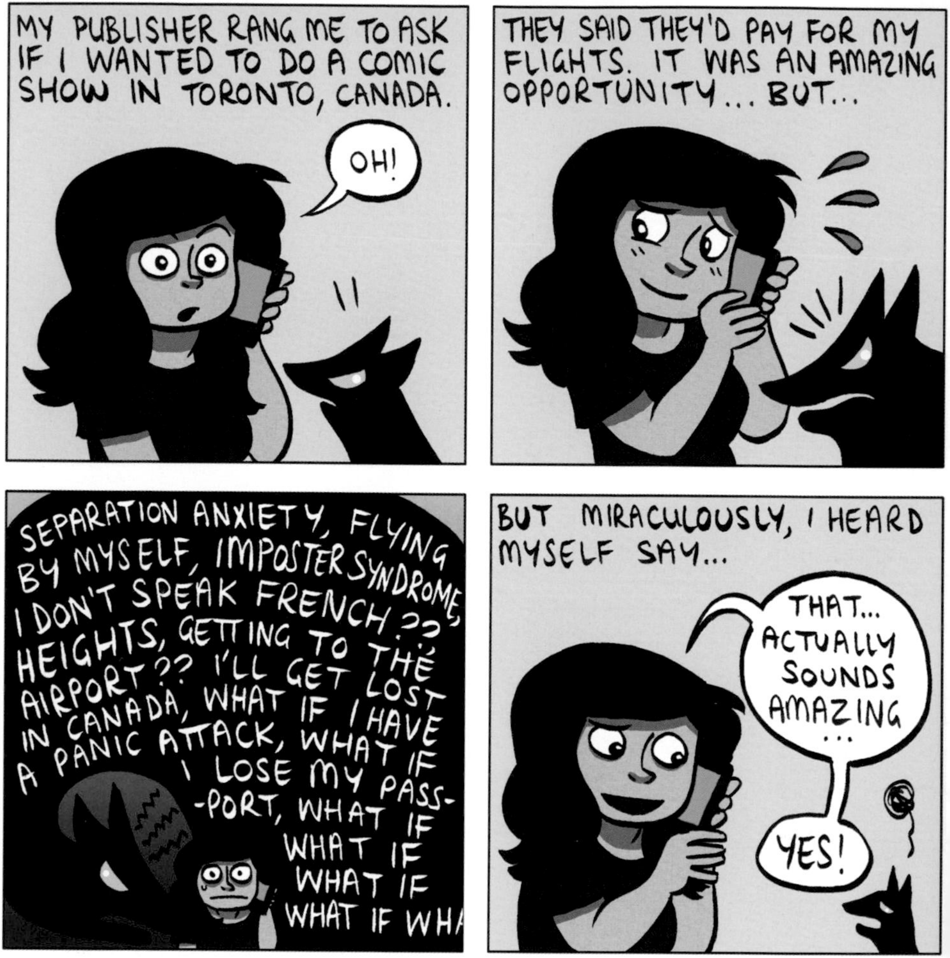
MY PUBLISHER RANG ME TO ASK IF I WANTED TO DO A COMIC SHOW IN TORONTO, CANADA.
OH!
THEY SAID THEY'D PAY FOR MY FLIGHTS. IT WAS AN AMAZING OPPORTUNITY... BUT...
SEPARATION ANXIETY, FLYING BY MYSELF, IMPOSTER SYNDROME, I DON'T SPEAK FRENCH?? HEIGHTS, GETTING TO THE AIRPORT?? I'LL GET LOST IN CANADA, WHAT IF I HAVE A PANIC ATTACK, WHAT IF I LOSE MY PASS-PORT, WHAT IF WHAT IF WHAT IF WHAT IF WHA
BUT MIRACULOUSLY, I HEARD MYSELF SAY...
THAT... ACTUALLY SOUNDS AMAZING ...
YES!

As you might be able to tell here, my publisher is awesome and is very patient with me!

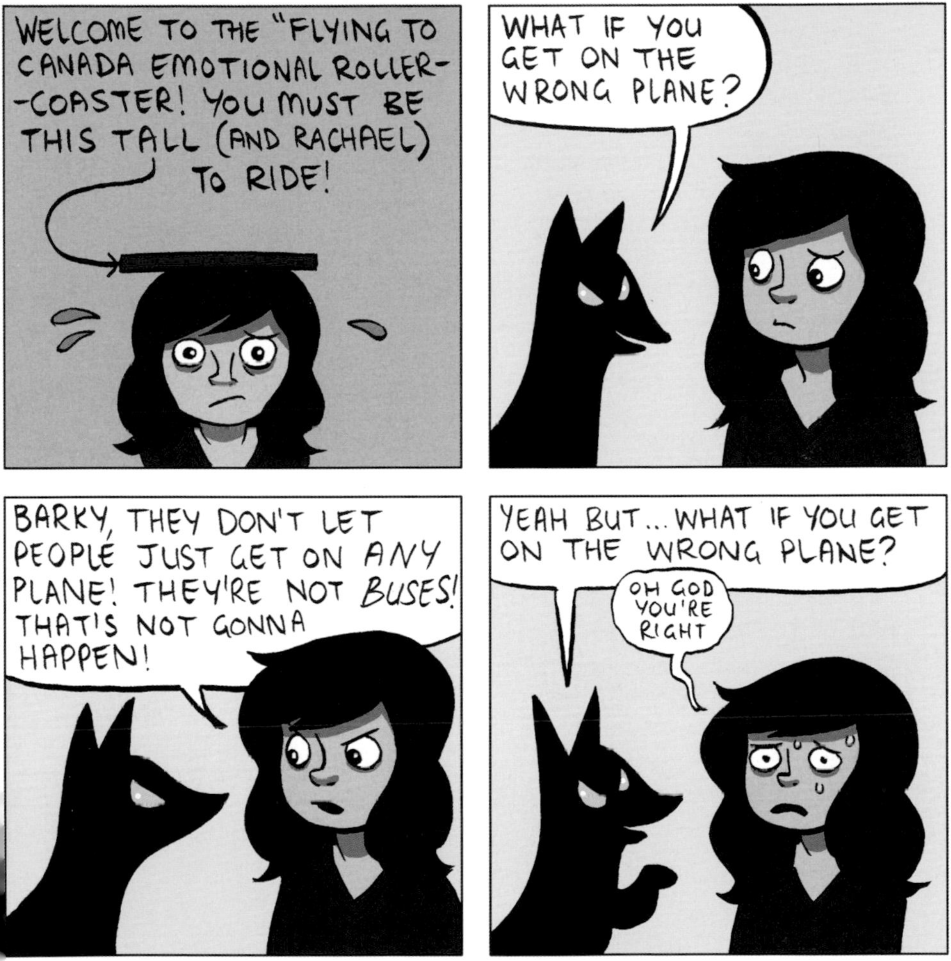
WELCOME TO THE "FLYING TO CANADA EMOTIONAL ROLLER-COASTER! YOU MUST BE THIS TALL (AND RACHAEL) TO RIDE!
WHAT IF YOU GET ON THE WRONG PLANE?
BARKY, THEY DON'T LET PEOPLE JUST GET ON *ANY* PLANE! THEY'RE NOT *BUSES*! THAT'S NOT GONNA HAPPEN!
YEAH BUT... WHAT IF YOU GET ON THE WRONG PLANE?
OH GOD YOU'RE RIGHT

Logic: 0. Repeating the exact same thing as if it is a new and different point: 1.

FLYING TO CANADA

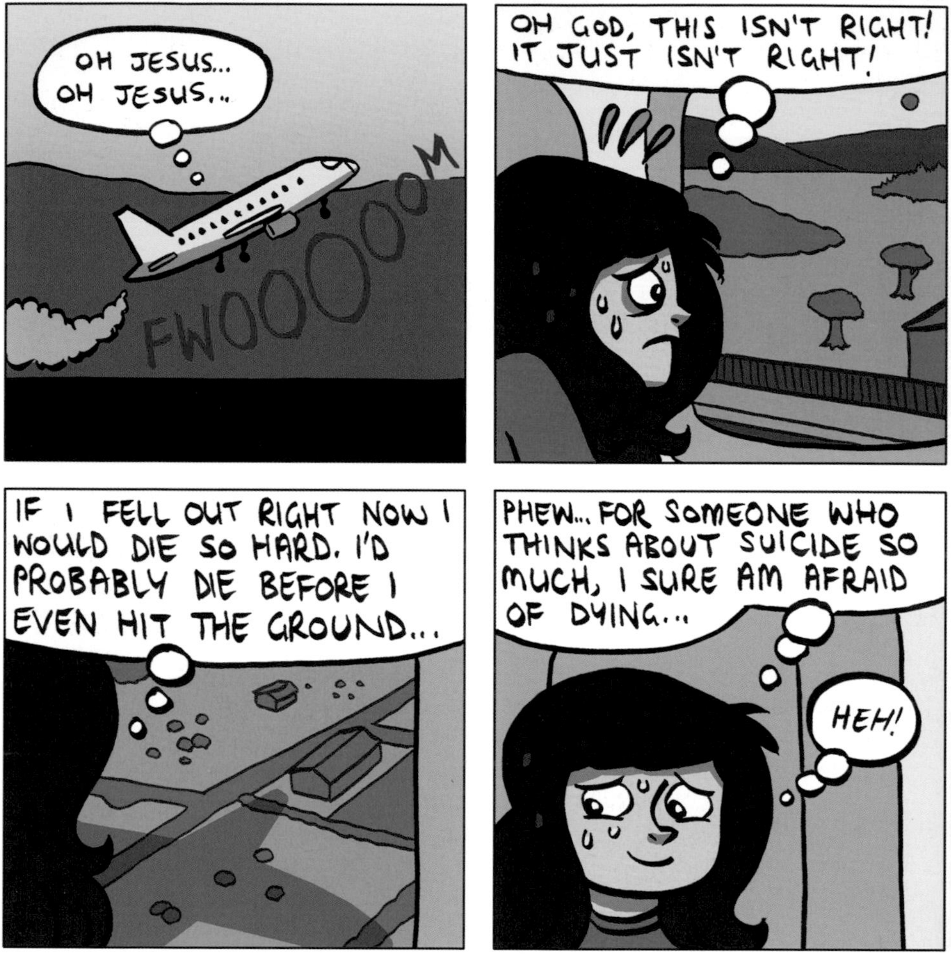
OH JESUS... OH JESUS...
FWOOOOOOOM
OH GOD, THIS ISN'T RIGHT! IT JUST ISN'T RIGHT!
IF I FELL OUT RIGHT NOW I WOULD DIE SO HARD. I'D PROBABLY DIE BEFORE I EVEN HIT THE GROUND...
PHEW... FOR SOMEONE WHO THINKS ABOUT SUICIDE SO MUCH, I SURE AM AFRAID OF DYING...
HEH!

'I Would Die So Hard' was a much less successful film.

I HAD ONE DAY IN CANADA ALL BY MYSELF. I THOUGHT I WOULD FREAK OUT BUT I ACTUALLY MADE THE MOST OF IT!
I TOOK MYSELF OUT TO A LOVELY BREAKFAST PLACE...

eggs
smoked salmon
avocado
lil cubes of potato!

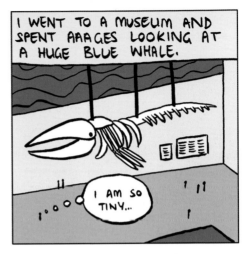

I WENT TO A MUSEUM AND SPENT AAAGES LOOKING AT A HUGE BLUE WHALE.

I AM SO TINY...

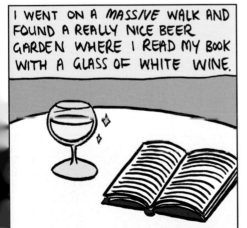

I WENT ON A *MASSIVE* WALK AND FOUND A REALLY NICE BEER GARDEN WHERE I READ MY BOOK WITH A GLASS OF WHITE WINE.

I KNOW IT DOESN'T SOUND LIKE MUCH, BUT I WAS PROUD OF MYSELF FOR NOT JUST HIDING IN MY HOTEL ROOM LIKE I THOUGHT I WOULD.

GO ME!

I totally cried at the blue whale exhibit. You might say ... I blubbered! (Sorry.)

LANDING IN MANCHESTER

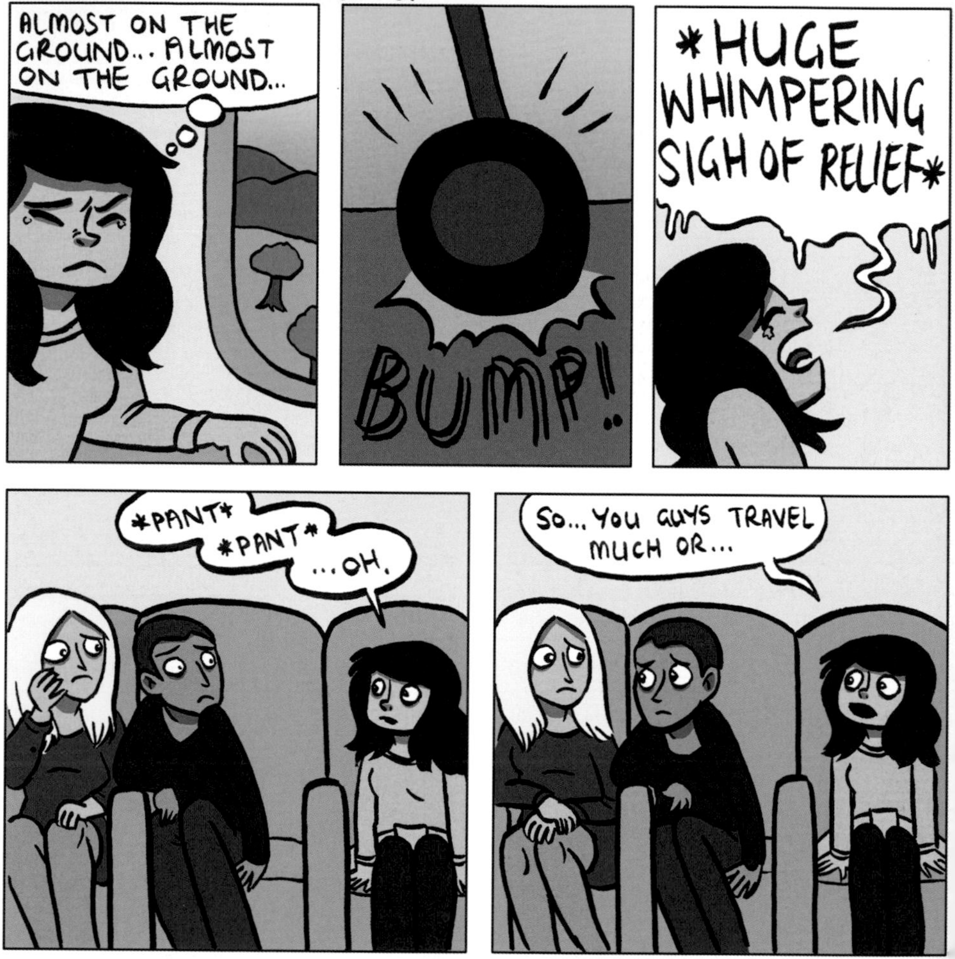
ALMOST ON THE GROUND... ALMOST ON THE GROUND...
BUMP!
HUGE WHIMPERING SIGH OF RELIEF
PANT *PANT* ...OH.
SO... YOU GUYS TRAVEL MUCH OR...

Because the second you land is the perfect time to start breaking the ice with the people you've been sat next to for 7 hours, right?

COMING HOME

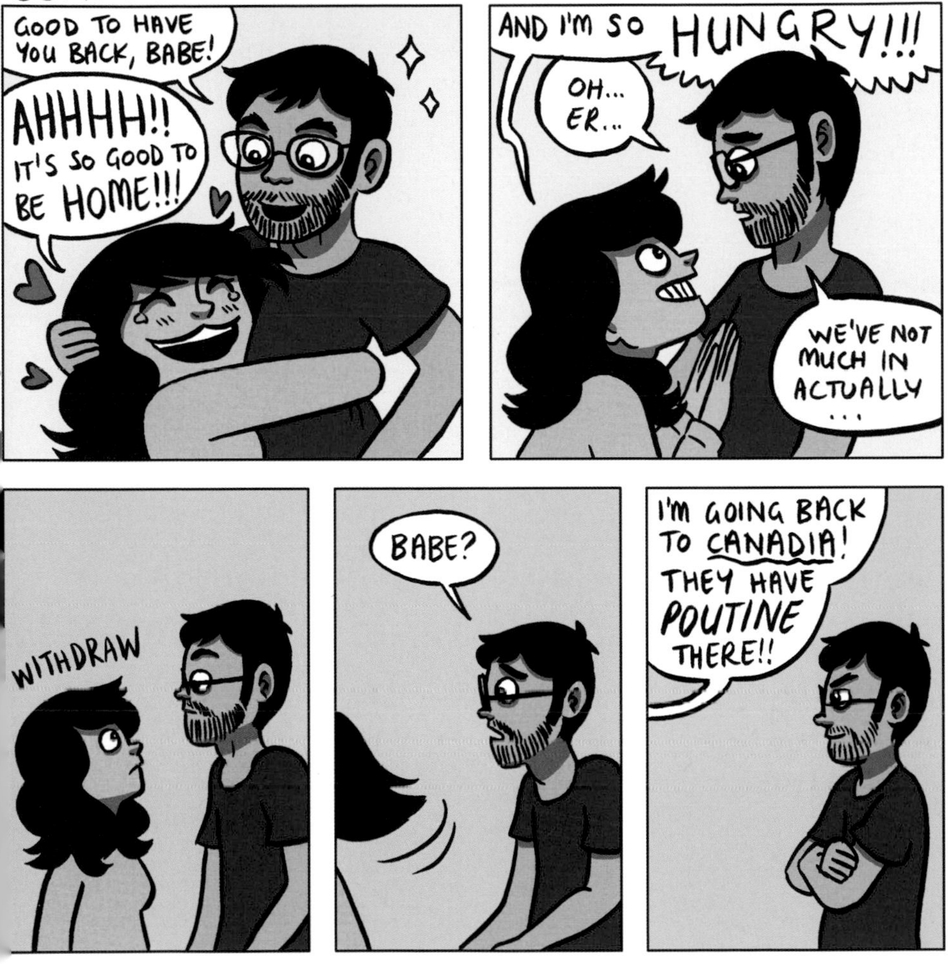
GOOD TO HAVE YOU BACK, BABE!
AHHHH!! IT'S SO GOOD TO BE HOME!!!
AND I'M SO HUNGRY!!!
OH... ER...
WE'VE NOT MUCH IN ACTUALLY ...
WITHDRAW
BABE?
I'M GOING BACK TO CANADIA! THEY HAVE POUTINE THERE!!

Adam is smug in that last panel because he knows I'm about to turn around and hug him again in 0.2 seconds.

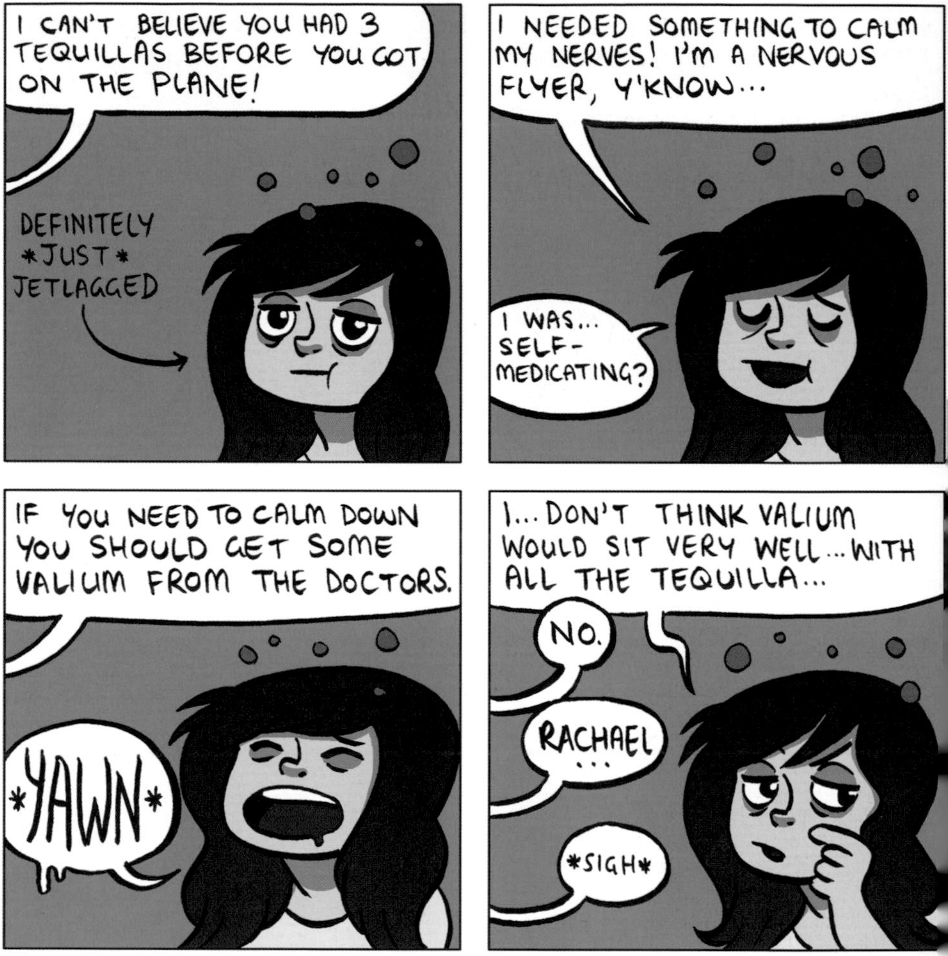
I CAN'T BELIEVE YOU HAD 3 TEQUILLAS BEFORE YOU GOT ON THE PLANE!
DEFINITELY *JUST* JETLAGGED
I NEEDED SOMETHING TO CALM MY NERVES! I'M A NERVOUS FLYER, Y'KNOW...
I WAS... SELF-MEDICATING?
IF YOU NEED TO CALM DOWN YOU SHOULD GET SOME VALIUM FROM THE DOCTORS.
YAWN
I... DON'T THINK VALIUM WOULD SIT VERY WELL... WITH ALL THE TEQUILLA...
NO.
RACHAEL...
SIGH

Go to bed, Rachael.

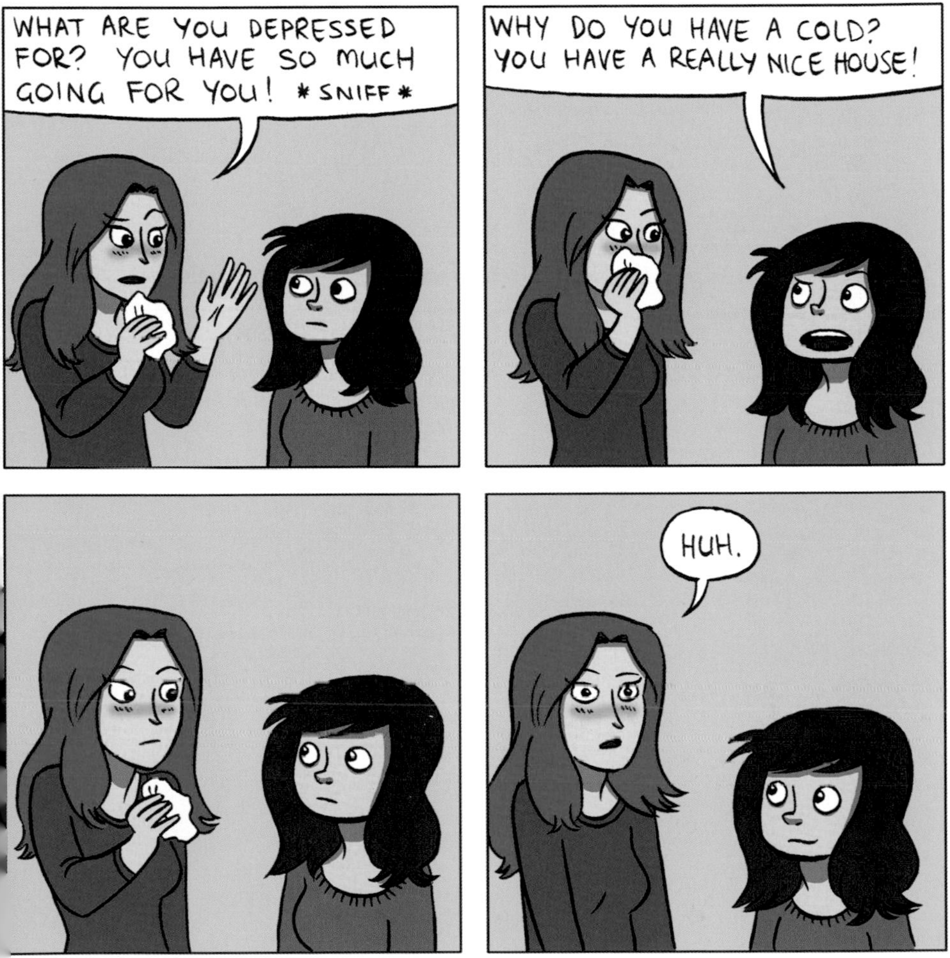
WHAT ARE YOU DEPRESSED FOR? YOU HAVE SO MUCH GOING FOR YOU! *SNIFF*
WHY DO YOU HAVE A COLD? YOU HAVE A REALLY NICE HOUSE!
HUH.

Usually closely followed by "Well have you tried being more positive?"

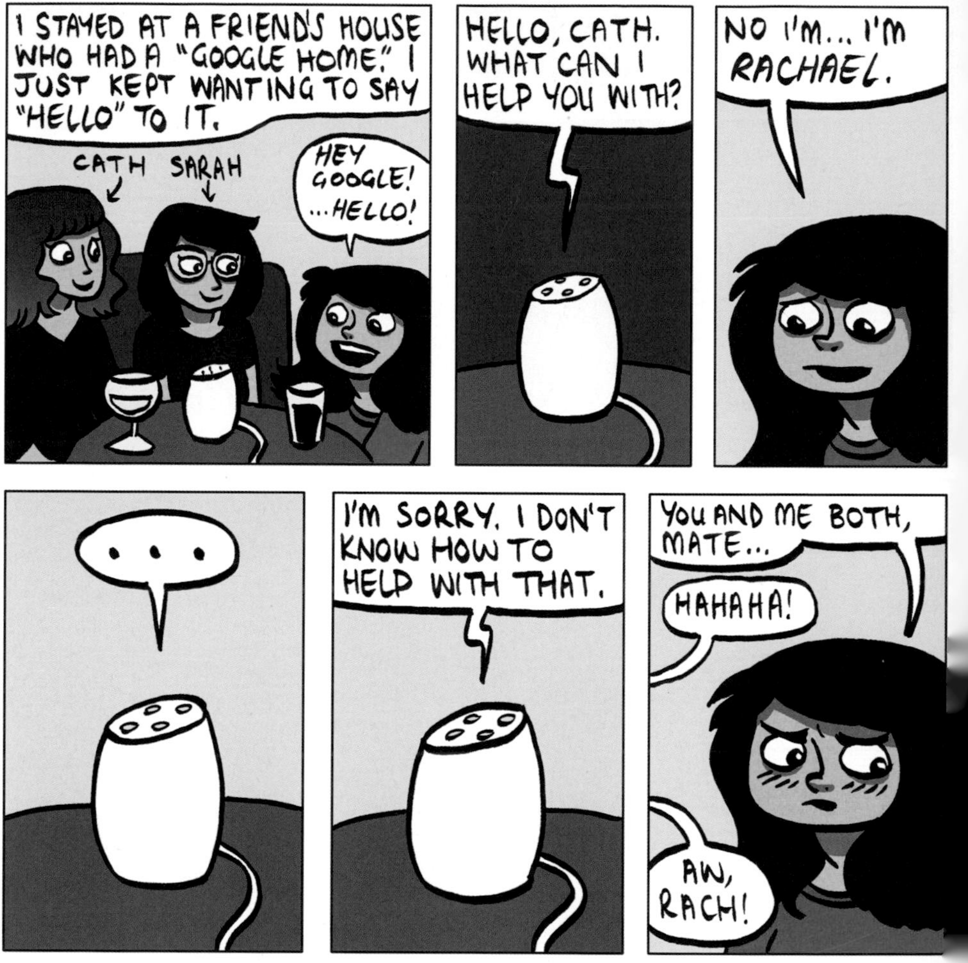
I STAYED AT A FRIEND'S HOUSE WHO HAD A "GOOGLE HOME." I JUST KEPT WANTING TO SAY "HELLO" TO IT.
CATH
SARAH
HEY GOOGLE! ...HELLO!
HELLO, CATH. WHAT CAN I HELP YOU WITH?
NO I'M... I'M RACHAEL.
...
I'M SORRY. I DON'T KNOW HOW TO HELP WITH THAT.
YOU AND ME BOTH, MATE...
HAHAHA!
AW, RACH!

"Hey Google, can you stop being a passive-aggressive dick? Thanks."

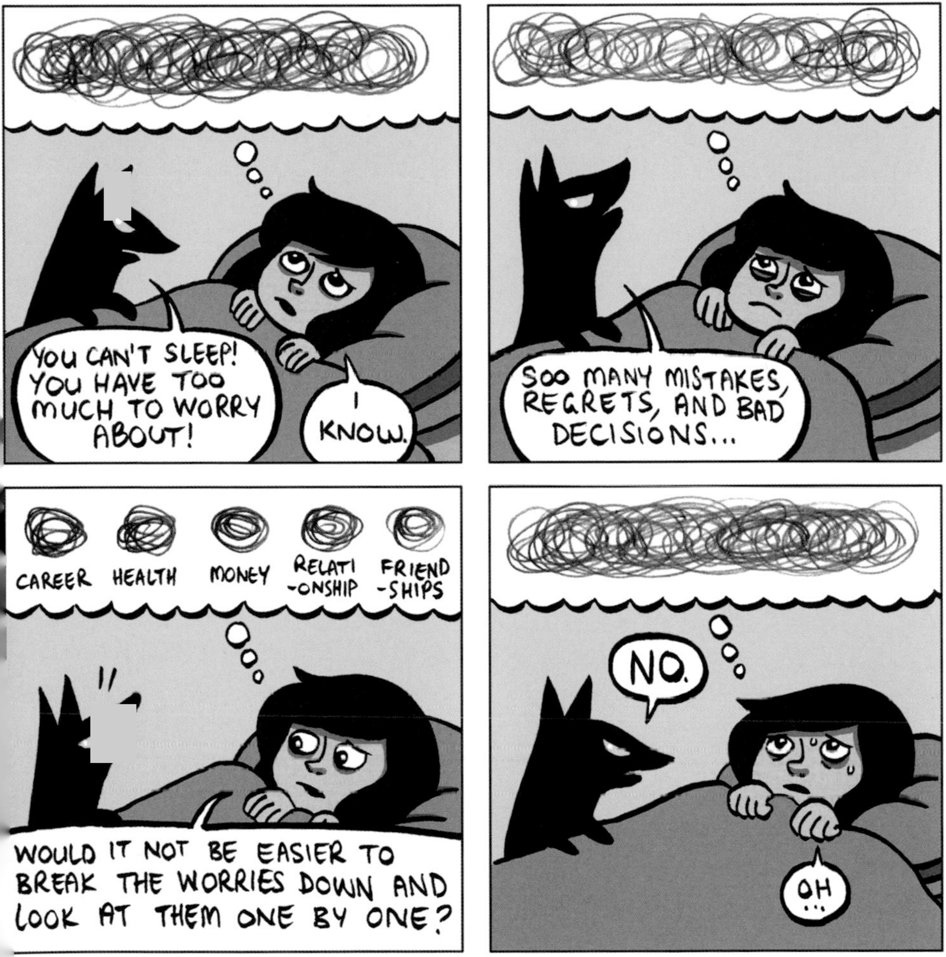
YOU CAN'T SLEEP! YOU HAVE TOO MUCH TO WORRY ABOUT!
I KNOW.
SOO MANY MISTAKES, REGRETS, AND BAD DECISIONS...
CAREER
HEALTH
MONEY
RELATI -ONSHIP
FRIEND -SHIPS
WOULD IT NOT BE EASIER TO BREAK THE WORRIES DOWN AND LOOK AT THEM ONE BY ONE?
NO.
OH ...

Sooooo many scribbly regrets ...

SELF HARM AVOIDANCE TECHNIQUES

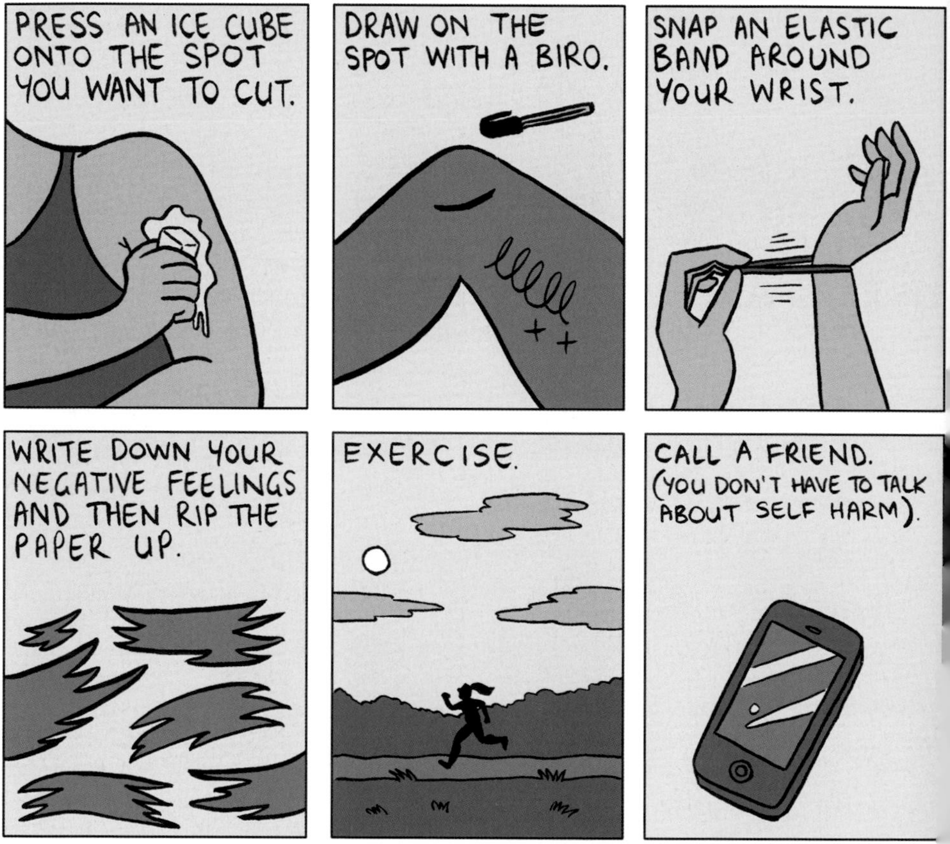
PRESS AN ICE CUBE ONTO THE SPOT YOU WANT TO CUT.
DRAW ON THE SPOT WITH A BIRO.
SNAP AN ELASTIC BAND AROUND YOUR WRIST.
WRITE DOWN YOUR NEGATIVE FEELINGS AND THEN RIP THE PAPER UP.
EXERCISE.
CALL A FRIEND. (YOU DON'T HAVE TO TALK ABOUT SELF HARM).

You’re not alone.

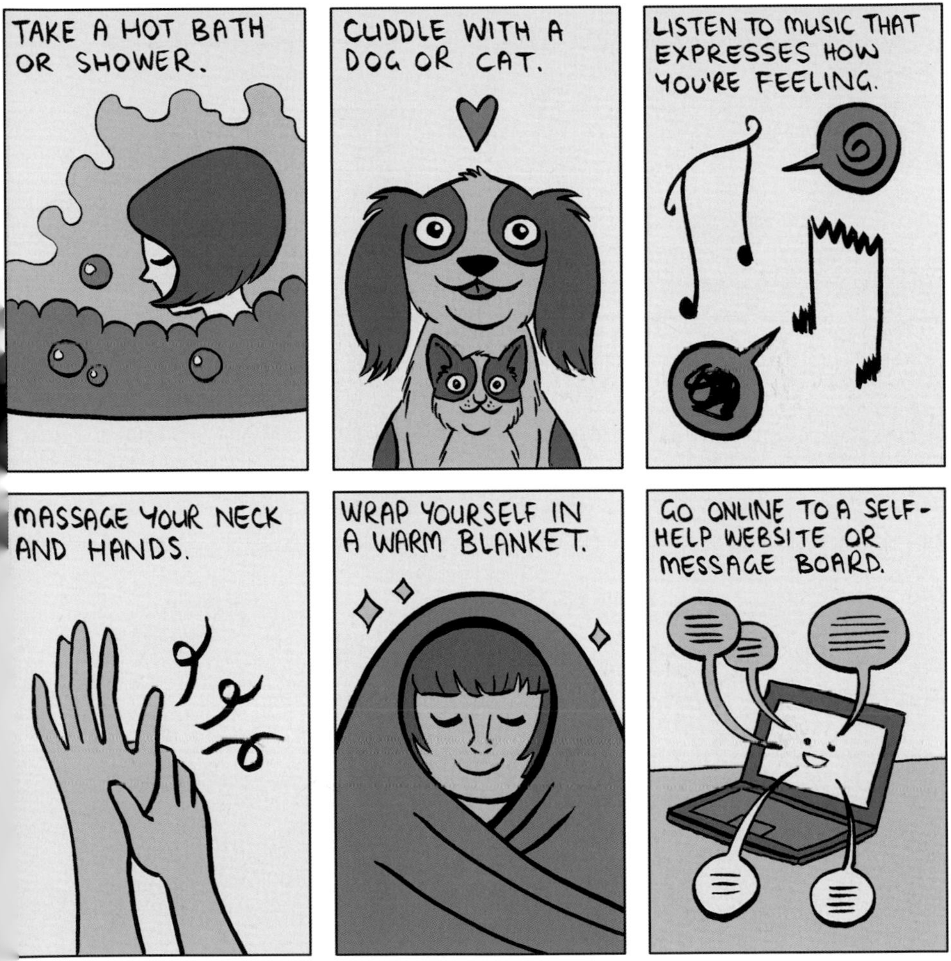
TAKE A HOT BATH OR SHOWER.
CUDDLE WITH A DOG OR CAT.
LISTEN TO MUSIC THAT EXPRESSES HOW YOU'RE FEELING.
MASSAGE YOUR NECK AND HANDS.
WRAP YOURSELF IN A WARM BLANKET.
GO ONLINE TO A SELF-HELP WEBSITE OR MESSAGE BOARD.

Mileage may vary. Find what works for you.
You got this.

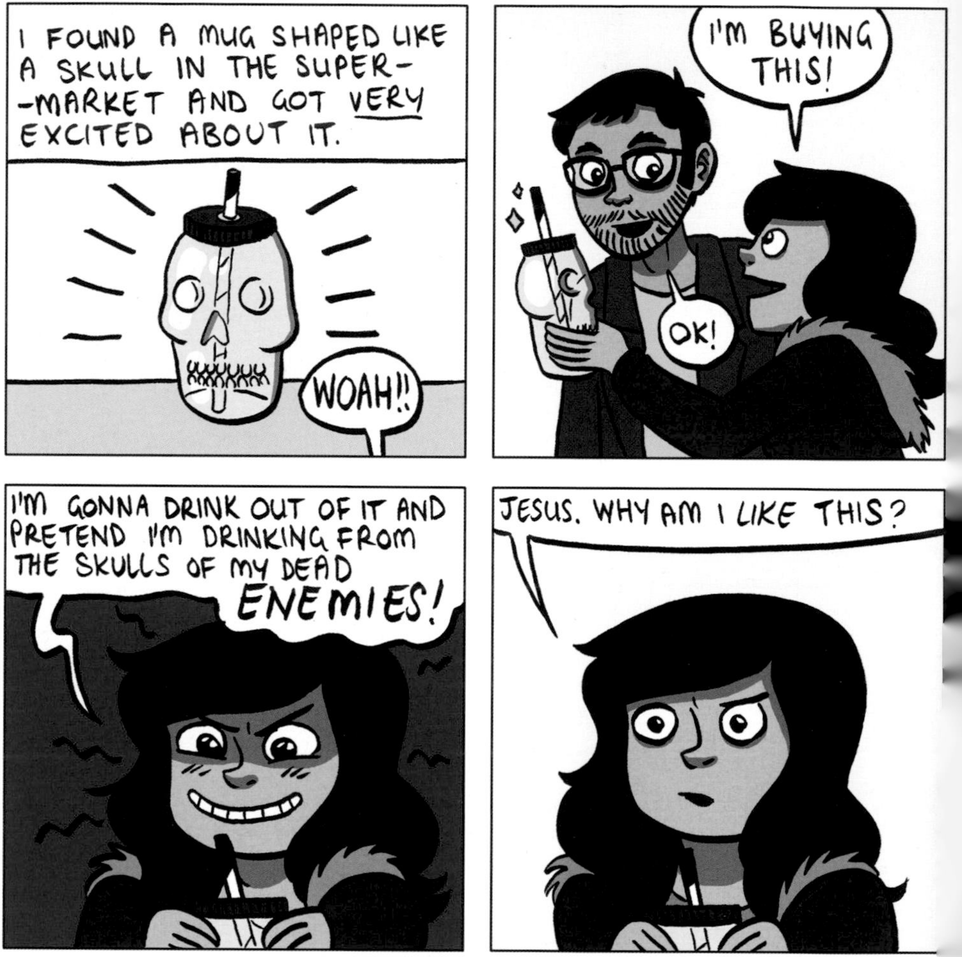
I FOUND A MUG SHAPED LIKE A SKULL IN THE SUPER--MARKET AND GOT VERY EXCITED ABOUT IT.
WOAH!!
I'M BUYING THIS!
OK!
I'M GONNA DRINK OUT OF IT AND PRETEND I'M DRINKING FROM THE SKULLS OF MY DEAD ENEMIES!
JESUS. WHY AM I LIKE THIS?

As opposed to drinking from the skulls of my LIVE enemies ...
which would be awkward I think.

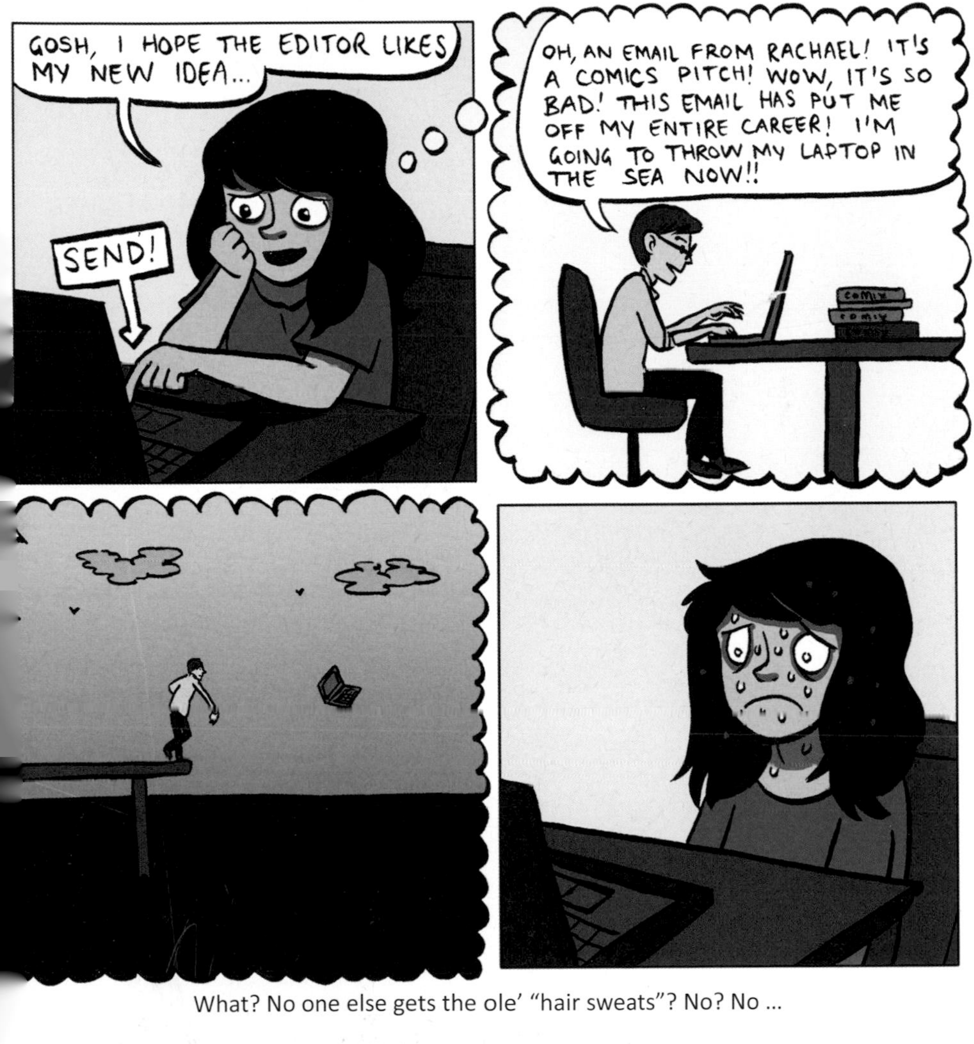
GOSH, I HOPE THE EDITOR LIKES MY NEW IDEA...
SEND!
OH, AN EMAIL FROM RACHAEL! IT'S A COMICS PITCH! WOW, IT'S SO BAD! THIS EMAIL HAS PUT ME OFF MY ENTIRE CAREER! I'M GOING TO THROW MY LAPTOP IN THE SEA NOW!!

What? No one else gets the ole' "hair sweats"? No? No ...

THE BAD TIMES

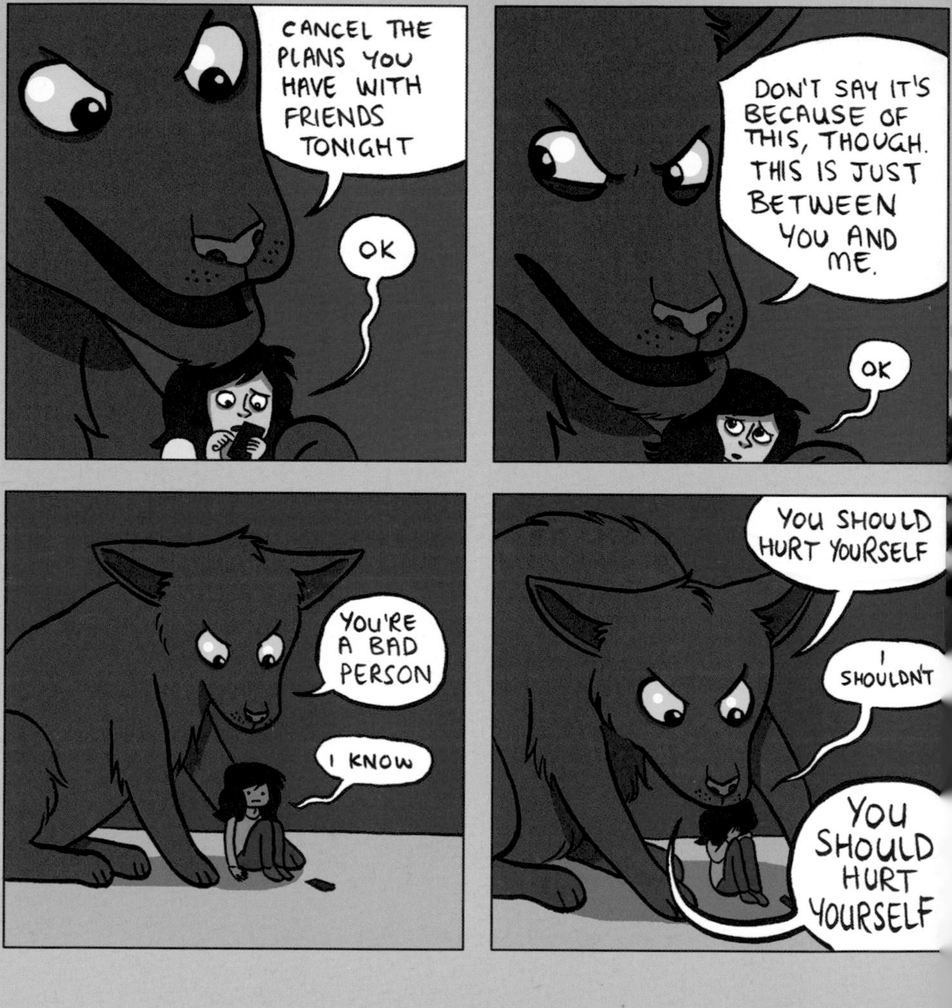
CANCEL THE PLANS YOU HAVE WITH FRIENDS TONIGHT
OK
DON'T SAY IT'S BECAUSE OF THIS, THOUGH. THIS IS JUST BETWEEN YOU AND ME.
OK
YOU'RE A BAD PERSON
I KNOW
YOU SHOULD HURT YOURSELF
I SHOULDN'T
YOU SHOULD HURT YOURSELF

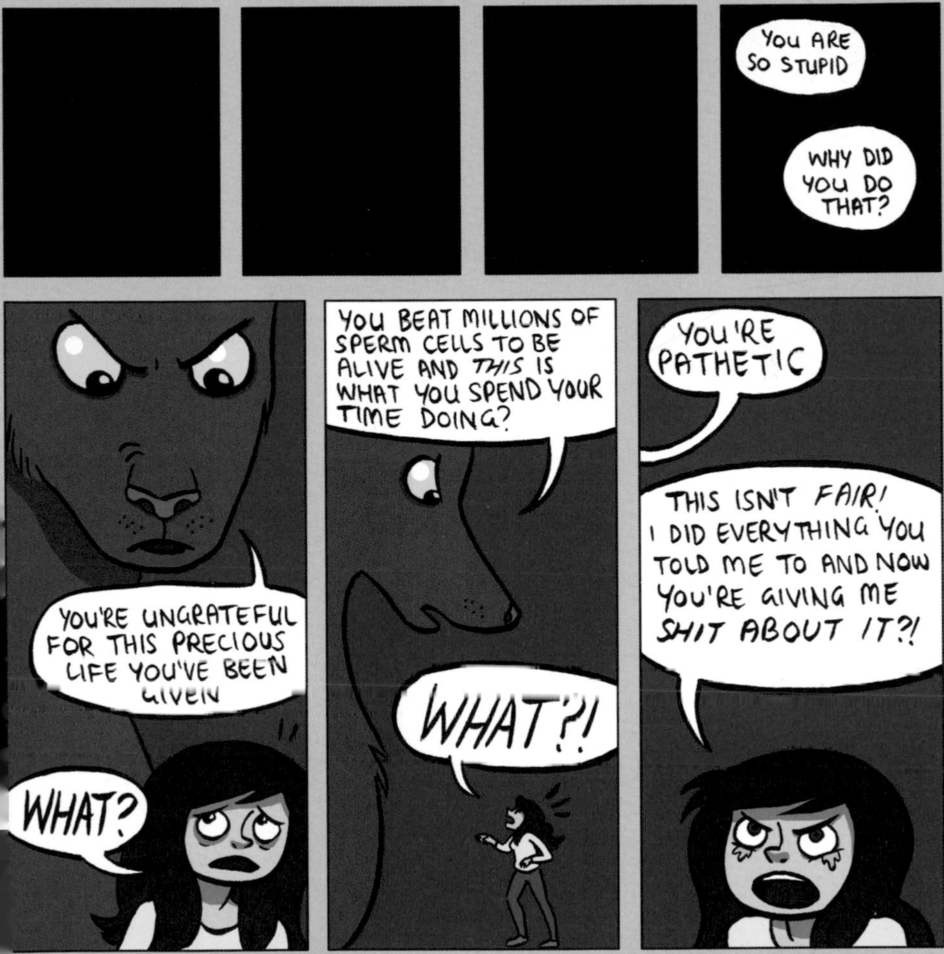

YOU ARE SO STUPID
WHY DID YOU DO THAT?
YOU'RE UNGRATEFUL FOR THIS PRECIOUS LIFE YOU'VE BEEN GIVEN
WHAT?
YOU BEAT MILLIONS OF SPERM CELLS TO BE ALIVE AND THIS IS WHAT YOU SPEND YOUR TIME DOING?
WHAT?!
YOU'RE PATHETIC
THIS ISN'T FAIR! I DID EVERYTHING YOU TOLD ME TO AND NOW YOU'RE GIVING ME SHIT ABOUT IT?!

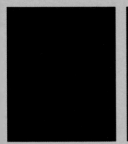

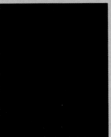

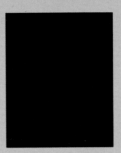

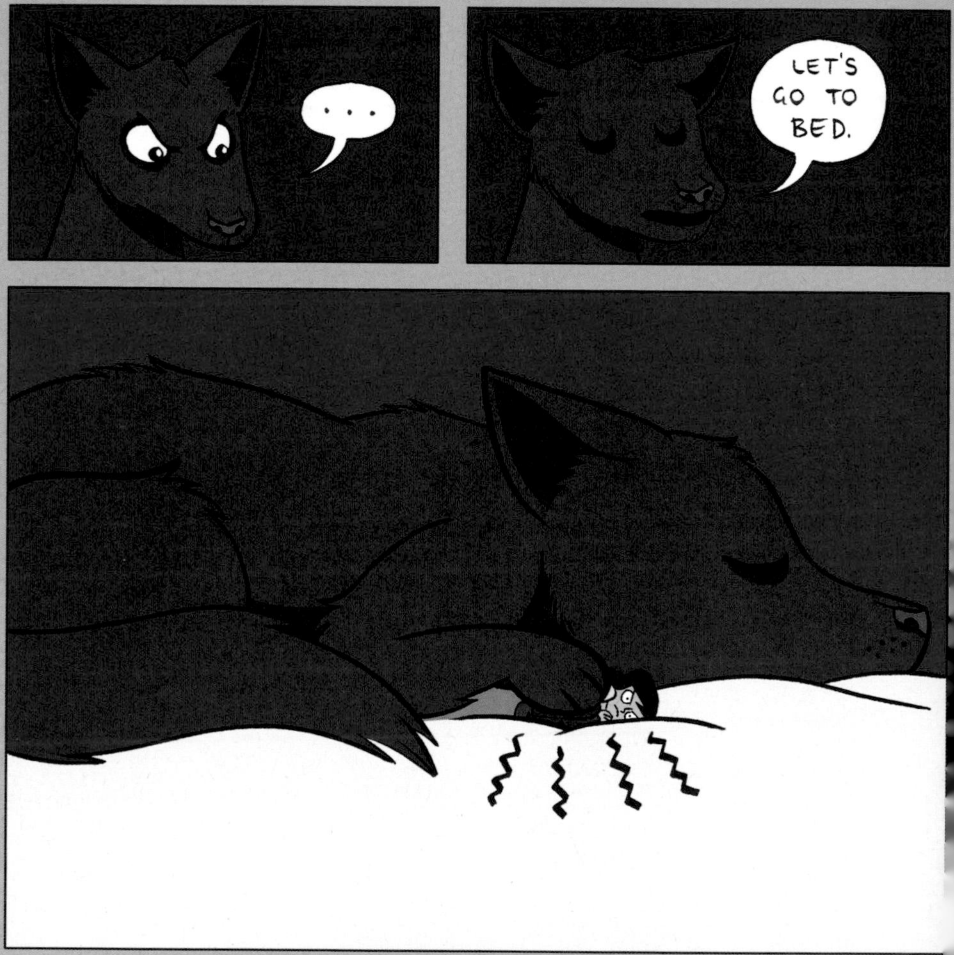
...
LET'S GO TO BED.

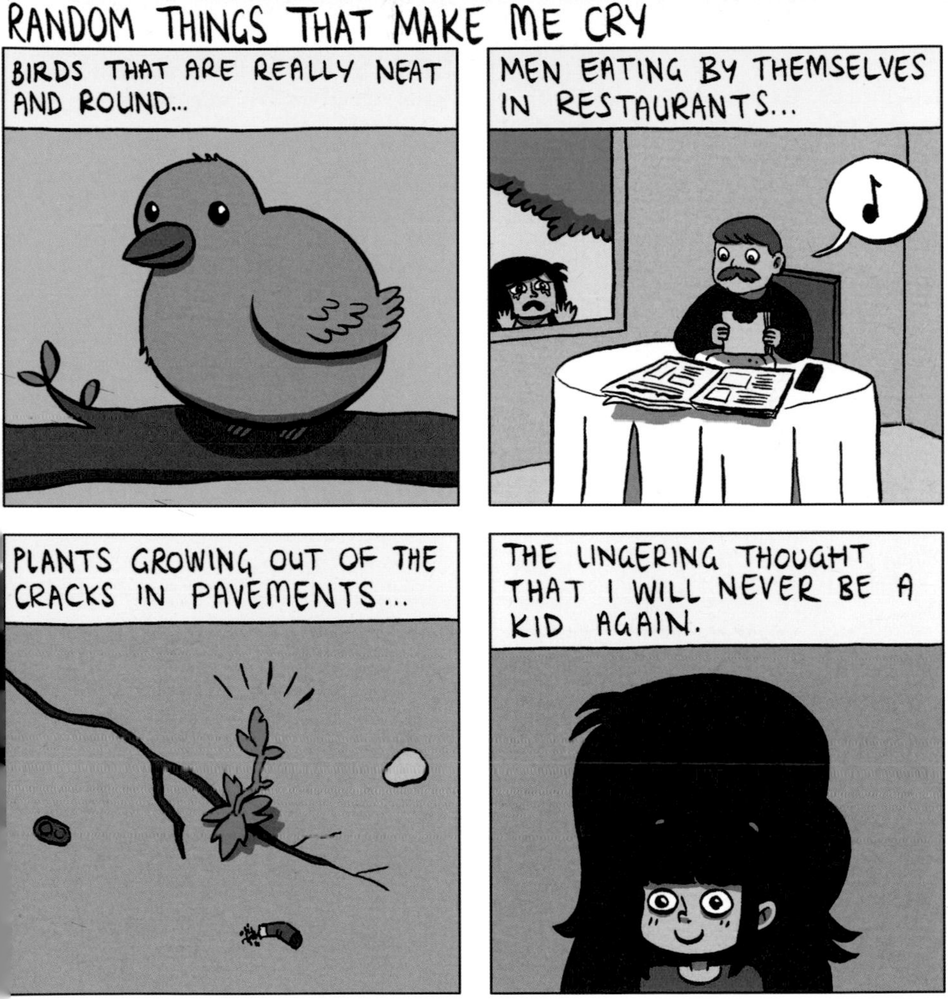
RANDOM THINGS THAT MAKE ME CRY
BIRDS THAT ARE REALLY NEAT AND ROUND...
MEN EATING BY THEMSELVES IN RESTAURANTS...
PLANTS GROWING OUT OF THE CRACKS IN PAVEMENTS...
THE LINGERING THOUGHT THAT I WILL NEVER BE A KID AGAIN.

Those plants, man ... they're just ... trying SO hard in such a harsh world ... *sob*.

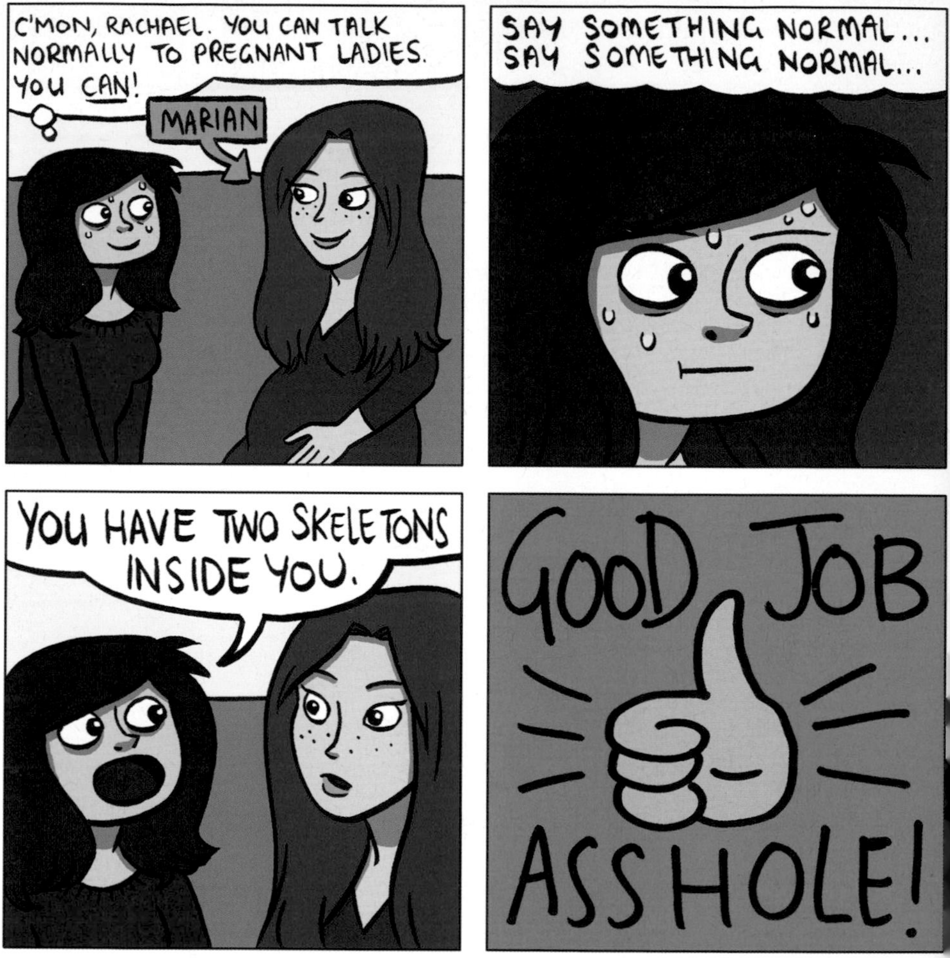
C'MON, RACHAEL. YOU CAN TALK NORMALLY TO PREGNANT LADIES. YOU CAN!
MARIAN
SAY SOMETHING NORMAL... SAY SOMETHING NORMAL...
YOU HAVE TWO SKELETONS INSIDE YOU.
GOOD JOB ASSHOLE!

I PANICKED!!

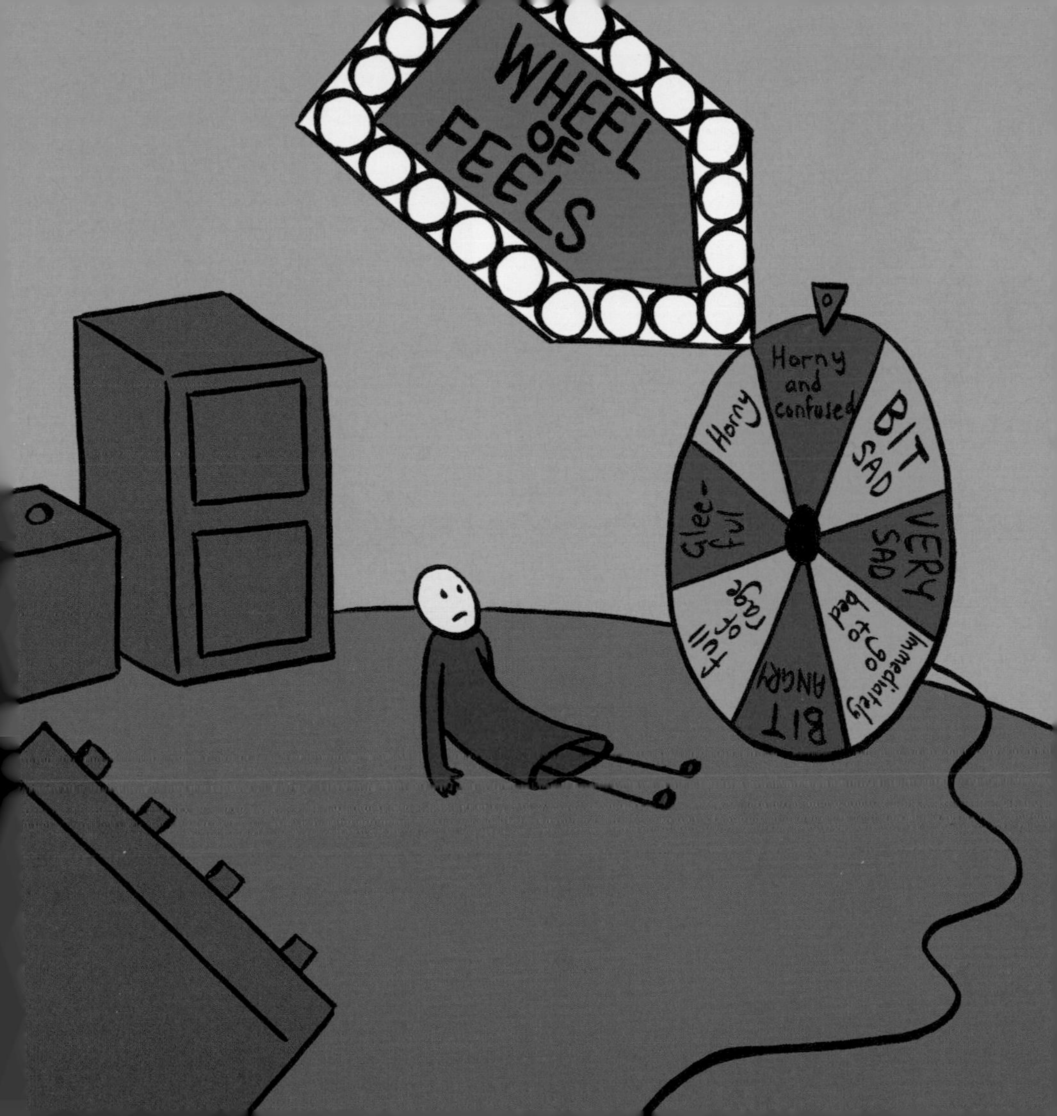
WHEEL OF FEELS
Horny and confused
BIT SAD
VERY SAD
Immediately go to bed
BIT ANGRY
full of rage
Glee-ful
Horny

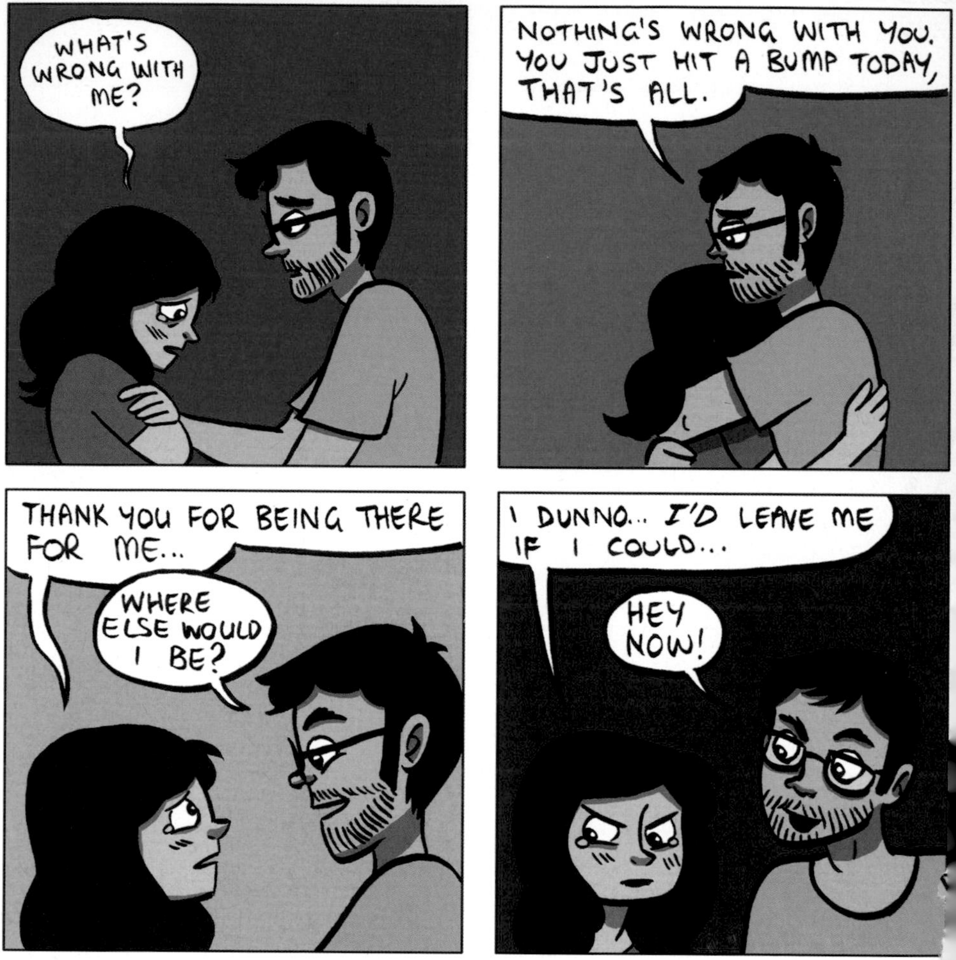
WHAT'S WRONG WITH ME?
NOTHING'S WRONG WITH YOU. YOU JUST HIT A BUMP TODAY, THAT'S ALL.
THANK YOU FOR BEING THERE FOR ME...
WHERE ELSE WOULD I BE?
I DUNNO... I'D LEAVE ME IF I COULD...
HEY NOW!

I hit a bump about once a week ...

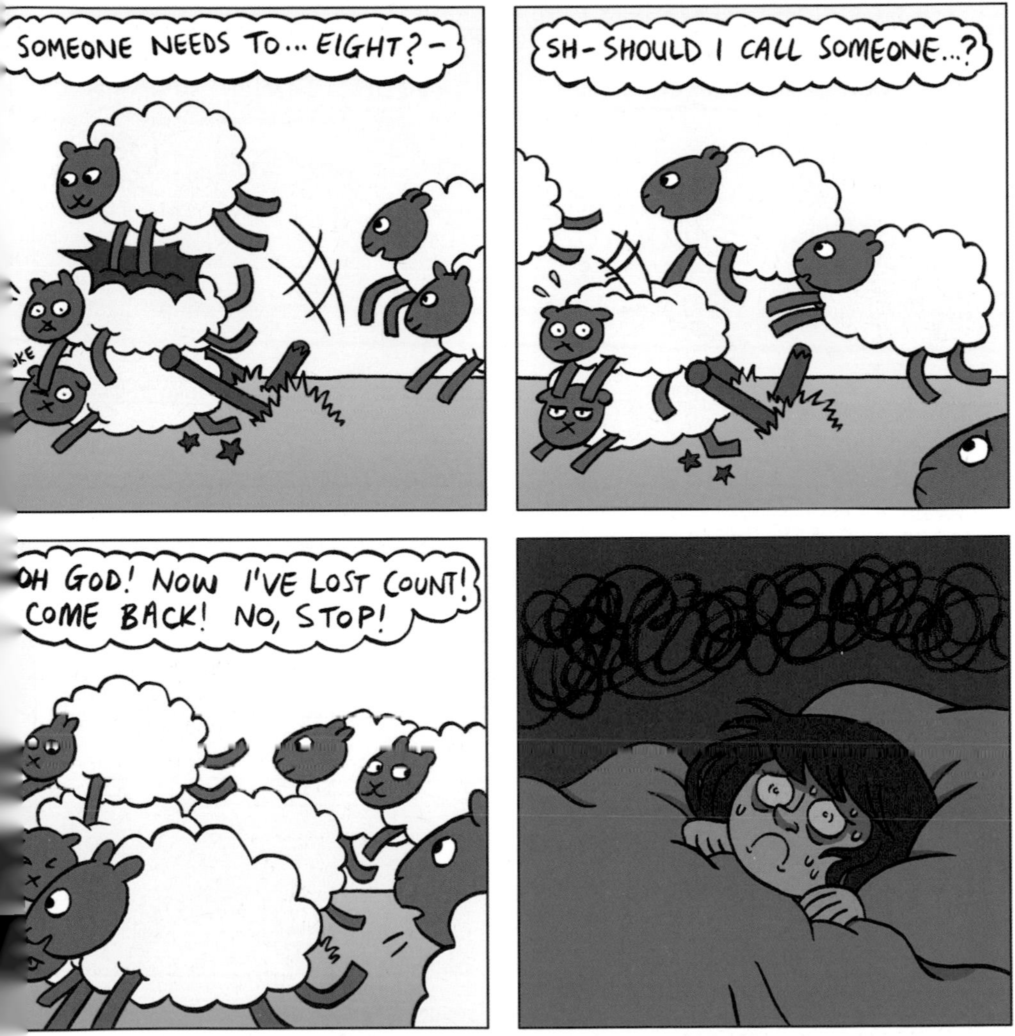
SOMEONE NEEDS TO... EIGHT?-
SH-SHOULD I CALL SOMEONE...?
OH GOD! NOW I'VE LOST COUNT! COME BACK! NO, STOP!

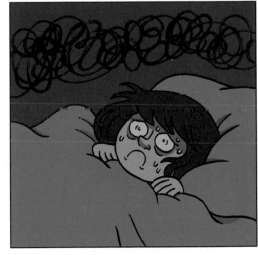

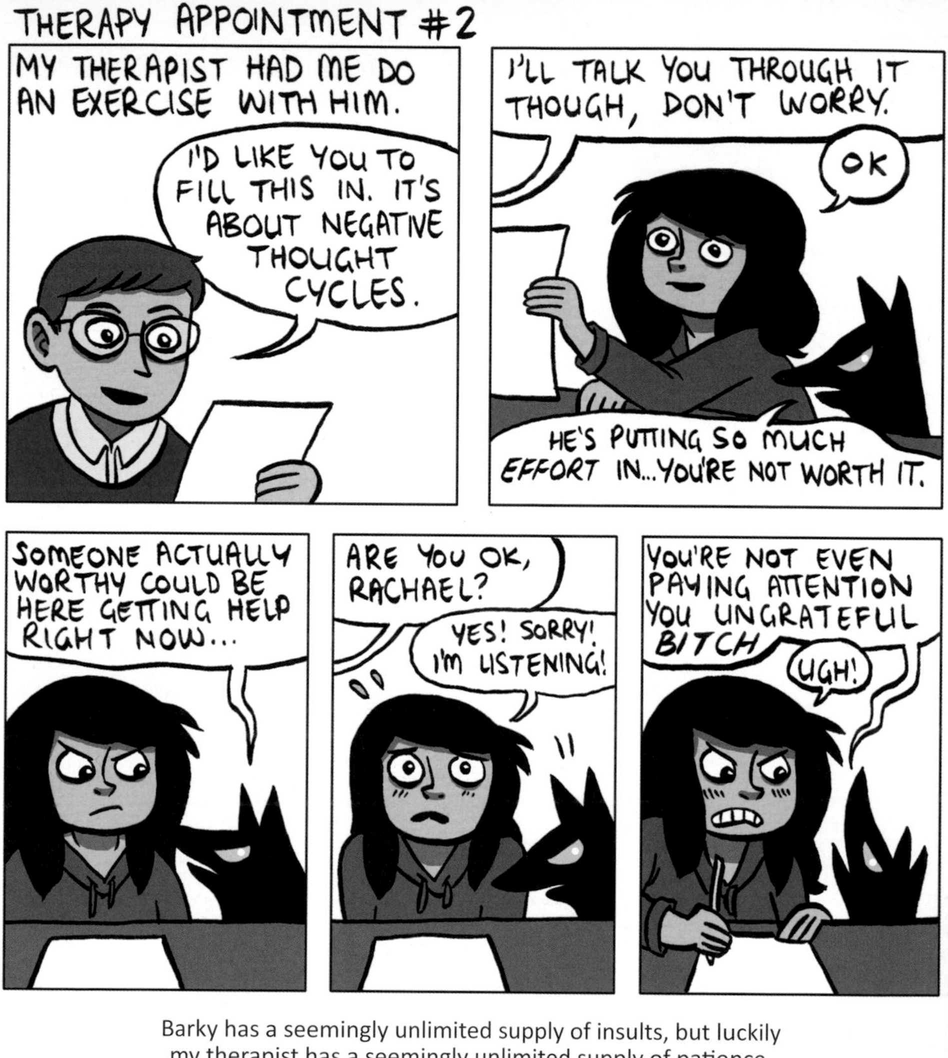
THERAPY APPOINTMENT #2
MY THERAPIST HAD ME DO AN EXERCISE WITH HIM.
I'D LIKE YOU TO FILL THIS IN. IT'S ABOUT NEGATIVE THOUGHT CYCLES.
I'LL TALK YOU THROUGH IT THOUGH, DON'T WORRY.
OK
HE'S PUTTING SO MUCH *EFFORT* IN...YOU'RE NOT WORTH IT.
SOMEONE ACTUALLY WORTHY COULD BE HERE GETTING HELP RIGHT NOW...
ARE YOU OK, RACHAEL?
YES! SORRY! I'M LISTENING!
YOU'RE NOT EVEN PAYING ATTENTION YOU UNGRATEFUL *BITCH*
UGH!

Barky has a seemingly unlimited supply of insults, but luckily my therapist has a seemingly unlimited supply of patience.

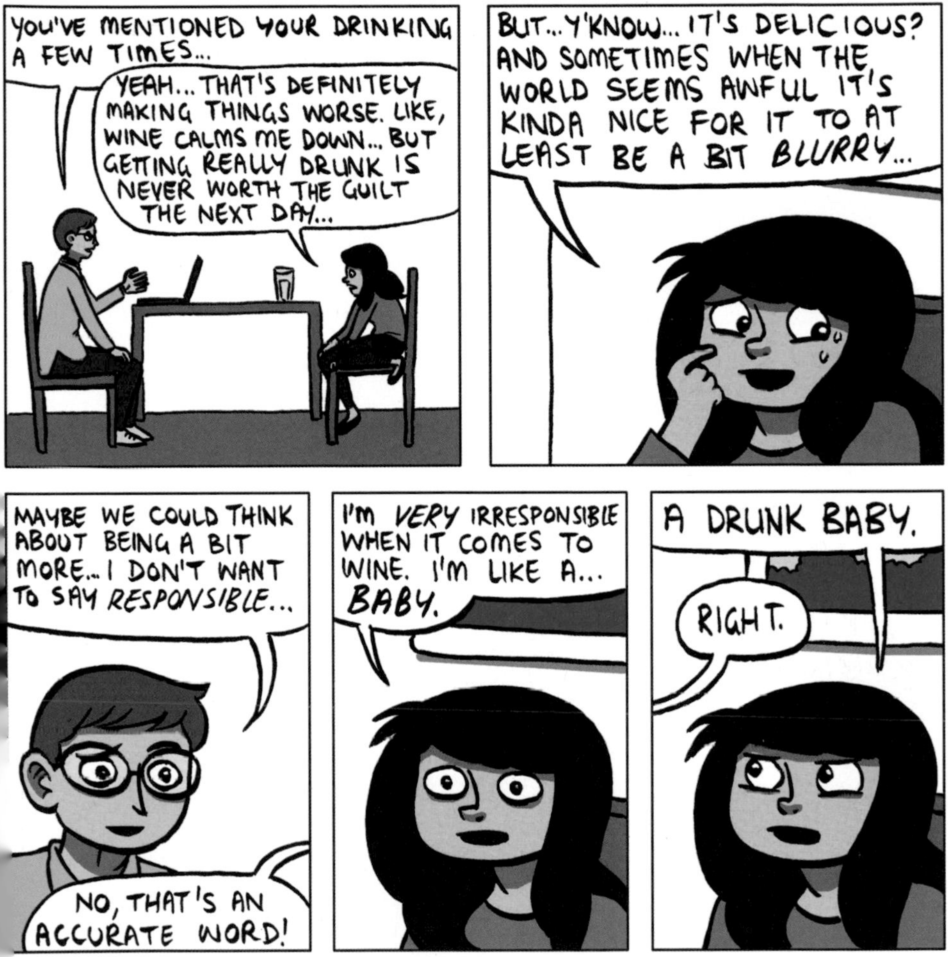
YOU'VE MENTIONED YOUR DRINKING A FEW TIMES...
YEAH... THAT'S DEFINITELY MAKING THINGS WORSE. LIKE, WINE CALMS ME DOWN... BUT GETTING REALLY DRUNK IS NEVER WORTH THE GUILT THE NEXT DAY...
BUT... Y'KNOW... IT'S DELICIOUS? AND SOMETIMES WHEN THE WORLD SEEMS AWFUL IT'S KINDA NICE FOR IT TO AT LEAST BE A BIT BLURRY...
MAYBE WE COULD THINK ABOUT BEING A BIT MORE... I DON'T WANT TO SAY RESPONSIBLE...
NO, THAT'S AN ACCURATE WORD!
I'M VERY IRRESPONSIBLE WHEN IT COMES TO WINE. I'M LIKE A... BABY.
A DRUNK BABY.
RIGHT.

Darn all those babies with their lack of responsibilities and love of alcohol!

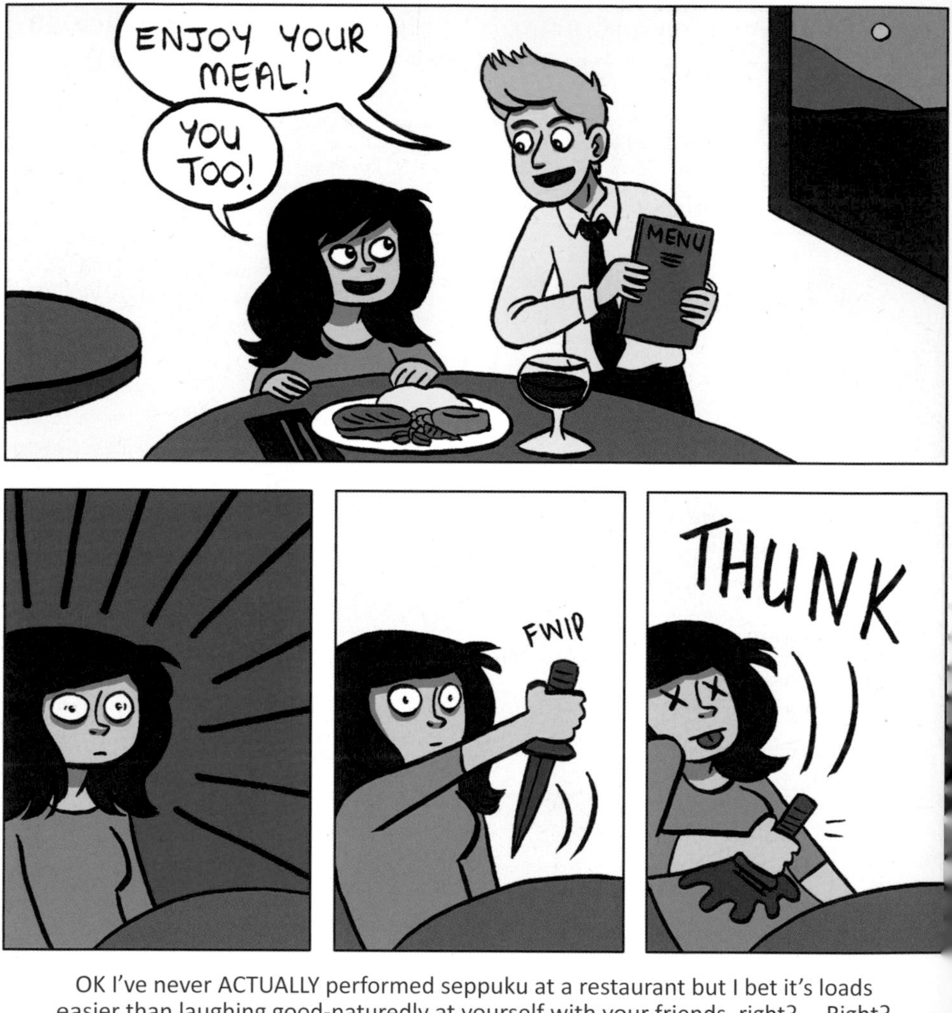
ENJOY YOUR MEAL!
YOU TOO!
MENU
FWIP
THUNK

OK I've never ACTUALLY performed seppuku at a restaurant but I bet it's loads easier than laughing good-naturedly at yourself with your friends, right? ... Right?

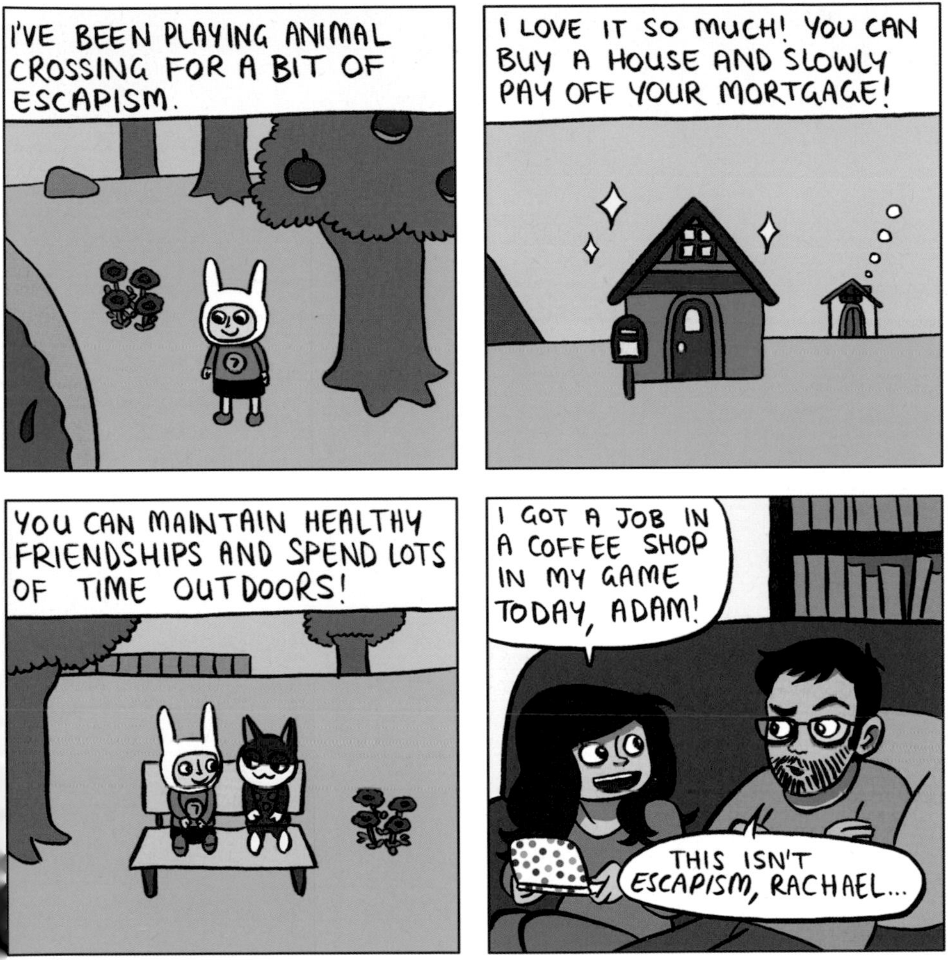
I'VE BEEN PLAYING ANIMAL CROSSING FOR A BIT OF ESCAPISM.
I LOVE IT SO MUCH! YOU CAN BUY A HOUSE AND SLOWLY PAY OFF YOUR MORTGAGE!
YOU CAN MAINTAIN HEALTHY FRIENDSHIPS AND SPEND LOTS OF TIME OUTDOORS!
I GOT A JOB IN A COFFEE SHOP IN MY GAME TODAY, ADAM!
THIS ISN'T ESCAPISM, RACHAEL...

My own house! A job! Fulfilling hobbies and manageable friendships!
It's a millennial's DREAM!

THE GOOD TIMES

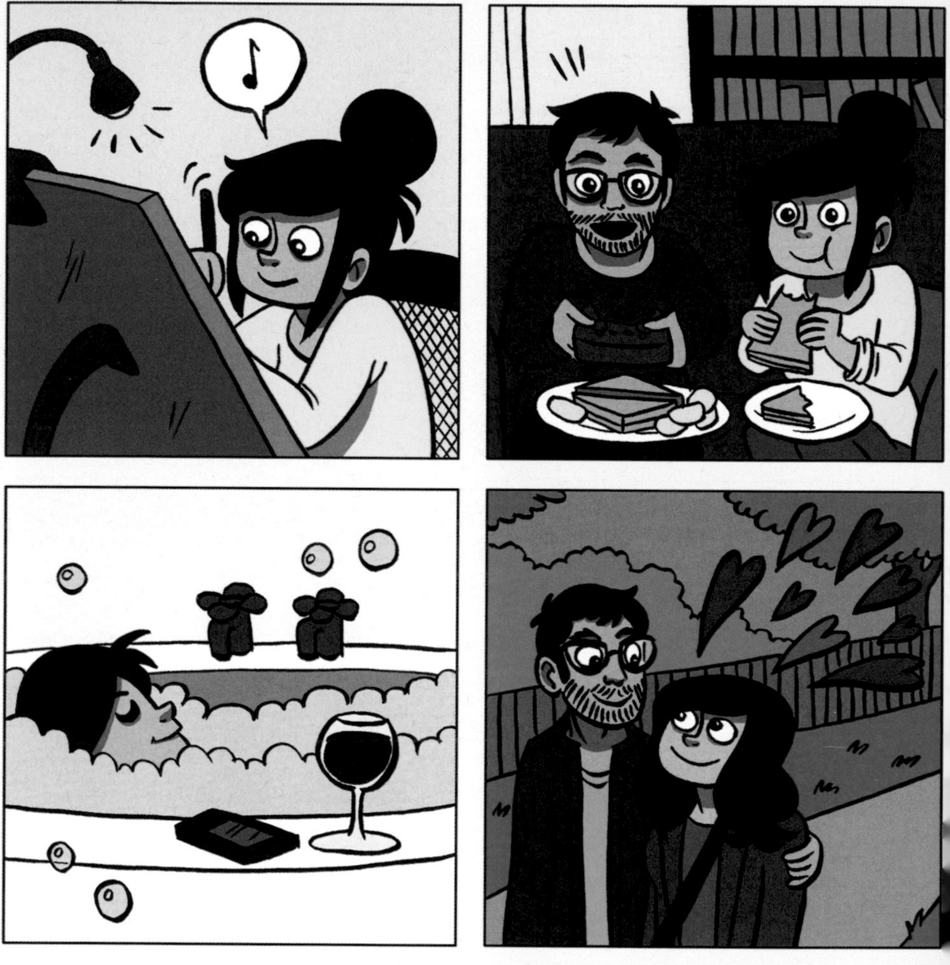

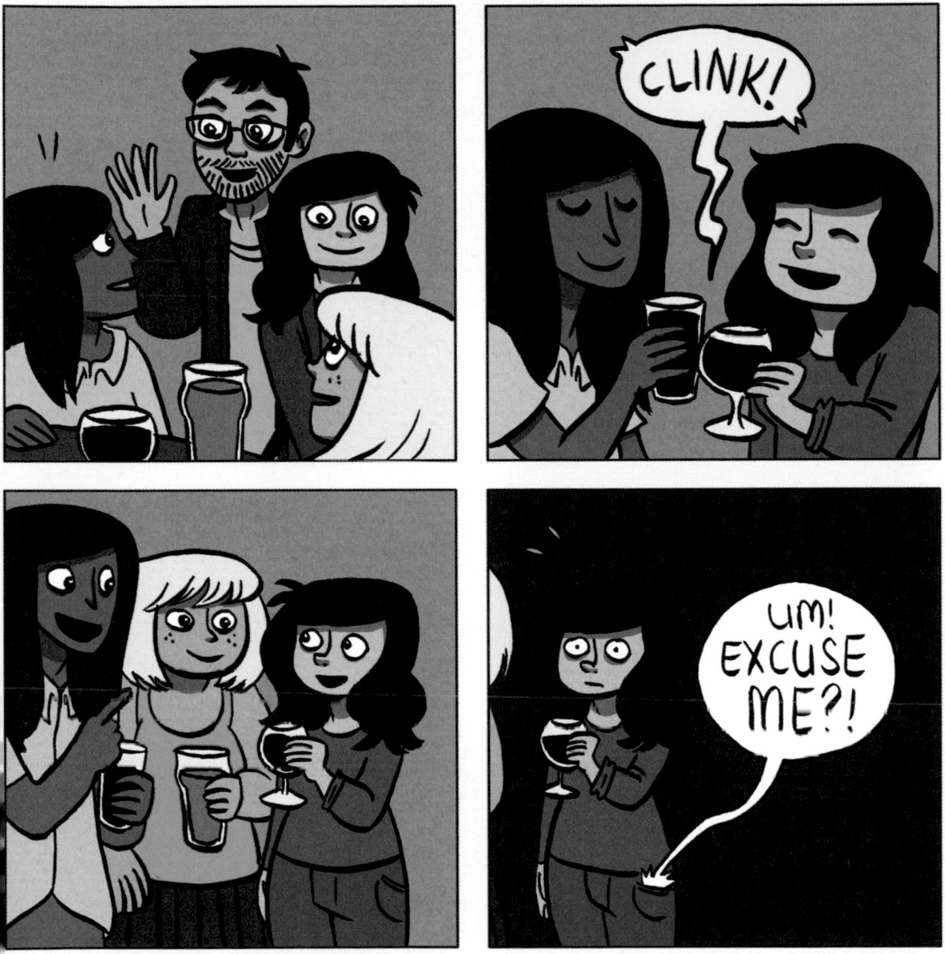
CLINK!
UM! EXCUSE ME?!

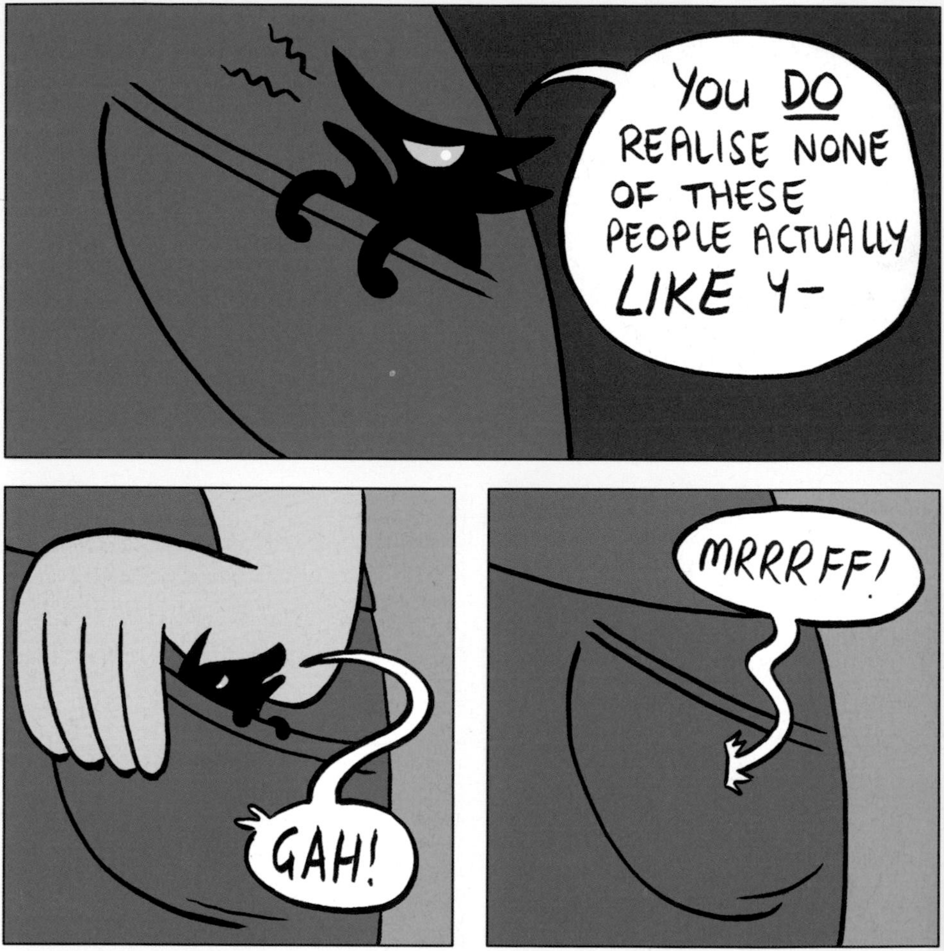

YOU DO REALISE NONE OF THESE PEOPLE ACTUALLY LIKE Y-
GAH!
MRRRFF!

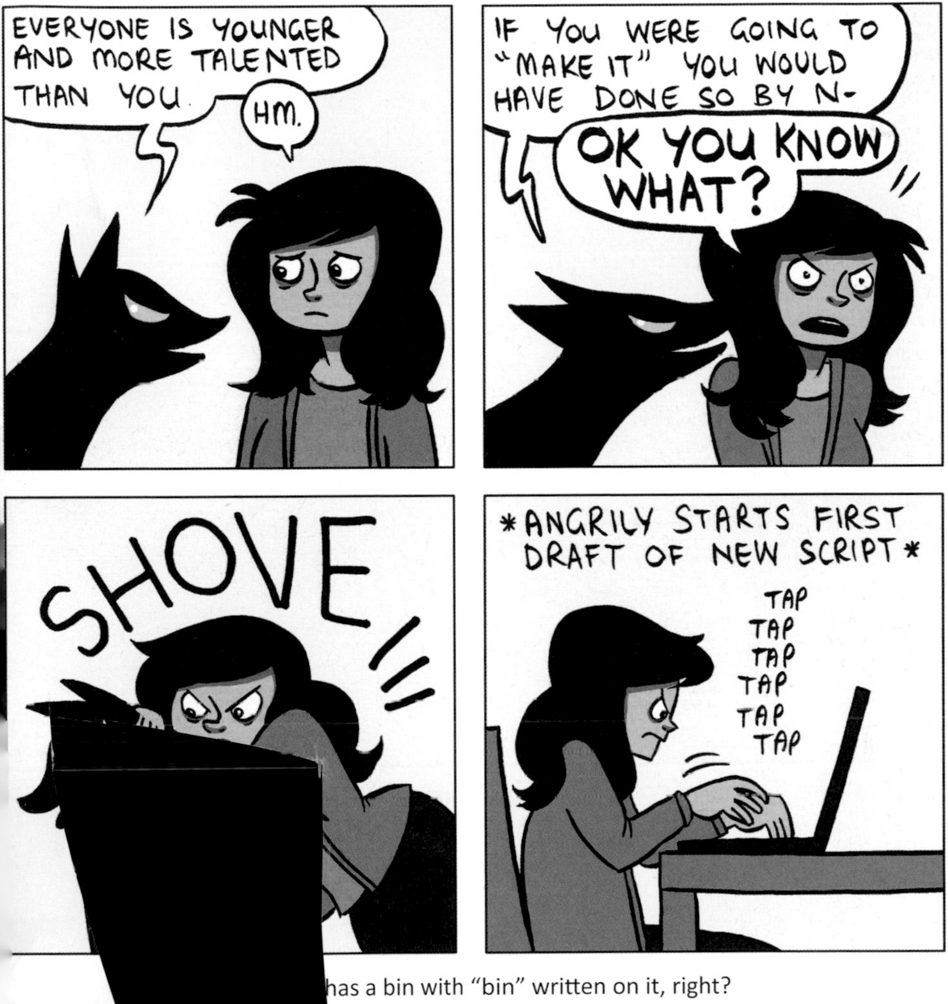
EVERYONE IS YOUNGER AND MORE TALENTED THAN YOU.
HM.
IF YOU WERE GOING TO "MAKE IT" YOU WOULD HAVE DONE SO BY N-
OK YOU KNOW WHAT?
SHOVE
ANGRILY STARTS FIRST DRAFT OF NEW SCRIPT
TAP
TAP
TAP
TAP
TAP
TAP

[redacted] has a bin with "bin" written on it, right?

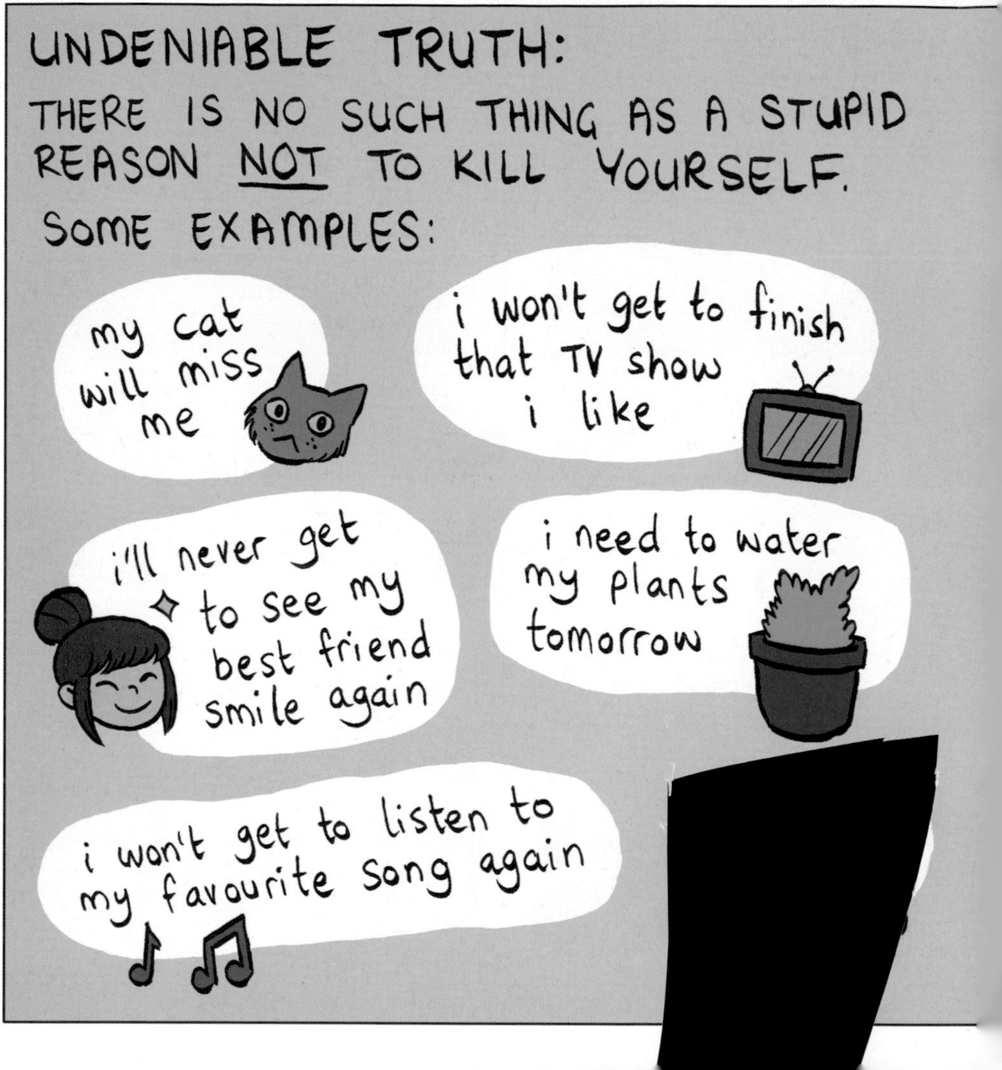
UNDENIABLE TRUTH:
THERE IS NO SUCH THING AS A STUPID REASON NOT TO KILL YOURSELF.
SOME EXAMPLES:
my cat will miss me
i won't get to finish that TV show i like
i'll never get to see my best friend smile again
i need to water my plants tomorrow
i won't get to listen to my favourite song again
[redacted]

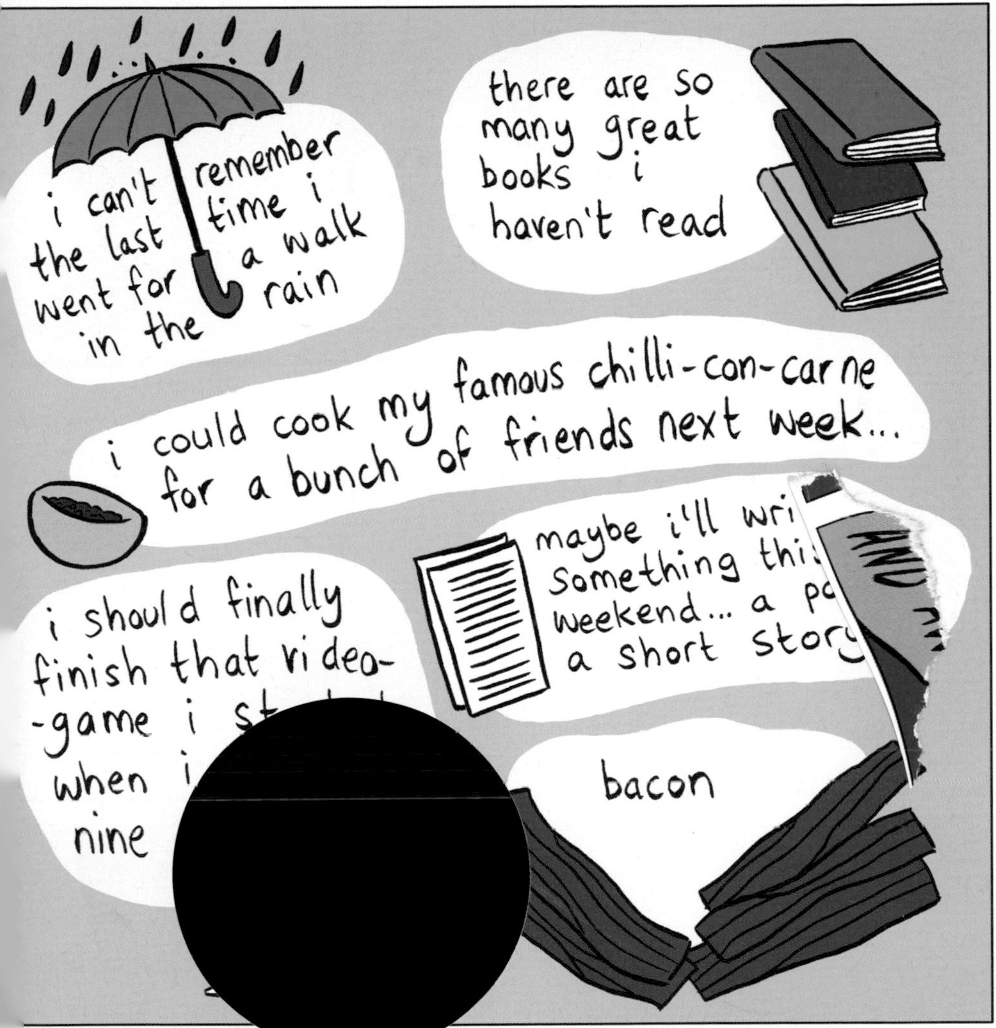
i can't remember the last time i went for a walk in the rain
there are so many great books i haven't read
i could cook my famous chilli-con-carne for a bunch of friends next week...
maybe i'll wri something thi weekend... a po a short stor
AND
i should finally finish that video-game i st [redacted] when i [redacted] nine
bacon

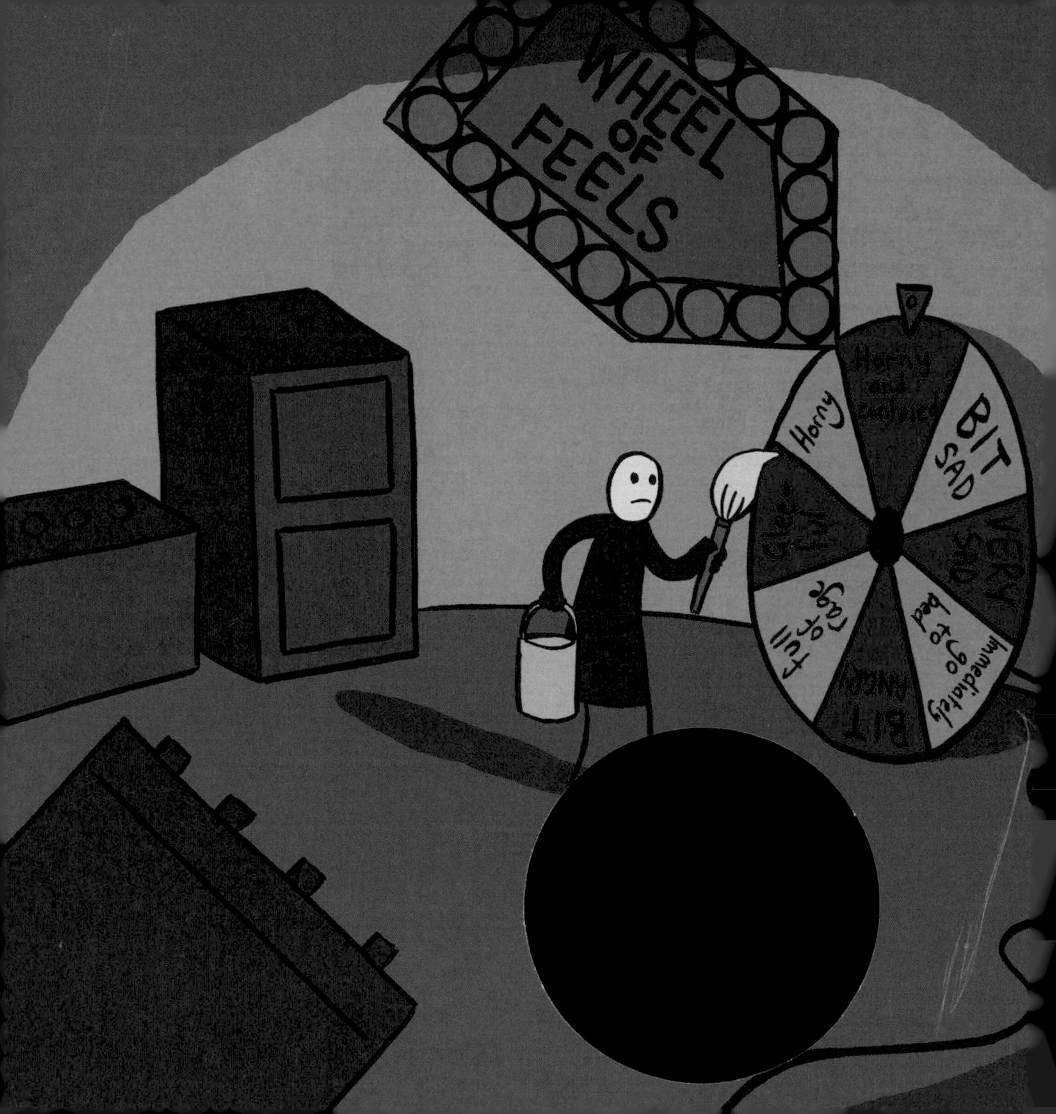
WHEEL OF FEELS
Horny
Horny and confused
BIT SAD
VERY SAD
Immediately go to bed
BIT ANGRY
full of rage
Glee-ful

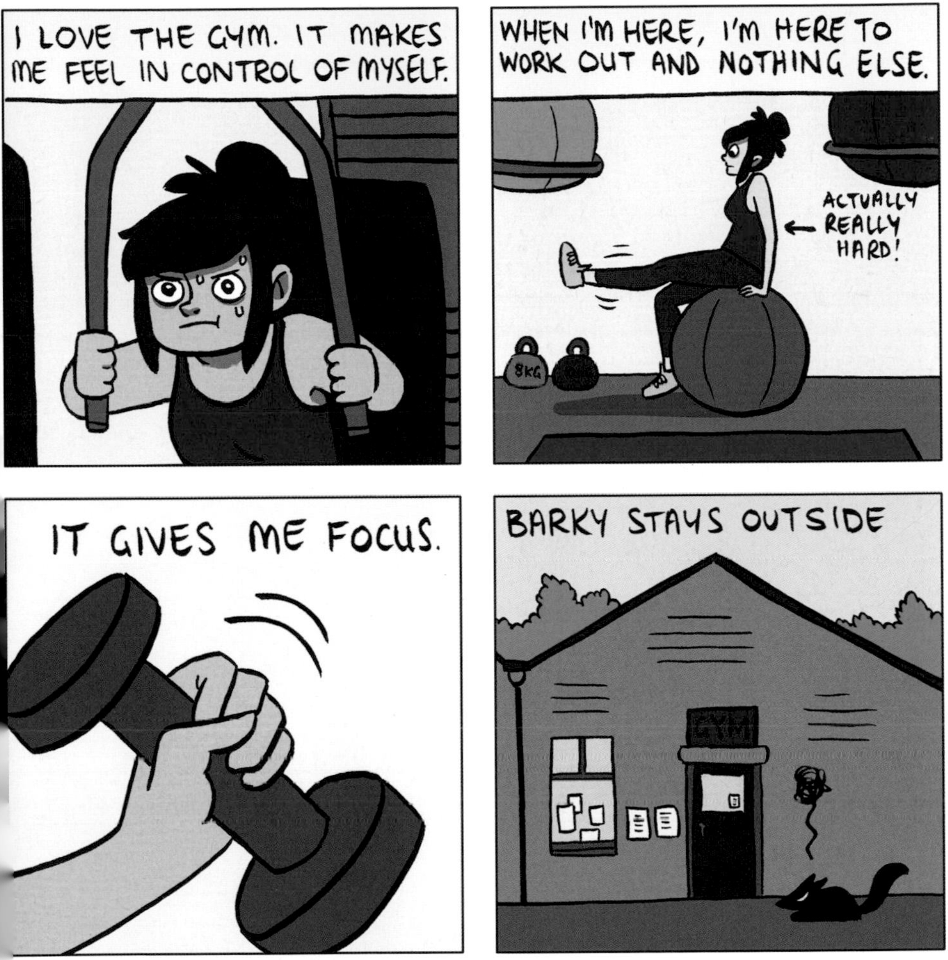
I LOVE THE GYM. IT MAKES ME FEEL IN CONTROL OF MYSELF.
WHEN I'M HERE, I'M HERE TO WORK OUT AND NOTHING ELSE.
ACTUALLY REALLY HARD!
8KG
IT GIVES ME FOCUS.
BARKY STAYS OUTSIDE

I've actually made myself look a lot better than I do working out in real life.
It is ... not a pretty sight. Sorry everyone who goes to my gym!!

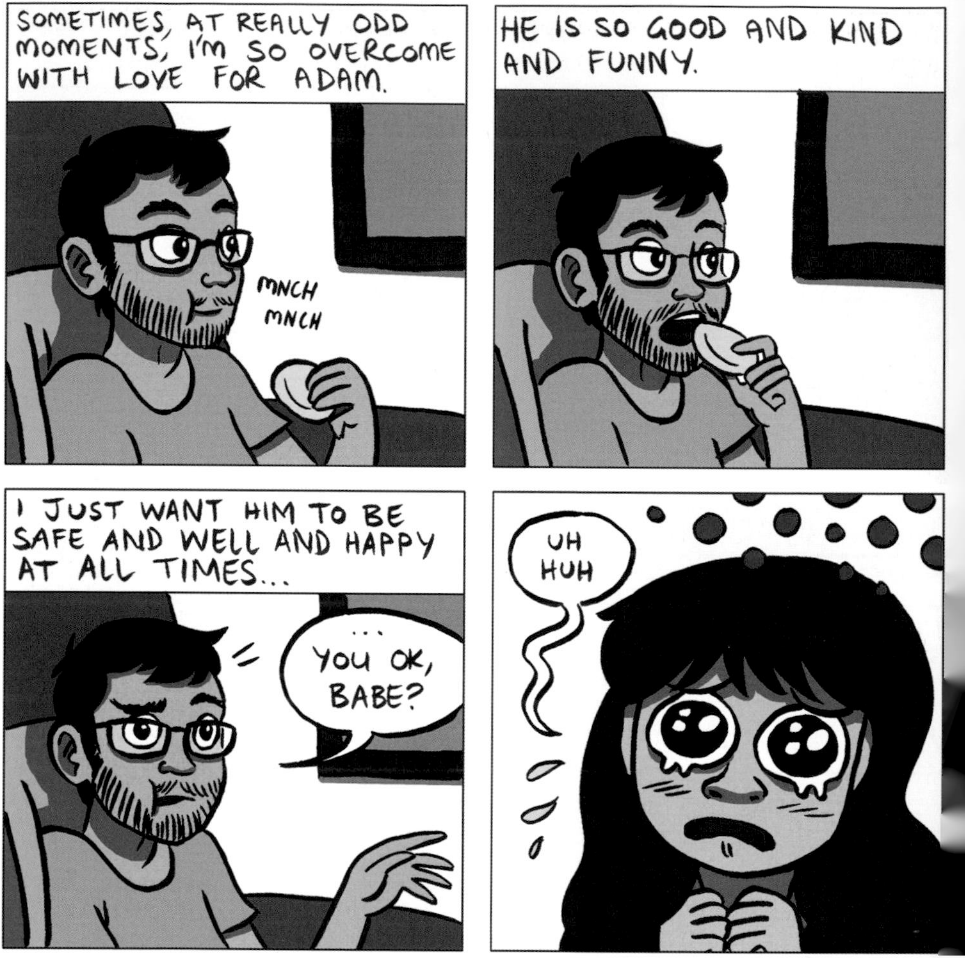
SOMETIMES, AT REALLY ODD MOMENTS, I'M SO OVERCOME WITH LOVE FOR ADAM.
MNCH MNCH
HE IS SO GOOD AND KIND AND FUNNY.
I JUST WANT HIM TO BE SAFE AND WELL AND HAPPY AT ALL TIMES...
... YOU OK, BABE?
UH HUH

Fun fact: Adam is eating a Pringle here, not a coaster, as my mum thought.

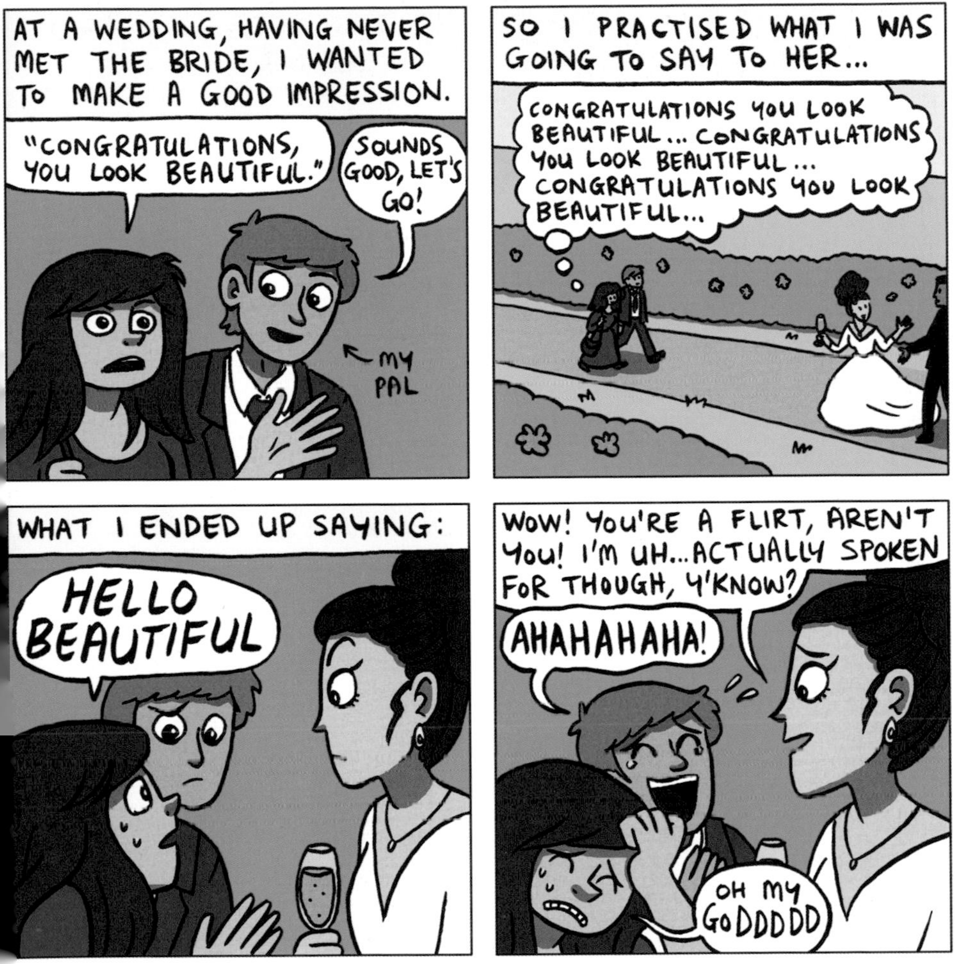

AT A WEDDING, HAVING NEVER MET THE BRIDE, I WANTED TO MAKE A GOOD IMPRESSION.
"CONGRATULATIONS, YOU LOOK BEAUTIFUL."
SOUNDS GOOD, LET'S GO!
MY PAL
SO I PRACTISED WHAT I WAS GOING TO SAY TO HER...
CONGRATULATIONS YOU LOOK BEAUTIFUL... CONGRATULATIONS YOU LOOK BEAUTIFUL... CONGRATULATIONS YOU LOOK BEAUTIFUL...
WHAT I ENDED UP SAYING:
HELLO BEAUTIFUL
WOW! YOU'RE A FLIRT, AREN'T YOU! I'M UH...ACTUALLY SPOKEN FOR THOUGH, Y'KNOW?
AHAHAHAHA!
OH MY GODDDDD

Practice makes perf- ... oh, never mind.

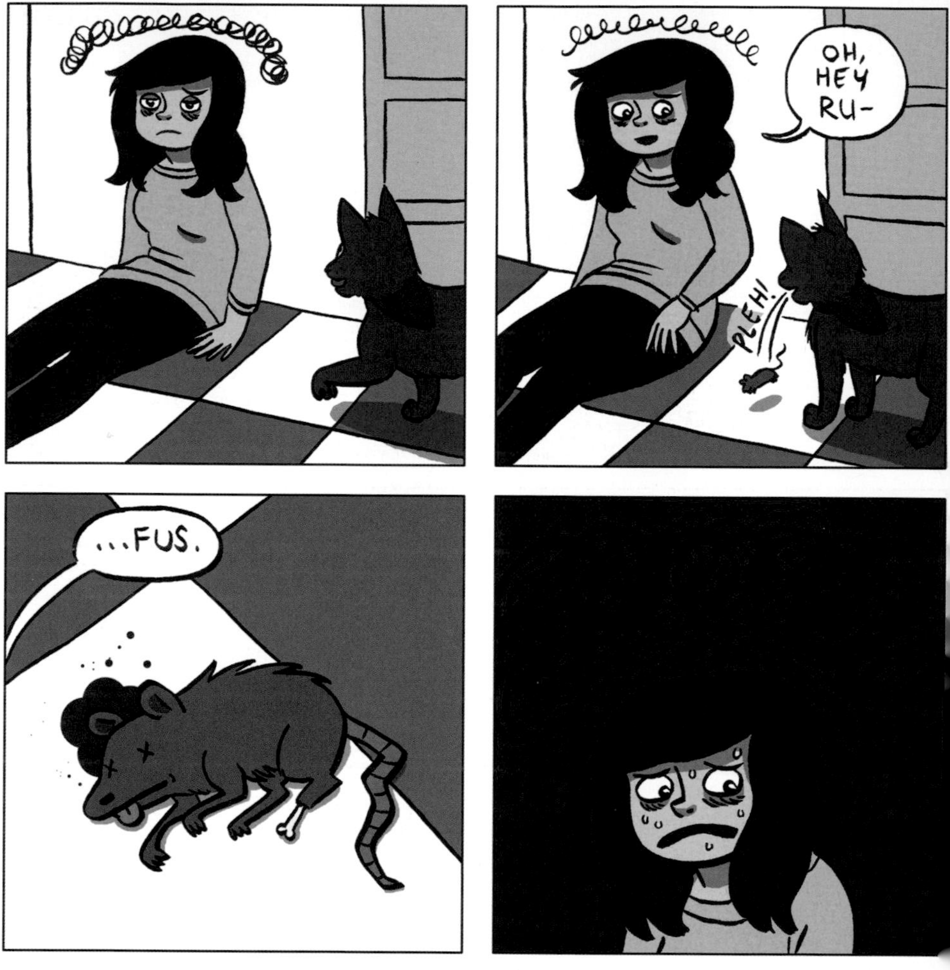
OH, HEY RU-
PLEH!
...FUS.

"Hey I know you're sad but at least you're not this mouse that I tortured for 20 minutes before brutally murdering ..." (is what I think Rufus was trying to communicate here).

Don't say "sorry" when you mean "thank you"! (Like I do all the bloody time.)

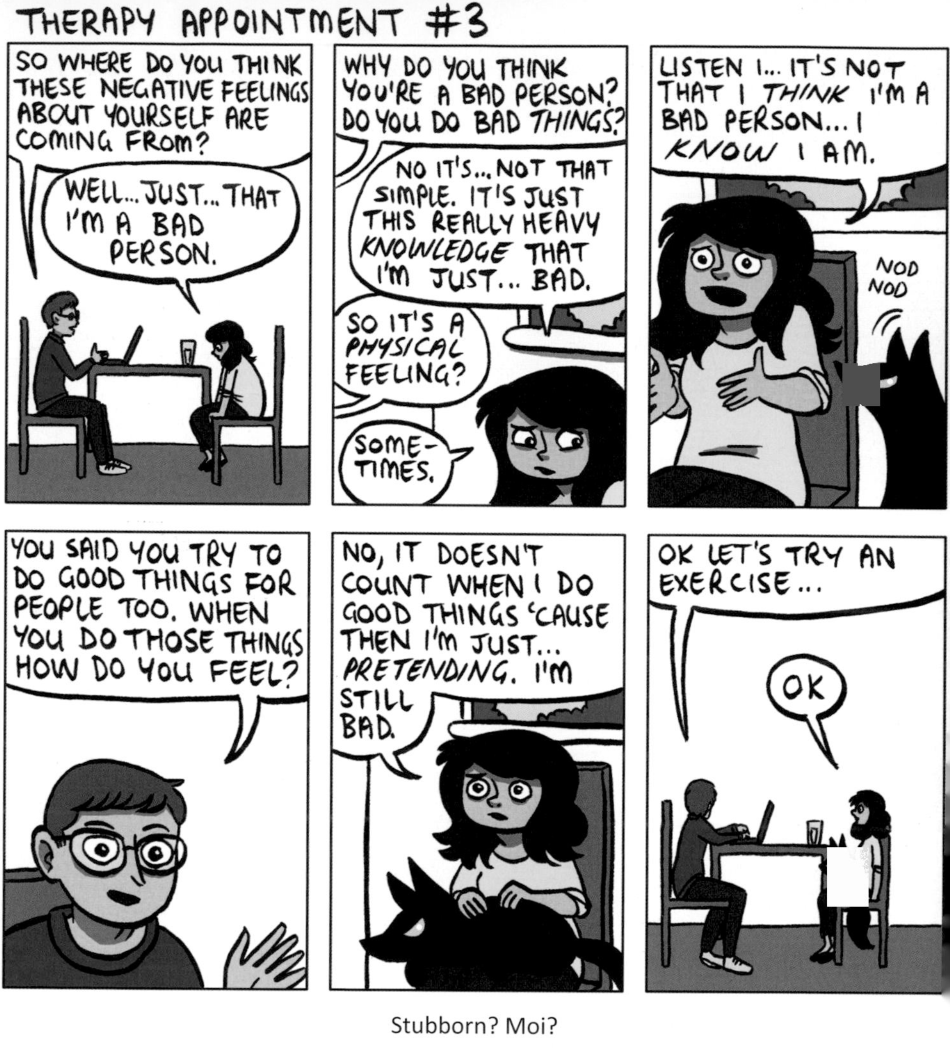
THERAPY APPOINTMENT #3
SO WHERE DO YOU THINK THESE NEGATIVE FEELINGS ABOUT YOURSELF ARE COMING FROM?
WELL... JUST... THAT I'M A BAD PERSON.
WHY DO YOU THINK YOU'RE A BAD PERSON? DO YOU DO BAD *THINGS*?
NO IT'S... NOT THAT SIMPLE. IT'S JUST THIS REALLY HEAVY *KNOWLEDGE* THAT I'M JUST... BAD.
SO IT'S A *PHYSICAL* FEELING?
SOME-TIMES.
LISTEN I... IT'S NOT THAT I *THINK* I'M A BAD PERSON... I *KNOW* I AM.
NOD NOD
YOU SAID YOU TRY TO DO GOOD THINGS FOR PEOPLE TOO. WHEN YOU DO THOSE THINGS HOW DO YOU FEEL?
NO, IT DOESN'T COUNT WHEN I DO GOOD THINGS 'CAUSE THEN I'M JUST... *PRETENDING*. I'M STILL BAD.
OK LET'S TRY AN EXERCISE...
OK

Stubborn? Moi?

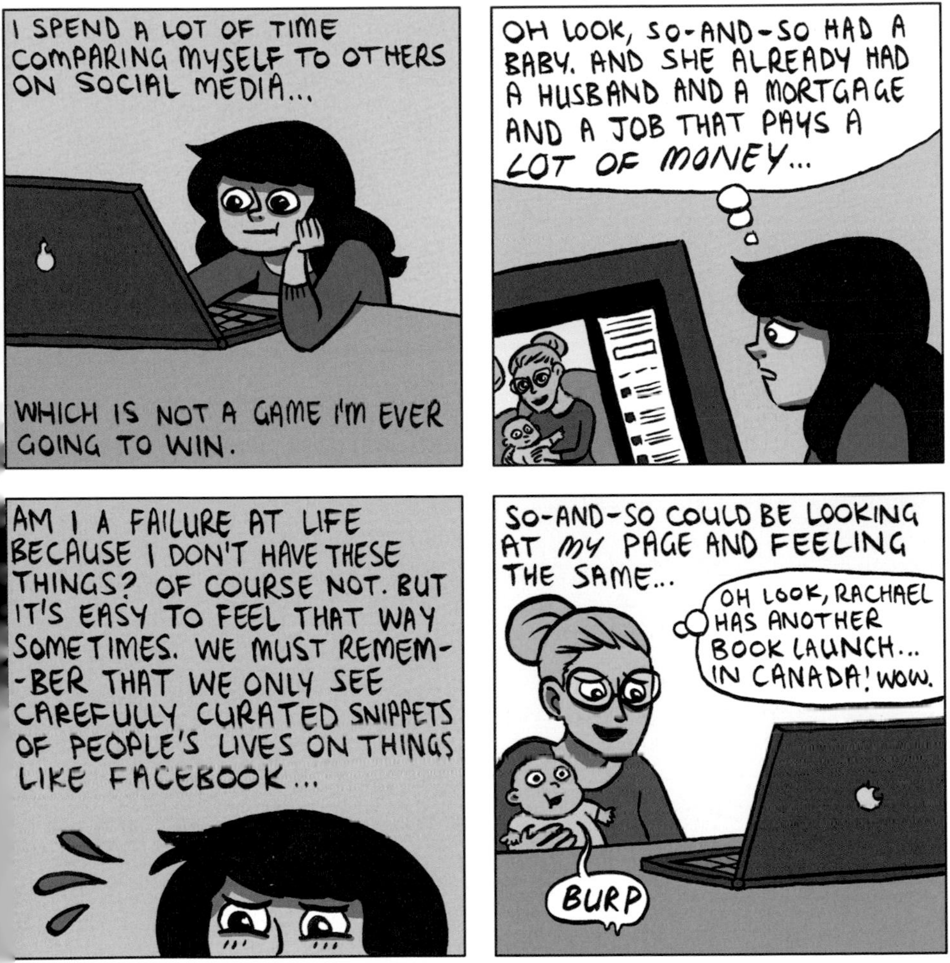
I SPEND A LOT OF TIME COMPARING MYSELF TO OTHERS ON SOCIAL MEDIA...
WHICH IS NOT A GAME I'M EVER GOING TO WIN.
OH LOOK, SO-AND-SO HAD A BABY. AND SHE ALREADY HAD A HUSBAND AND A MORTGAGE AND A JOB THAT PAYS A LOT OF MONEY...
AM I A FAILURE AT LIFE BECAUSE I DON'T HAVE THESE THINGS? OF COURSE NOT. BUT IT'S EASY TO FEEL THAT WAY SOMETIMES. WE MUST REMEM--BER THAT WE ONLY SEE CAREFULLY CURATED SNIPPETS OF PEOPLE'S LIVES ON THINGS LIKE FACEBOOK...
SO-AND-SO COULD BE LOOKING AT MY PAGE AND FEELING THE SAME...
OH LOOK, RACHAEL HAS ANOTHER BOOK LAUNCH... IN CANADA! WOW.
BURP

I hope I do have a baby one day because
LOOK HOW AMAZING I AM AT DRAWING THEM!

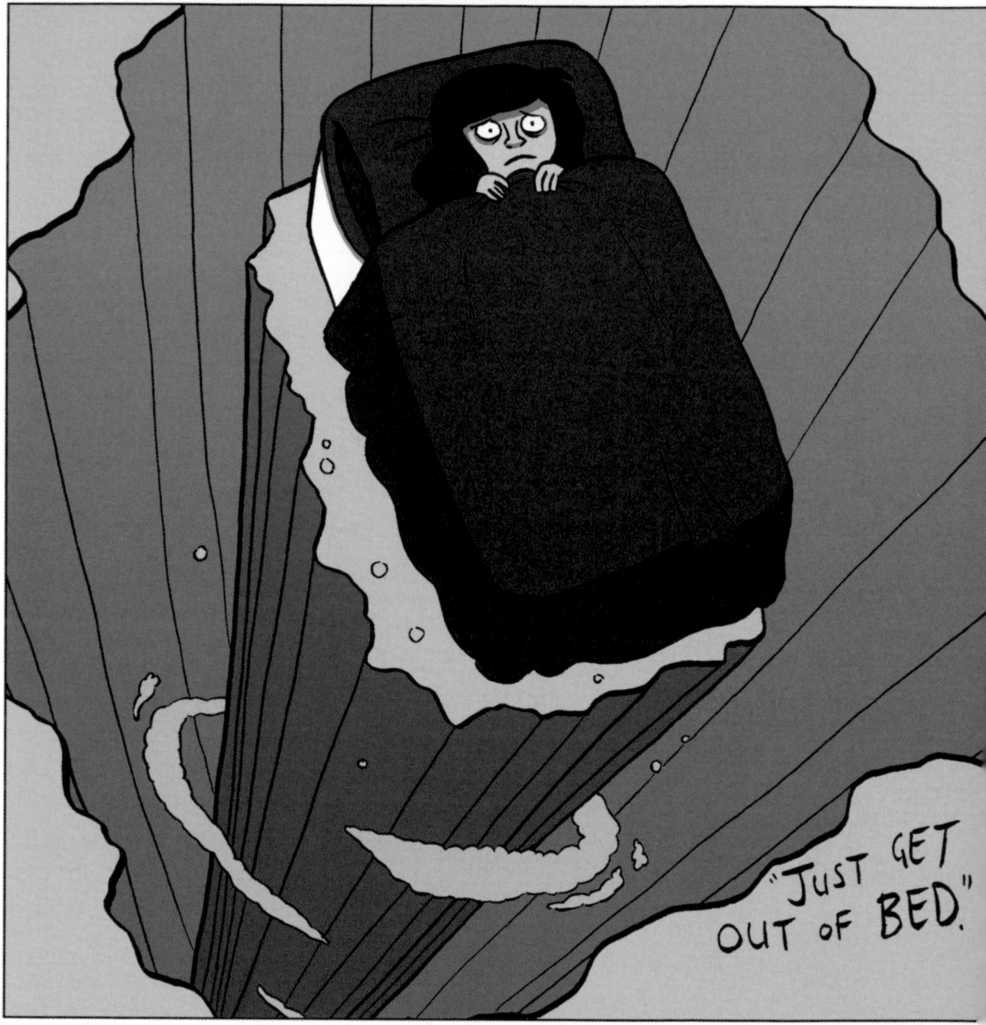
"JUST GET OUT OF BED."

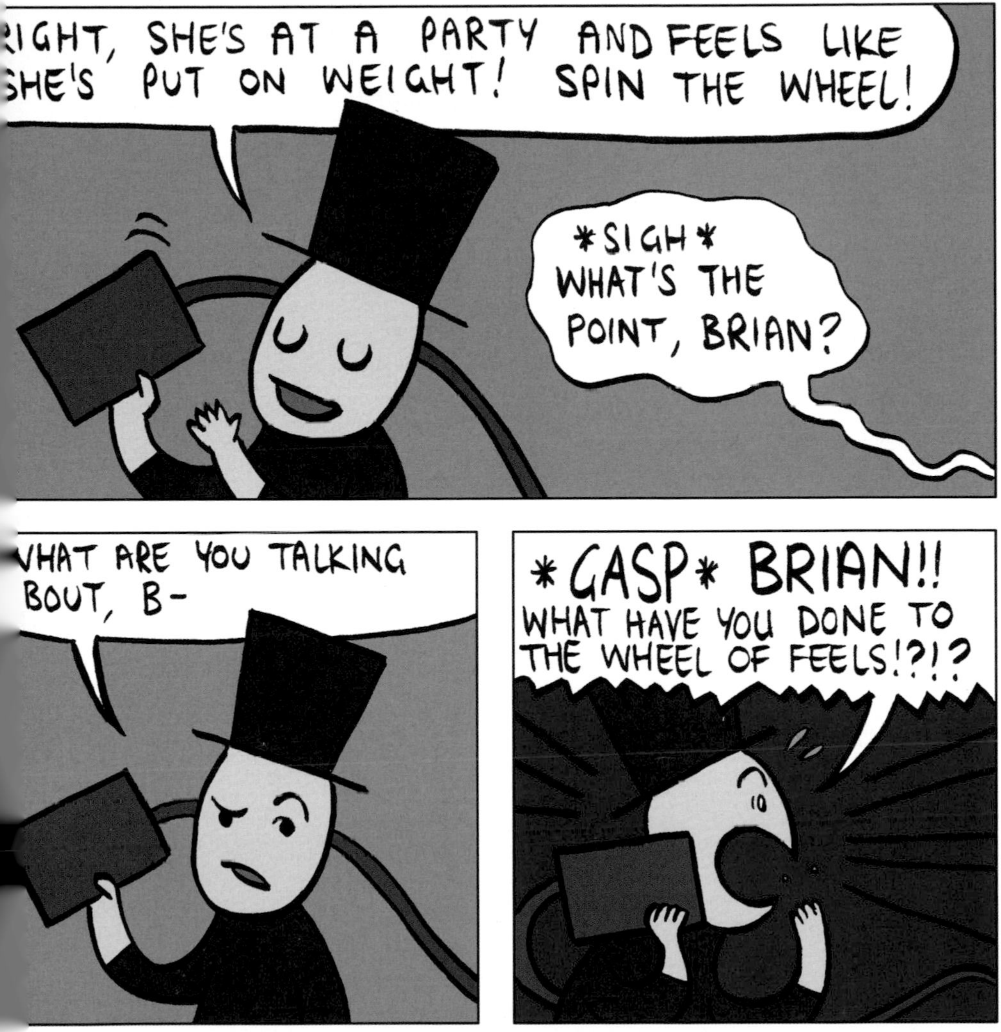
RIGHT, SHE'S AT A PARTY AND FEELS LIKE SHE'S PUT ON WEIGHT! SPIN THE WHEEL!
SIGH WHAT'S THE POINT, BRIAN?
WHAT ARE YOU TALKING ABOUT, B-
GASP BRIAN!! WHAT HAVE YOU DONE TO THE WHEEL OF FEELS!?!?

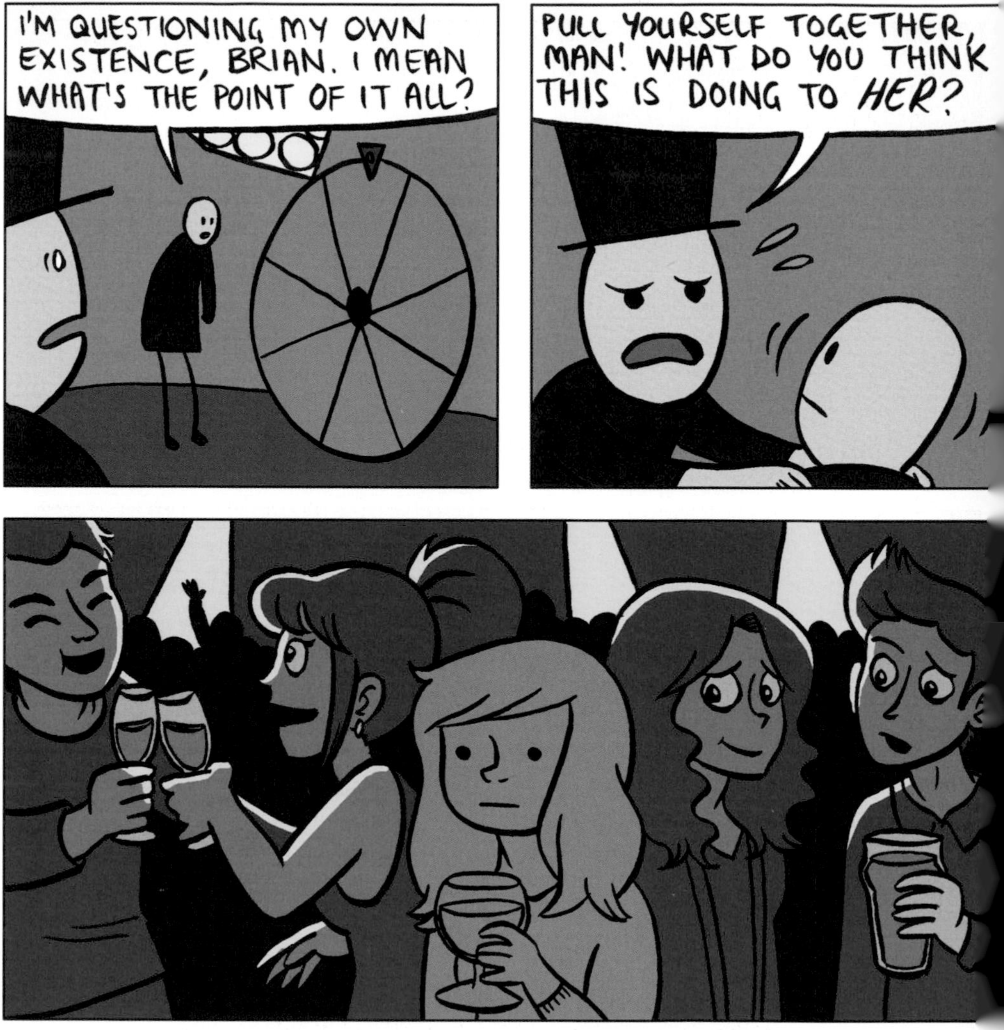
I'M QUESTIONING MY OWN EXISTENCE, BRIAN. I MEAN WHAT'S THE POINT OF IT ALL?
PULL YOURSELF TOGETHER, MAN! WHAT DO YOU THINK THIS IS DOING TO *HER*?

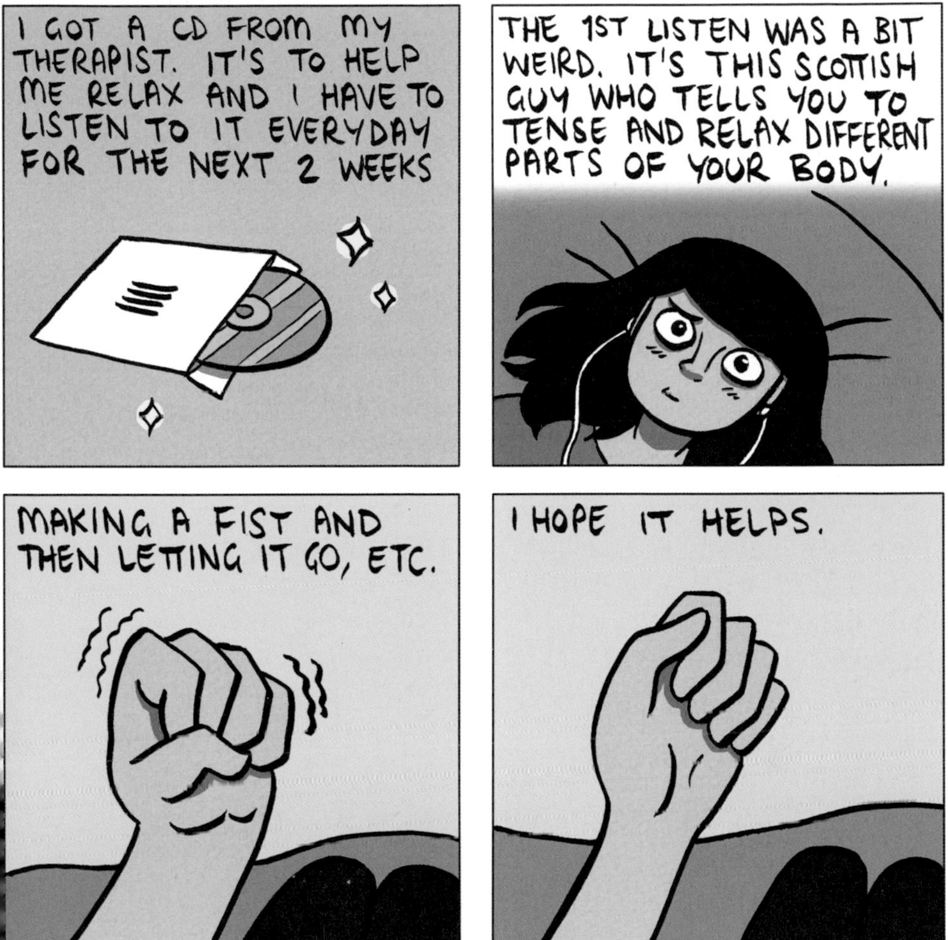
I GOT A CD FROM MY THERAPIST. IT'S TO HELP ME RELAX AND I HAVE TO LISTEN TO IT EVERYDAY FOR THE NEXT 2 WEEKS
THE 1ST LISTEN WAS A BIT WEIRD. IT'S THIS SCOTTISH GUY WHO TELLS YOU TO TENSE AND RELAX DIFFERENT PARTS OF YOUR BODY.
MAKING A FIST AND THEN LETTING IT GO, ETC.
I HOPE IT HELPS.

The track is called "Stresspac Deep Relaxation" and you can totally find it on YouTube if you want to try it too :).

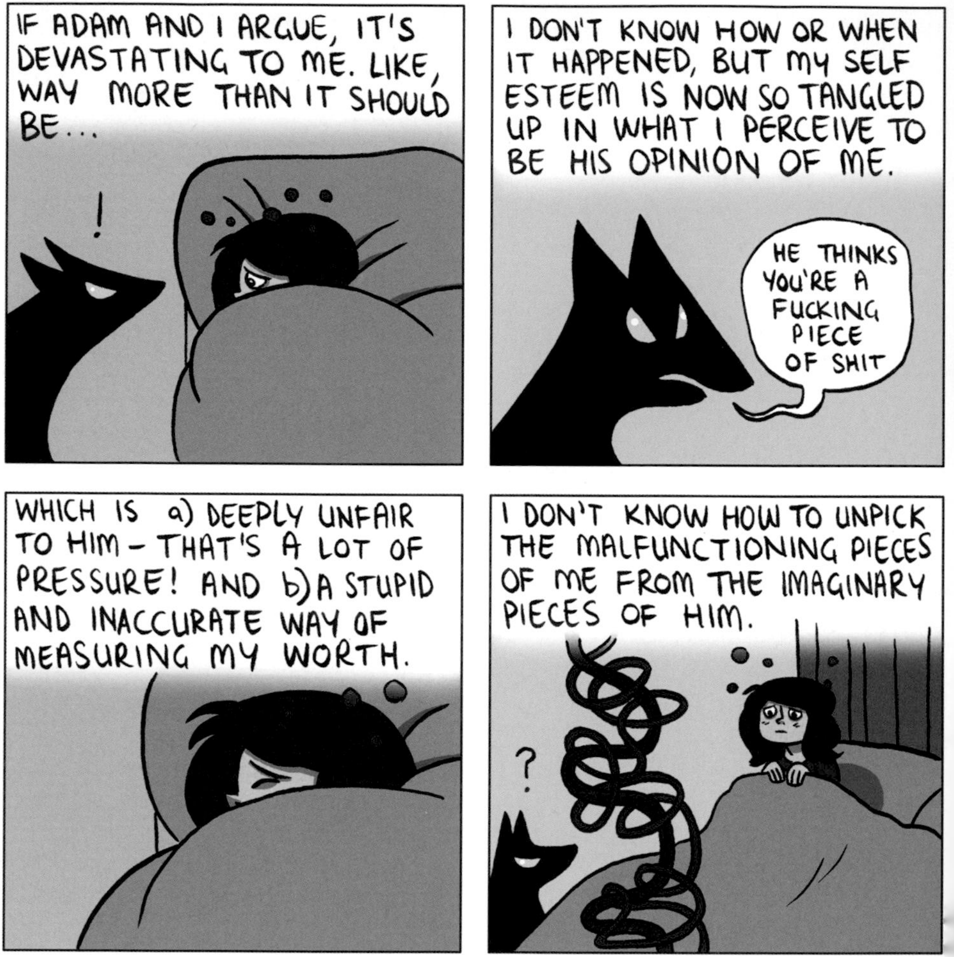
IF ADAM AND I ARGUE, IT'S DEVASTATING TO ME. LIKE, WAY MORE THAN IT SHOULD BE...
!
I DON'T KNOW HOW OR WHEN IT HAPPENED, BUT MY SELF ESTEEM IS NOW SO TANGLED UP IN WHAT I PERCEIVE TO BE HIS OPINION OF ME.
HE THINKS YOU'RE A FUCKING PIECE OF SHIT
WHICH IS a) DEEPLY UNFAIR TO HIM - THAT'S A LOT OF PRESSURE! AND b) A STUPID AND INACCURATE WAY OF MEASURING MY WORTH.
I DON'T KNOW HOW TO UNPICK THE MALFUNCTIONING PIECES OF ME FROM THE IMAGINARY PIECES OF HIM.
?

I think I need a *map* to that last sentence, jeeez ...

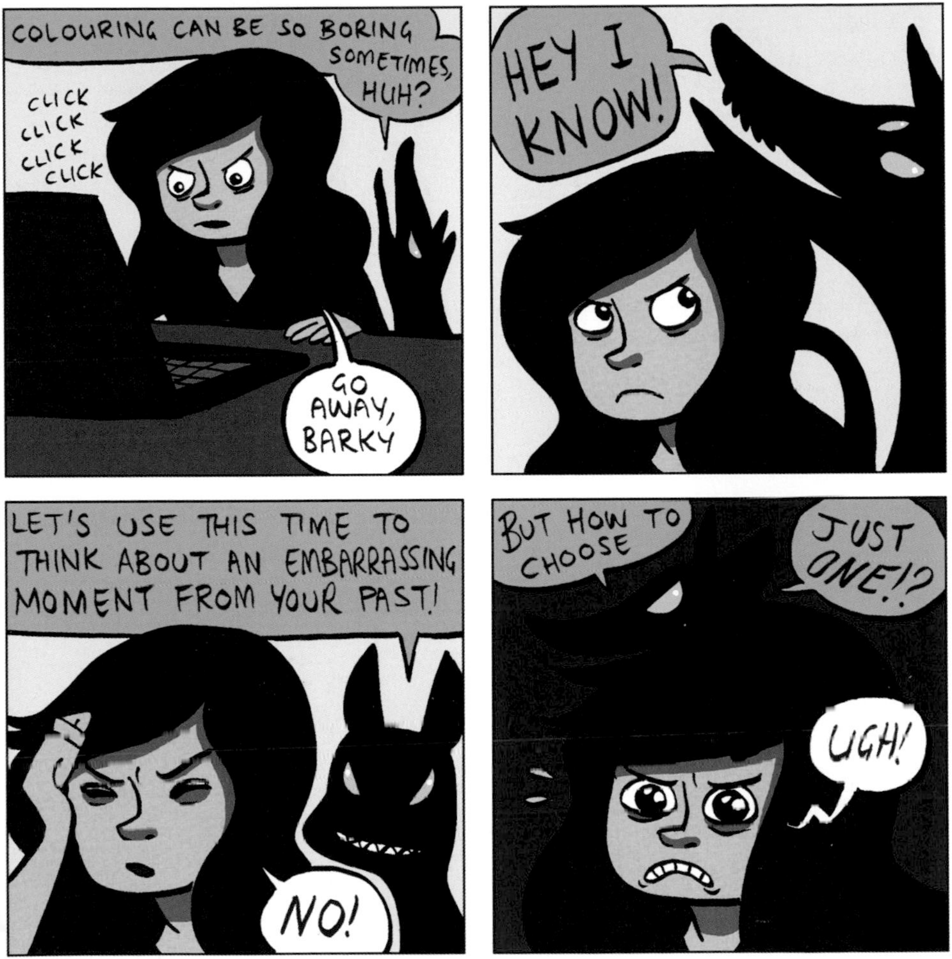
COLOURING CAN BE SO BORING SOMETIMES, HUH?
CLICK CLICK CLICK CLICK
GO AWAY, BARKY
HEY I KNOW!
LET'S USE THIS TIME TO THINK ABOUT AN EMBARRASSING MOMENT FROM YOUR PAST!
NO!
BUT HOW TO CHOOSE
JUST ONE!?
UGH!

It was weird colouring this strip.

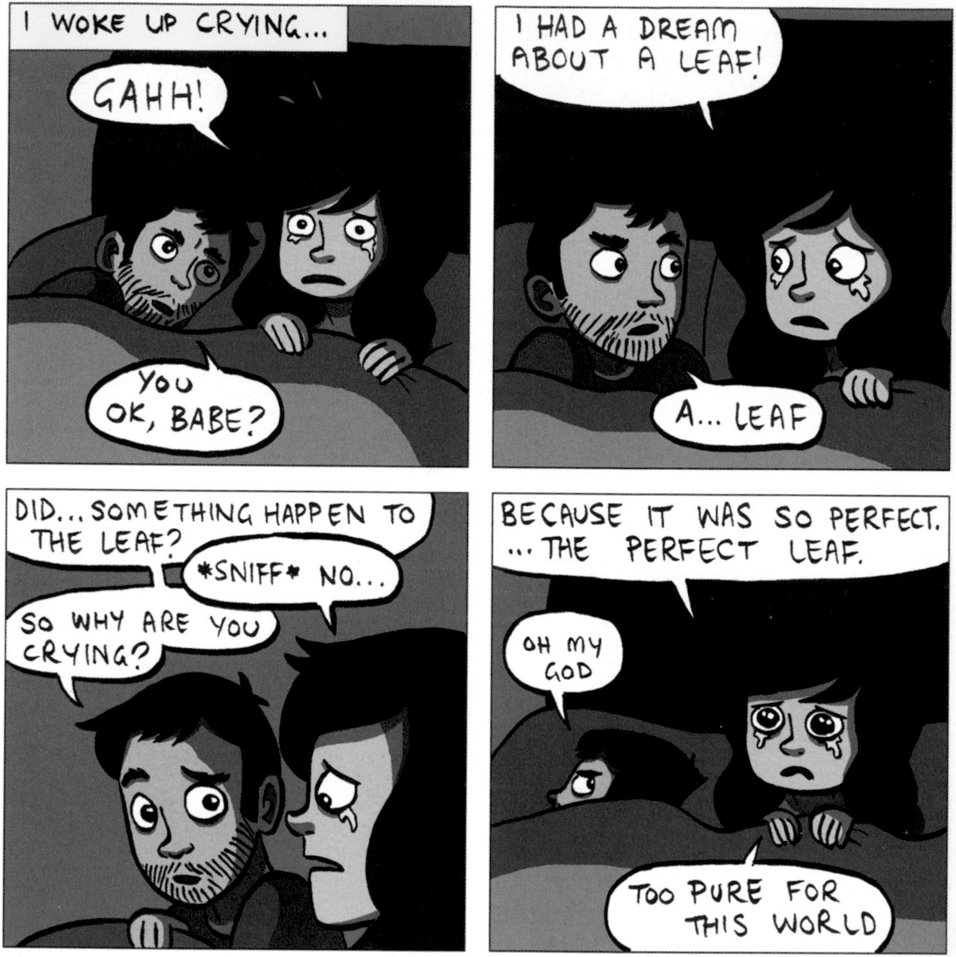
I WOKE UP CRYING...
GAHH!
YOU OK, BABE?
I HAD A DREAM ABOUT A LEAF!
A... LEAF
DID... SOMETHING HAPPEN TO THE LEAF?
SNIFF NO...
SO WHY ARE YOU CRYING?
BECAUSE IT WAS SO PERFECT. ... THE PERFECT LEAF.
OH MY GOD
TOO PURE FOR THIS WORLD

Don’t give me that look – you’d have cried too, OK?

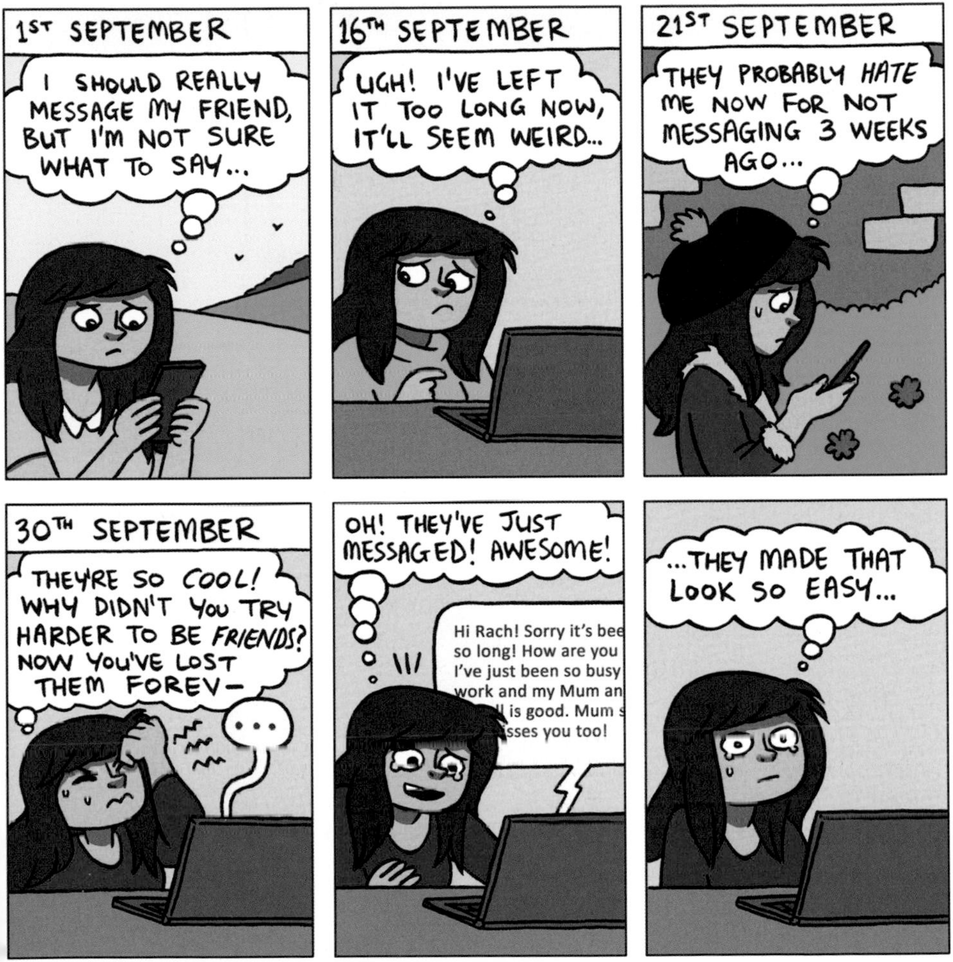

1ST SEPTEMBER
I SHOULD REALLY MESSAGE MY FRIEND, BUT I'M NOT SURE WHAT TO SAY...
16TH SEPTEMBER
UGH! I'VE LEFT IT TOO LONG NOW, IT'LL SEEM WEIRD...
21ST SEPTEMBER
THEY PROBABLY HATE ME NOW FOR NOT MESSAGING 3 WEEKS AGO...
30TH SEPTEMBER
THEY'RE SO COOL! WHY DIDN'T YOU TRY HARDER TO BE FRIENDS? NOW YOU'VE LOST THEM FOREV–
...
OH! THEY'VE JUST MESSAGED! AWESOME!
Hi Rach! Sorry it's bee
so long! How are you
I've just been so busy
work and my Mum an
is good. Mum
sses you too!
...THEY MADE THAT LOOK SO EASY...

SEND THE DAMN MESSAGE, RACHAEL

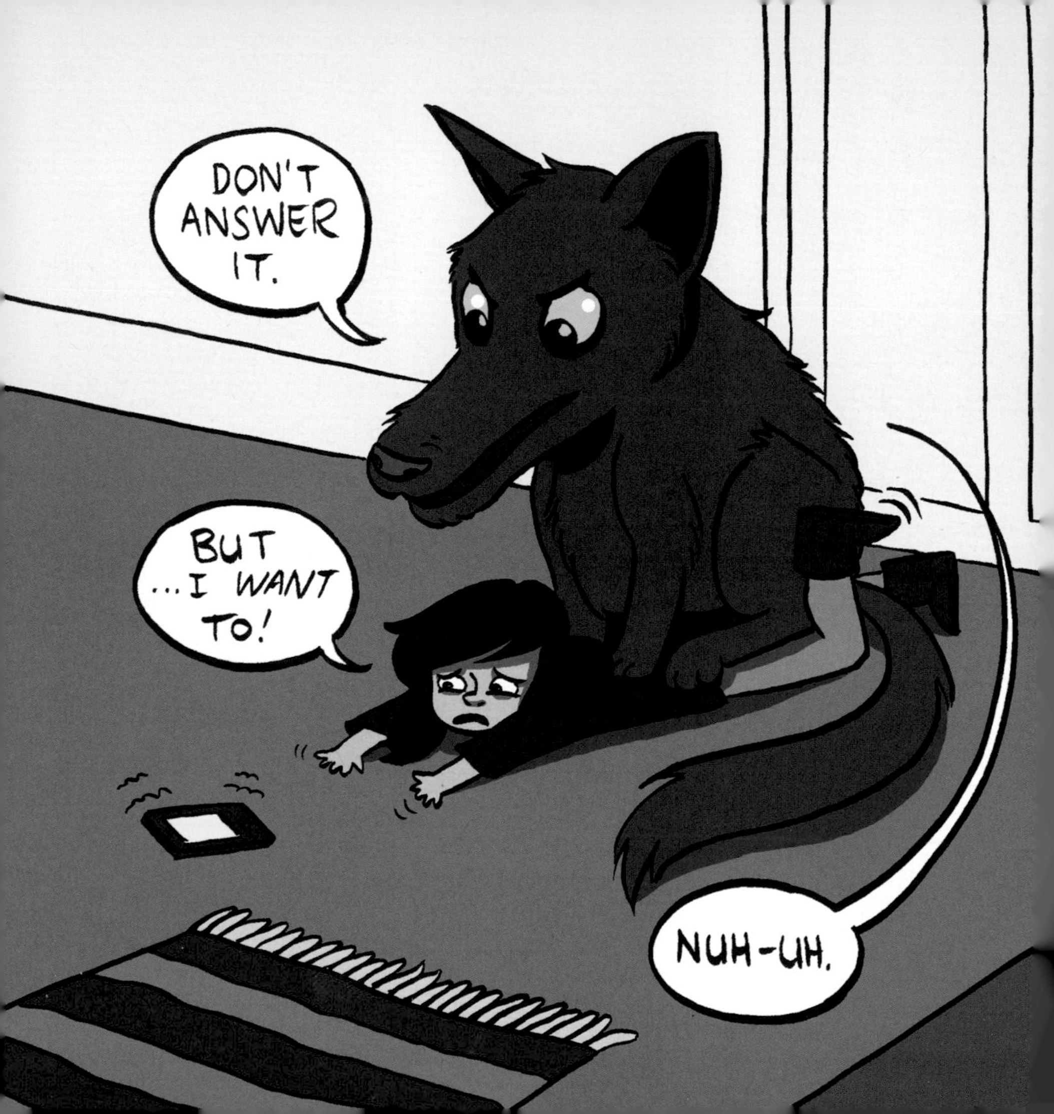
DON'T ANSWER IT.
BUT ...I WANT TO!
NUH-UH.

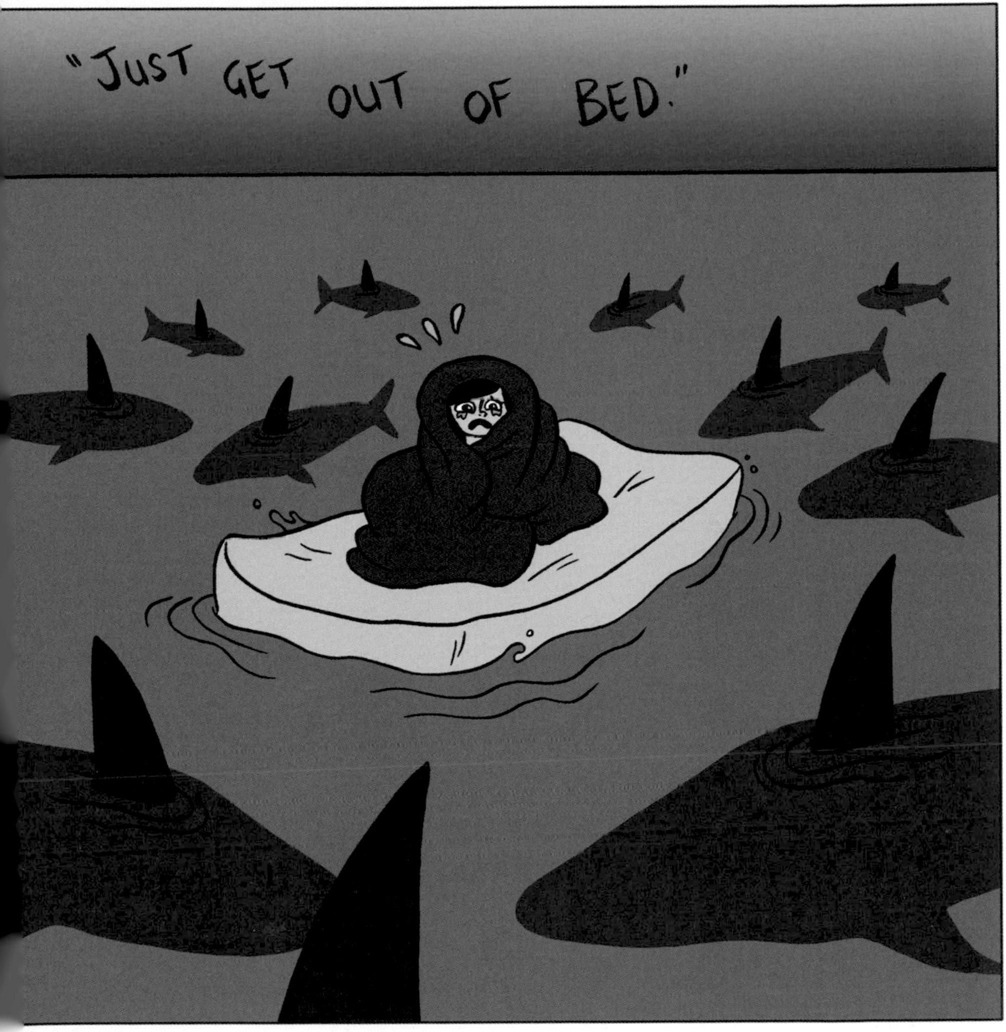
"JUST GET OUT OF BED."

THE NEXT 10 PAGES ARE A TRUE STORY ABOUT
MY 1ST EXPERIENCE OF HARASSMENT. THE
PAGE BORDERS OF THE STORY ARE GREEN, SO IF
YOU WANT TO SKIP IT, JUST FLIP TO WHERE
THE PAGES ARE WHITE AGAIN. *HUGS*

I WASN'T GOING TO TELL THIS STORY, BUT THE
RECENT #METOO MOVEMENT GAVE ME THE
BRAVERY I NEEDED TO DO SO. THE SADDEST
THING ABOUT THIS STORY IS THE FACT THAT
IT REALLY ISN'T THAT UNUSUAL, AND THAT
IN THE END, I WAS ONE OF THE LUCKY ONES.

I'M TELLING IT NOW IN THE HOPES THAT IT
MAY MAKE OTHERS FEEL LESS ALONE, AND
TO TRY TO LIFT SOME OF THE THINGS THAT
HAVE SAT IN THE CORNERS OF MY MIND FOR
17 YEARS.

— Rachael xxx

"ALL THINGS CONSIDERED" by Rachael Smith

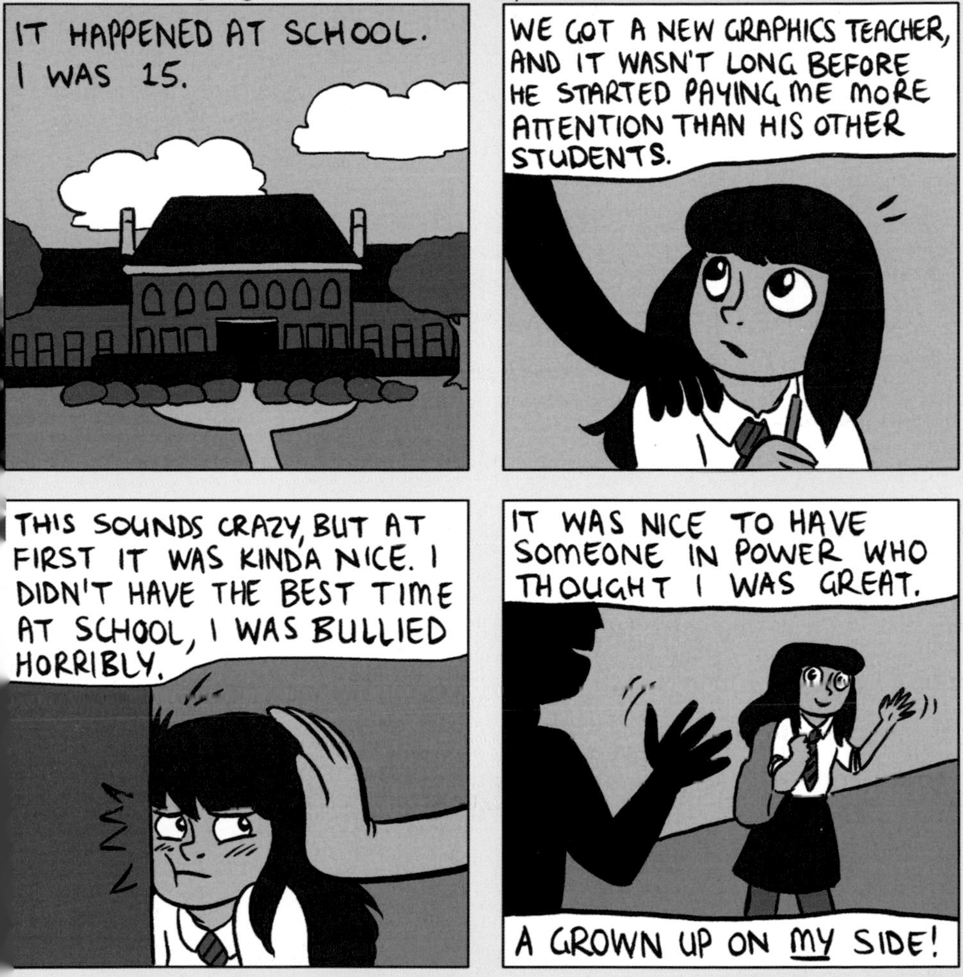
IT HAPPENED AT SCHOOL. I WAS 15.
WE GOT A NEW GRAPHICS TEACHER, AND IT WASN'T LONG BEFORE HE STARTED PAYING ME MORE ATTENTION THAN HIS OTHER STUDENTS.
THIS SOUNDS CRAZY, BUT AT FIRST IT WAS KINDA NICE. I DIDN'T HAVE THE BEST TIME AT SCHOOL, I WAS BULLIED HORRIBLY.
IT WAS NICE TO HAVE SOMEONE IN POWER WHO THOUGHT I WAS GREAT.
A GROWN UP ON MY SIDE!

THINKING ABOUT IT NOW, THINGS HAPPENED SO SLOWLY I BARELY NOTICED THEM BECOMING INAPPROPRIATE...

HE'D COMMENT ON HOW I WORE MY HAIR... AND THEN ASK WHETHER I'D HAD A SHOWER OR A BATH TO GET IT THAT WAY.

HE'D WRITE ME POEMS, THEN FOLLOW ME HOME FROM SCHOOL TO GIVE THEM TO ME ON MY DOORSTEP.

...MAKING IT CLEAR HE NOW KNEW WHERE I LIVED.

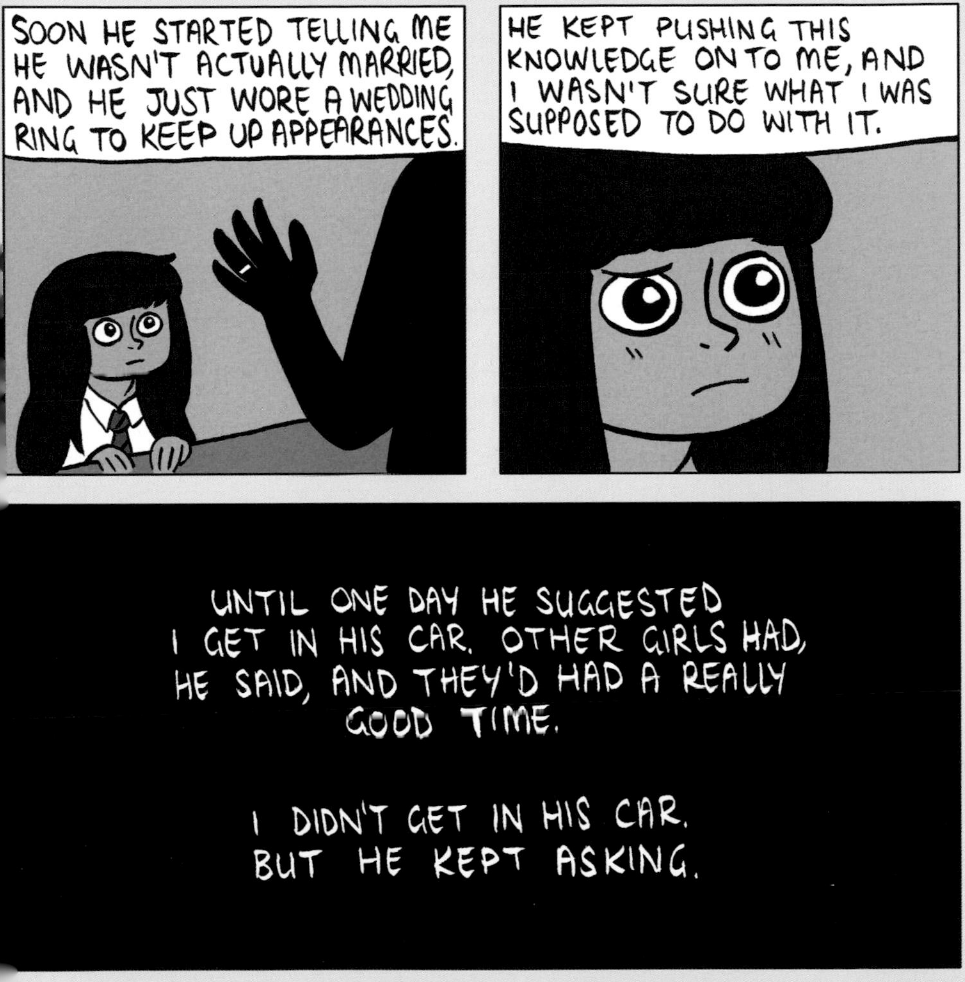
SOON HE STARTED TELLING ME HE WASN'T ACTUALLY MARRIED, AND HE JUST WORE A WEDDING RING TO KEEP UP APPEARANCES.
HE KEPT PUSHING THIS KNOWLEDGE ON TO ME, AND I WASN'T SURE WHAT I WAS SUPPOSED TO DO WITH IT.
UNTIL ONE DAY HE SUGGESTED I GET IN HIS CAR. OTHER GIRLS HAD, HE SAID, AND THEY'D HAD A REALLY GOOD TIME.
I DIDN'T GET IN HIS CAR. BUT HE KEPT ASKING.

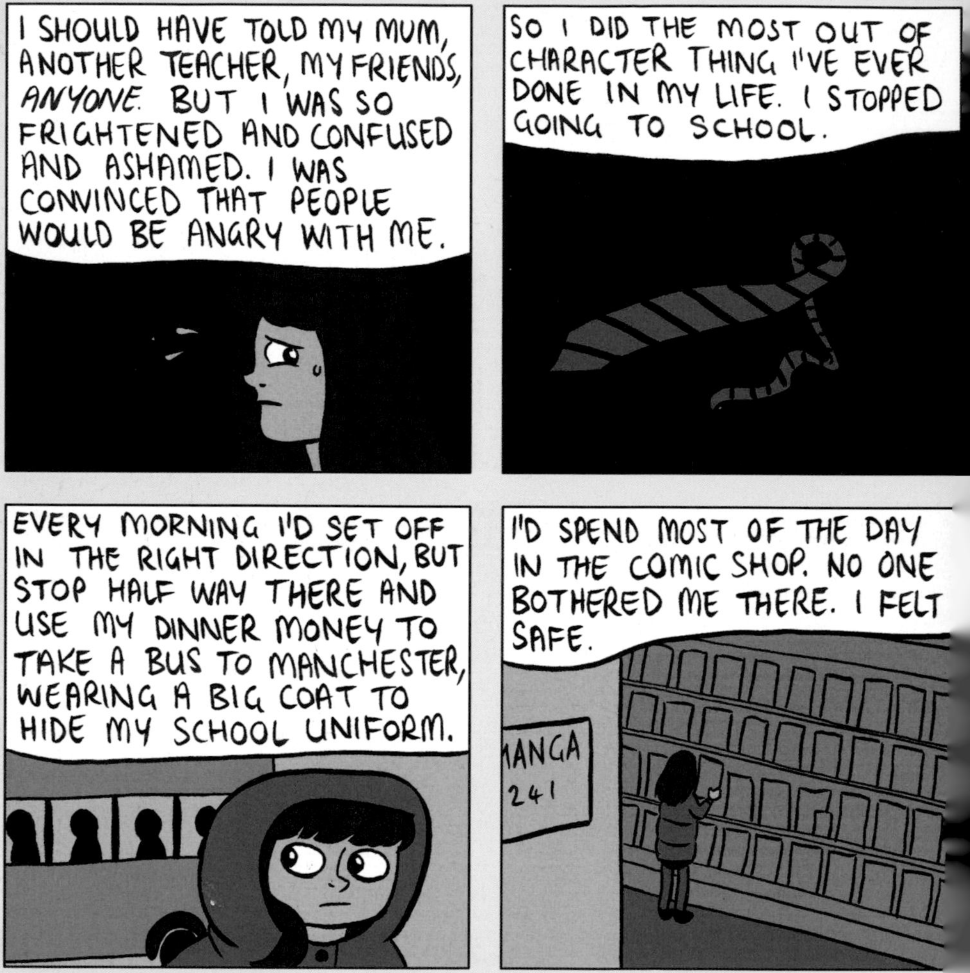
I SHOULD HAVE TOLD MY MUM, ANOTHER TEACHER, MY FRIENDS, *ANYONE*. BUT I WAS SO FRIGHTENED AND CONFUSED AND ASHAMED. I WAS CONVINCED THAT PEOPLE WOULD BE ANGRY WITH ME.
SO I DID THE MOST OUT OF CHARACTER THING I'VE EVER DONE IN MY LIFE. I STOPPED GOING TO SCHOOL.
EVERY MORNING I'D SET OFF IN THE RIGHT DIRECTION, BUT STOP HALF WAY THERE AND USE MY DINNER MONEY TO TAKE A BUS TO MANCHESTER, WEARING A BIG COAT TO HIDE MY SCHOOL UNIFORM.
I'D SPEND MOST OF THE DAY IN THE COMIC SHOP. NO ONE BOTHERED ME THERE. I FELT SAFE.
MANGA
241

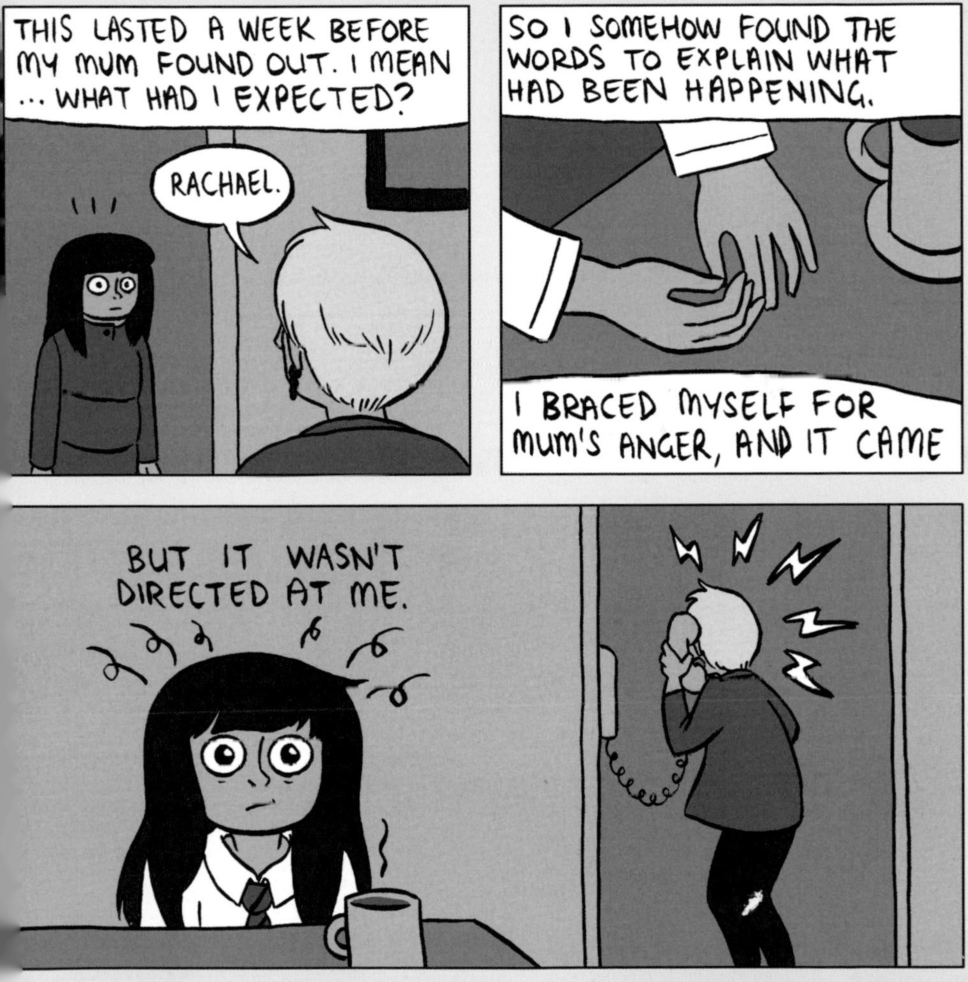
THIS LASTED A WEEK BEFORE MY MUM FOUND OUT. I MEAN ... WHAT HAD I EXPECTED?
RACHAEL.
SO I SOMEHOW FOUND THE WORDS TO EXPLAIN WHAT HAD BEEN HAPPENING.
I BRACED MYSELF FOR MUM'S ANGER, AND IT CAME
BUT IT WASN'T DIRECTED AT ME.

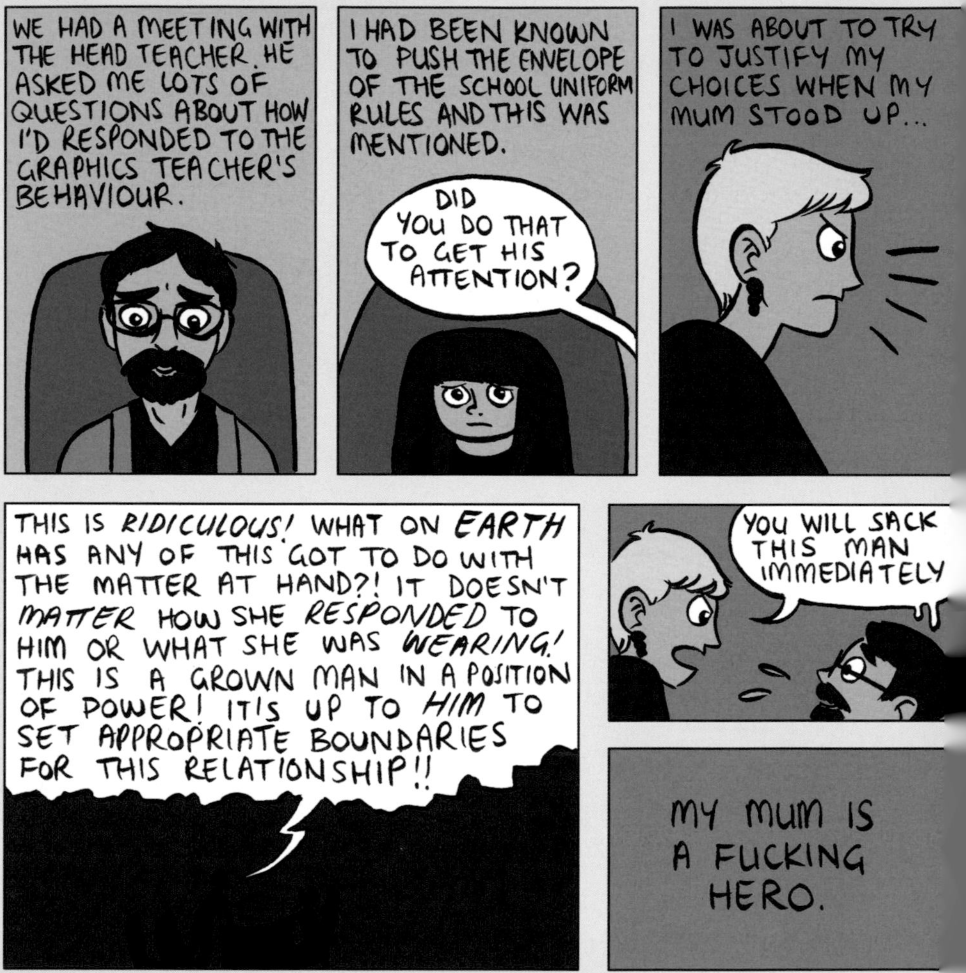
WE HAD A MEETING WITH THE HEAD TEACHER. HE ASKED ME LOTS OF QUESTIONS ABOUT HOW I'D RESPONDED TO THE GRAPHICS TEACHER'S BEHAVIOUR.
I HAD BEEN KNOWN TO PUSH THE ENVELOPE OF THE SCHOOL UNIFORM RULES AND THIS WAS MENTIONED.
DID YOU DO THAT TO GET HIS ATTENTION?
I WAS ABOUT TO TRY TO JUSTIFY MY CHOICES WHEN MY MUM STOOD UP...
THIS IS RIDICULOUS! WHAT ON EARTH HAS ANY OF THIS GOT TO DO WITH THE MATTER AT HAND?! IT DOESN'T MATTER HOW SHE RESPONDED TO HIM OR WHAT SHE WAS WEARING! THIS IS A GROWN MAN IN A POSITION OF POWER! IT'S UP TO HIM TO SET APPROPRIATE BOUNDARIES FOR THIS RELATIONSHIP!!
YOU WILL SACK THIS MAN IMMEDIATELY
MY MUM IS A FUCKING HERO.

THE GRAPHICS TEACHER WAS SACKED.
I WENT BACK TO SCHOOL.
I DID PRETTY WELL IN MY GCSEs.

ALL THINGS CONSIDERED.

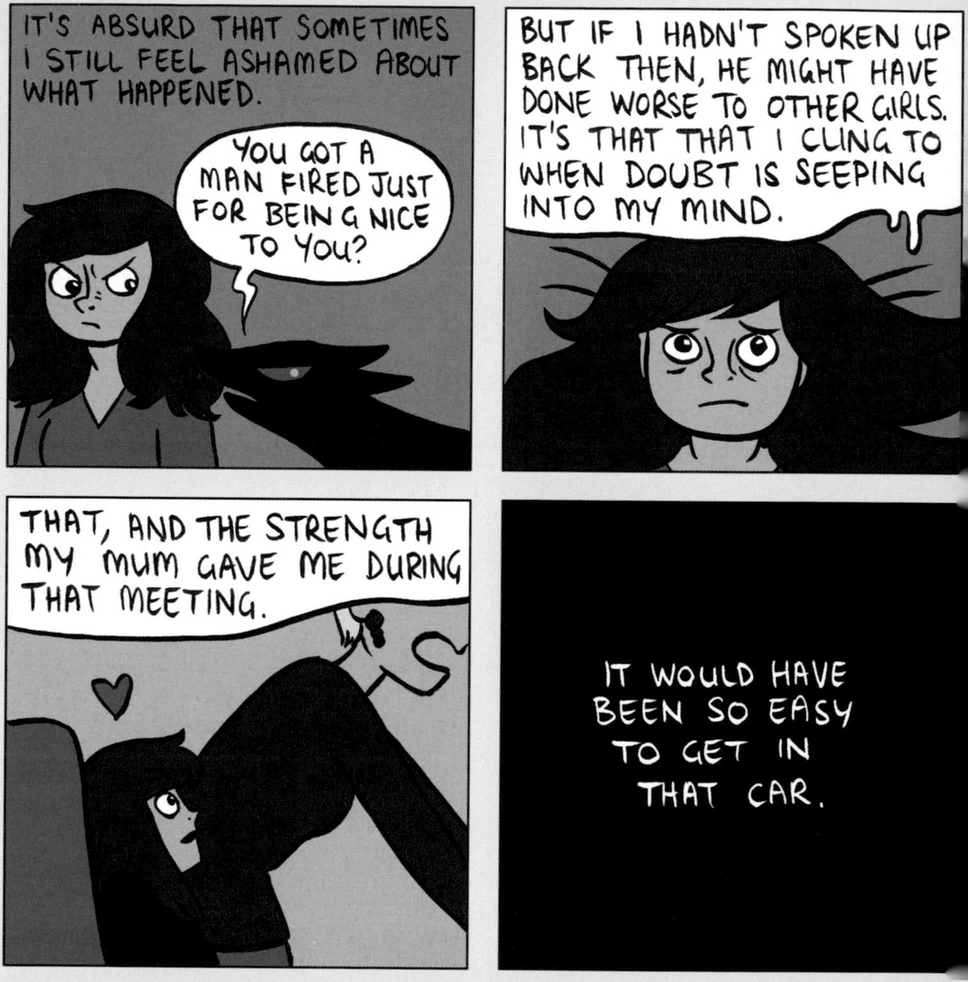
IT'S ABSURD THAT SOMETIMES I STILL FEEL ASHAMED ABOUT WHAT HAPPENED.
YOU GOT A MAN FIRED JUST FOR BEING NICE TO YOU?
BUT IF I HADN'T SPOKEN UP BACK THEN, HE MIGHT HAVE DONE WORSE TO OTHER GIRLS. IT'S THAT THAT I CLING TO WHEN DOUBT IS SEEPING INTO MY MIND.
THAT, AND THE STRENGTH MY MUM GAVE ME DURING THAT MEETING.
IT WOULD HAVE BEEN SO EASY TO GET IN THAT CAR.

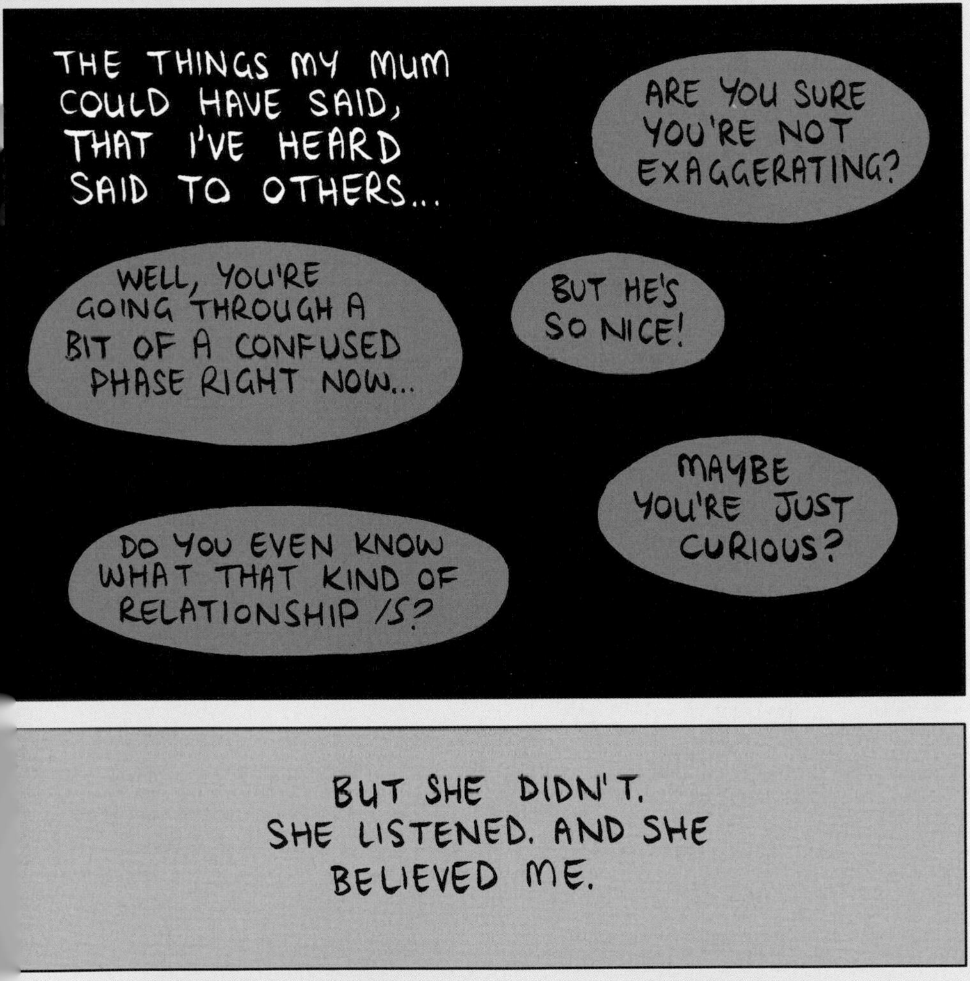
THE THINGS MY MUM COULD HAVE SAID, THAT I'VE HEARD SAID TO OTHERS...
ARE YOU SURE YOU'RE NOT EXAGGERATING?
WELL, YOU'RE GOING THROUGH A BIT OF A CONFUSED PHASE RIGHT NOW...
BUT HE'S SO NICE!
MAYBE YOU'RE JUST CURIOUS?
DO YOU EVEN KNOW WHAT THAT KIND OF RELATIONSHIP *IS*?
BUT SHE DIDN'T.
SHE LISTENED. AND SHE BELIEVED ME.

SHE'S THE ONLY GROWN UP I'VE
EVER NEEDED ON MY SIDE.

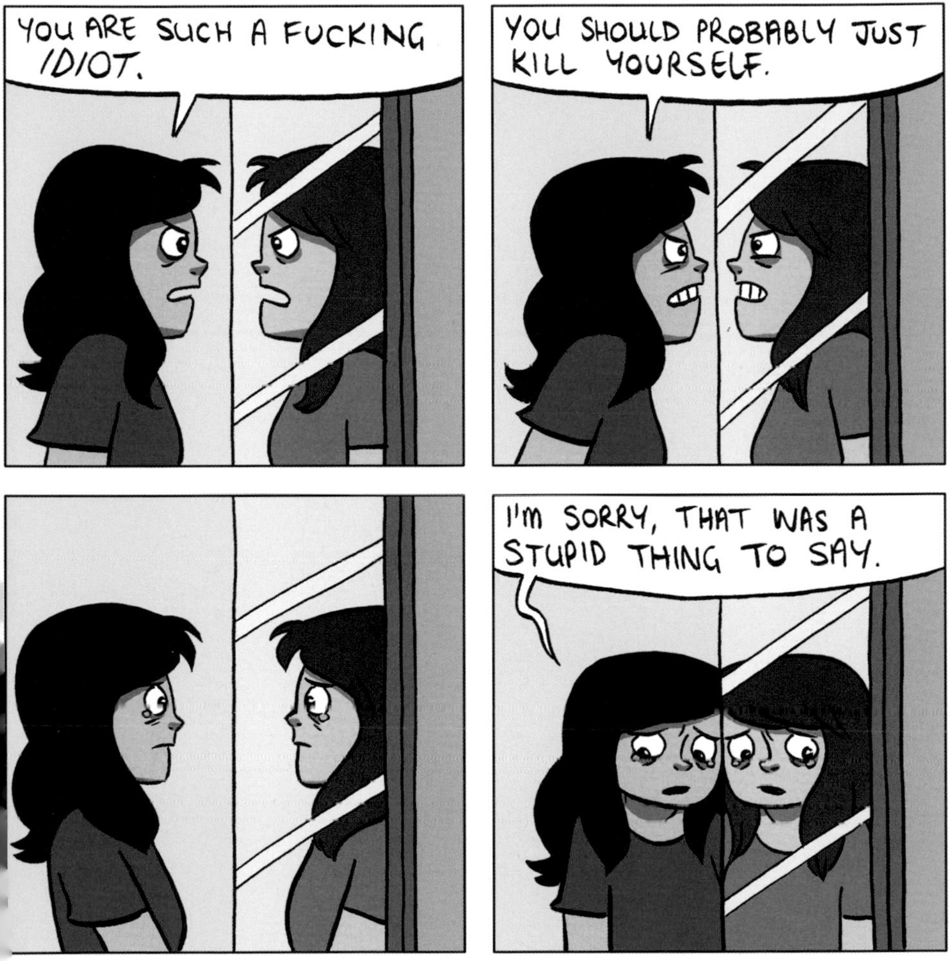
YOU ARE SUCH A FUCKING IDIOT.
YOU SHOULD PROBABLY JUST KILL YOURSELF.
I'M SORRY, THAT WAS A STUPID THING TO SAY.

Wine may have been involved in this v intelligent conversation.

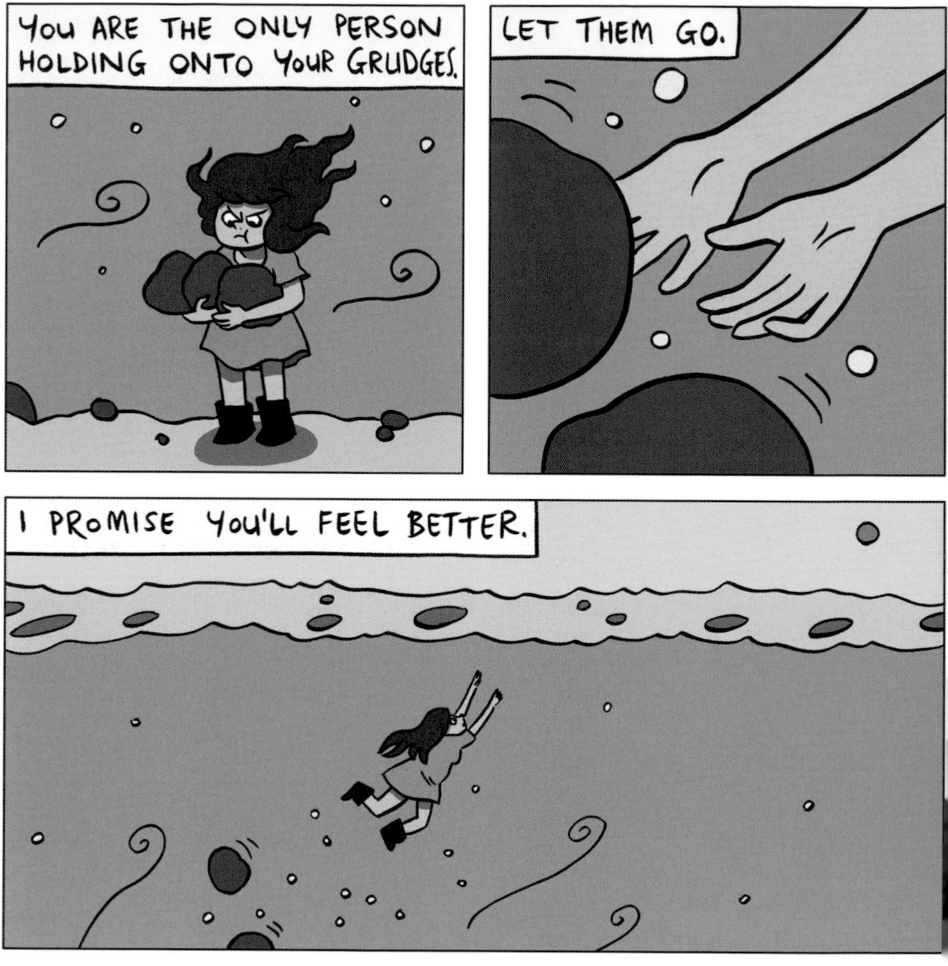
YOU ARE THE ONLY PERSON HOLDING ONTO YOUR GRUDGES.
LET THEM GO.
I PROMISE YOU'LL FEEL BETTER.

What? You don’t go swimming in a dress and boots?

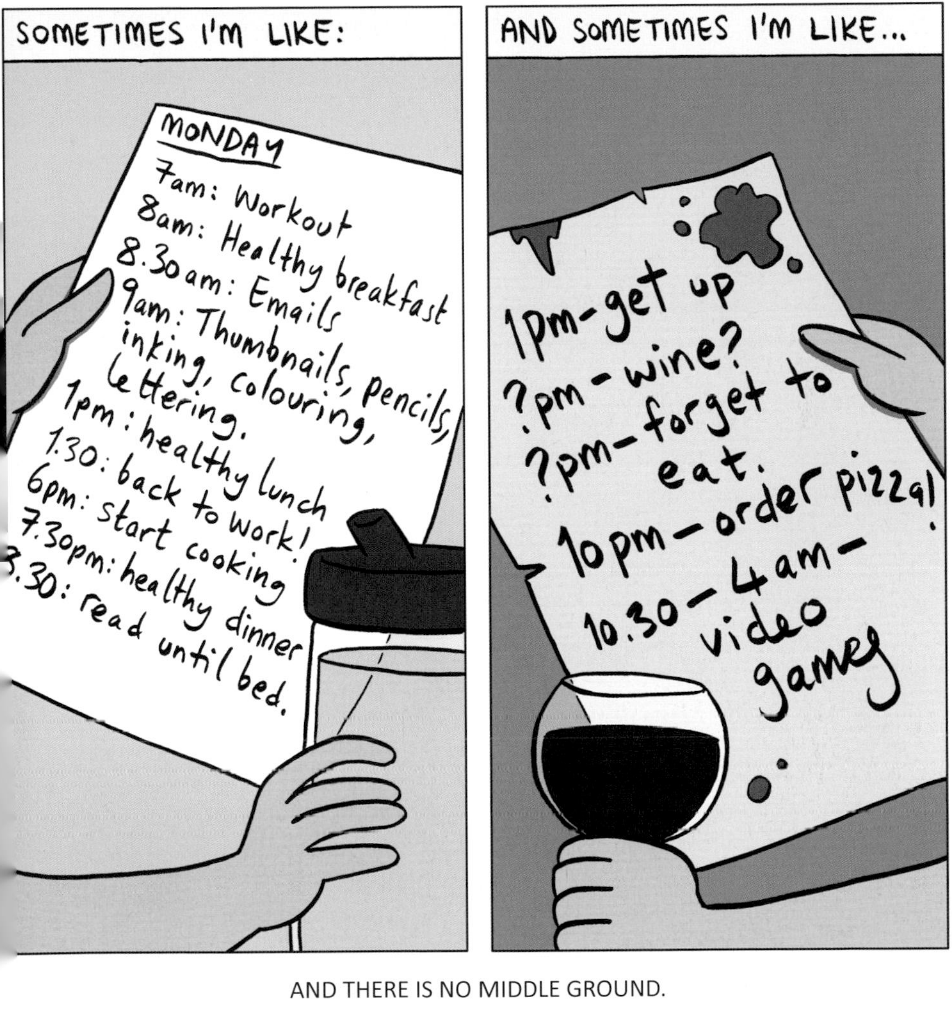
SOMETIMES I'M LIKE:
MONDAY
7am: Workout
8am: Healthy breakfast
8.30am: Emails
9am: Thumbnails, pencils, inking, colouring, lettering.
1pm: healthy lunch
1.30: back to work!
6pm: start cooking
7.30pm: healthy dinner
8.30: read until bed.
AND SOMETIMES I'M LIKE...
1pm - get up
?pm - wine?
?pm - forget to eat.
10pm - order pizza!
10.30 - 4am - video games

AND THERE IS NO MIDDLE GROUND.

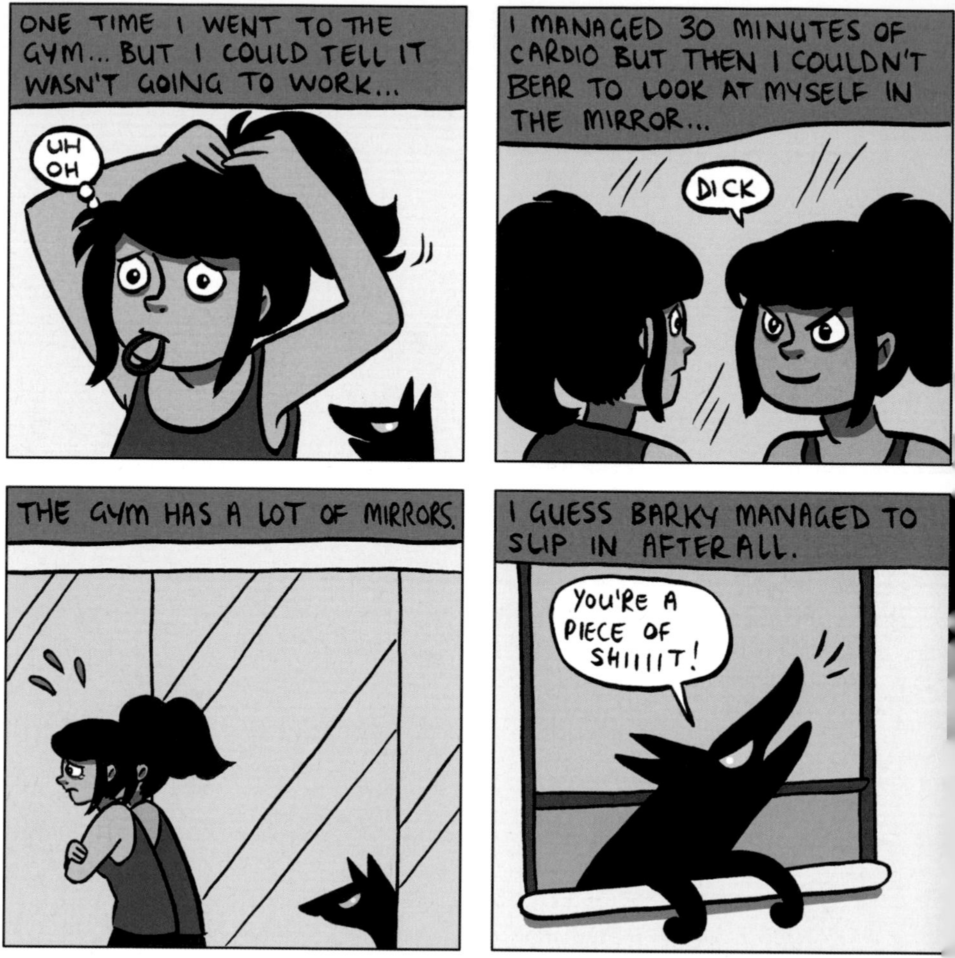
ONE TIME I WENT TO THE GYM... BUT I COULD TELL IT WASN'T GOING TO WORK...
UH OH
I MANAGED 30 MINUTES OF CARDIO BUT THEN I COULDN'T BEAR TO LOOK AT MYSELF IN THE MIRROR...
DICK
THE GYM HAS A LOT OF MIRRORS.
I GUESS BARKY MANAGED TO SLIP IN AFTER ALL.
YOU'RE A PIECE OF SHIIIIT!

Sometimes nothing can stop a bad day. You just gotta ride it out.
The gym will work next time.

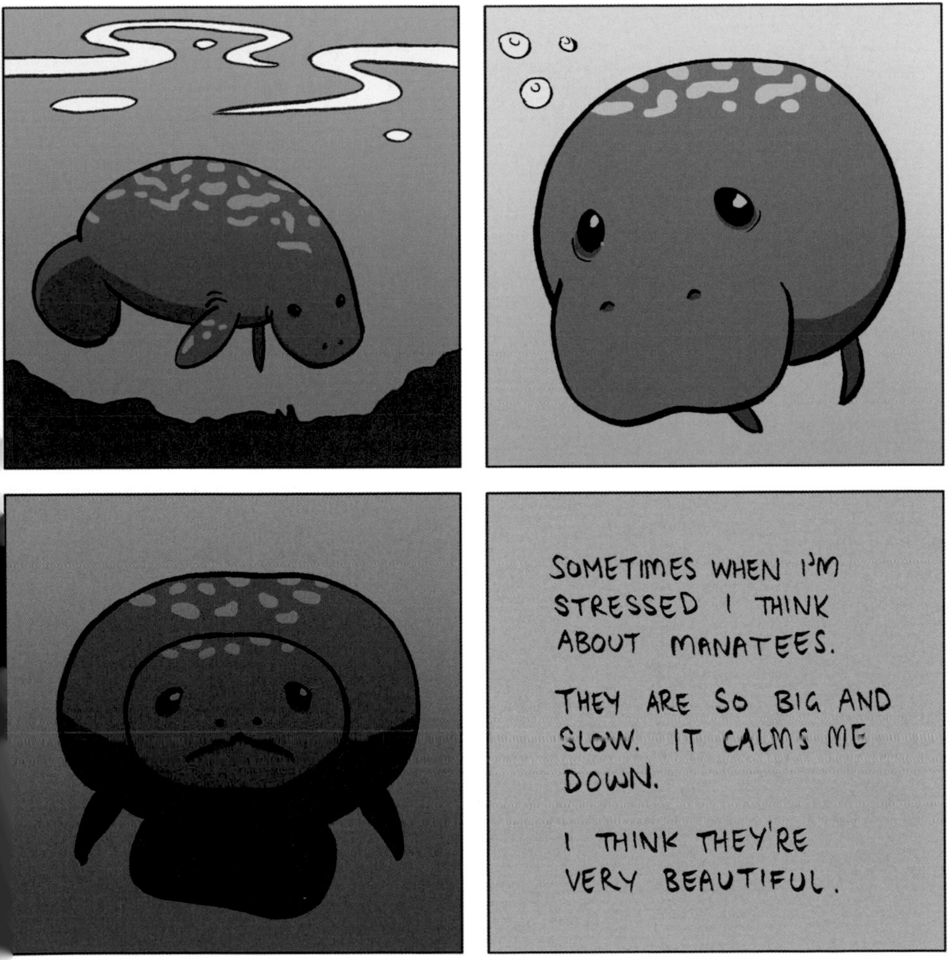
SOMETIMES WHEN I'M STRESSED I THINK ABOUT MANATEES.
THEY ARE SO BIG AND SLOW. IT CALMS ME DOWN.
I THINK THEY'RE VERY BEAUTIFUL.

In these turbulent times, let us all try to be more manatee.

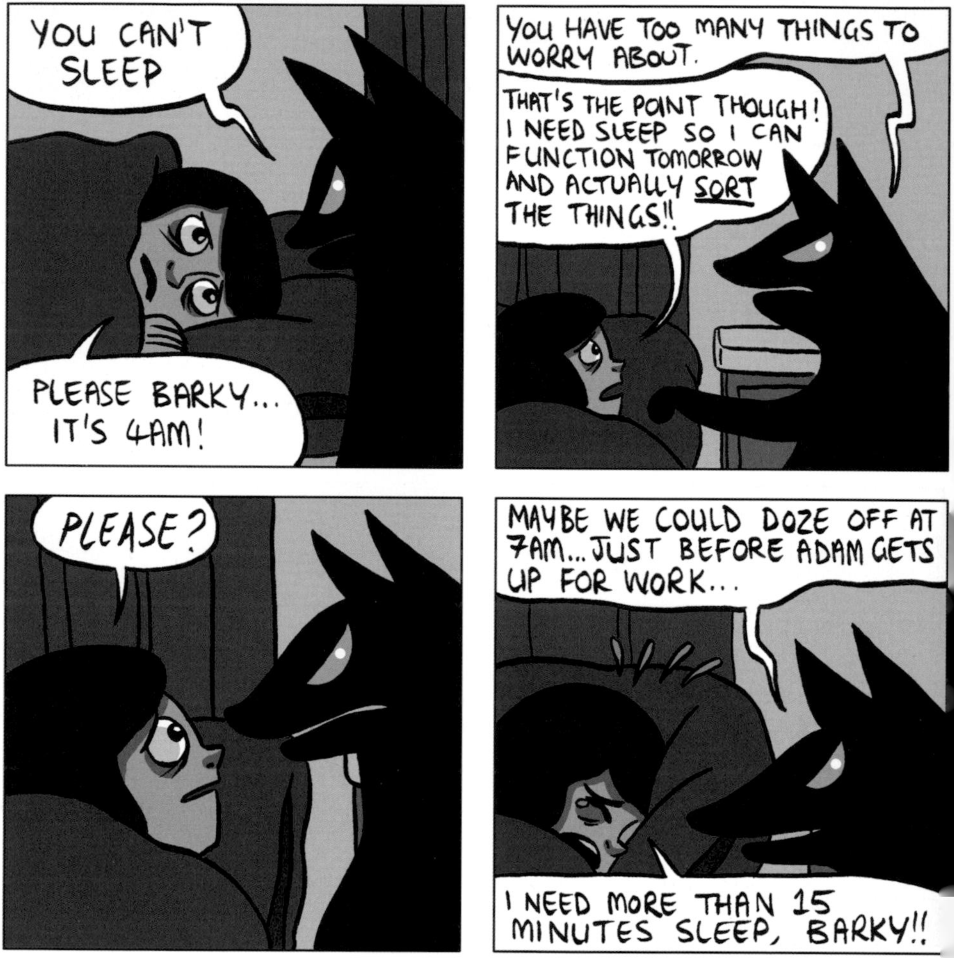
YOU CAN'T SLEEP
PLEASE BARKY... IT'S 4AM!
YOU HAVE TOO MANY THINGS TO WORRY ABOUT.
THAT'S THE POINT THOUGH! I NEED SLEEP SO I CAN FUNCTION TOMORROW AND ACTUALLY SORT THE THINGS!!
PLEASE?
MAYBE WE COULD DOZE OFF AT 7AM... JUST BEFORE ADAM GETS UP FOR WORK...
I NEED MORE THAN 15 MINUTES SLEEP, BARKY!!

If it wasn't the worrying then Barky's dog breath would definitely have kept me awake. You wanna back up a little there, pal??

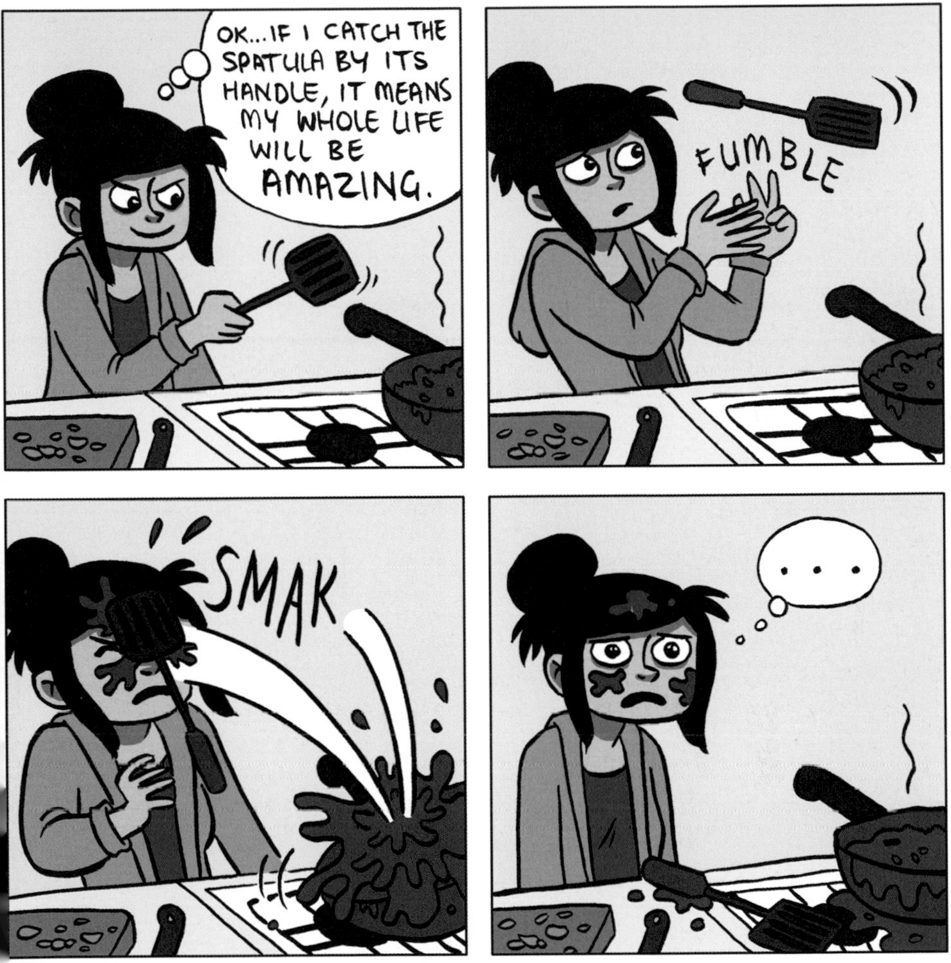
OK...IF I CATCH THE SPATULA BY ITS HANDLE, IT MEANS MY WHOLE LIFE WILL BE AMAZING.
FUMBLE
SMAK
. . .

Please tell me other people do crap like this?

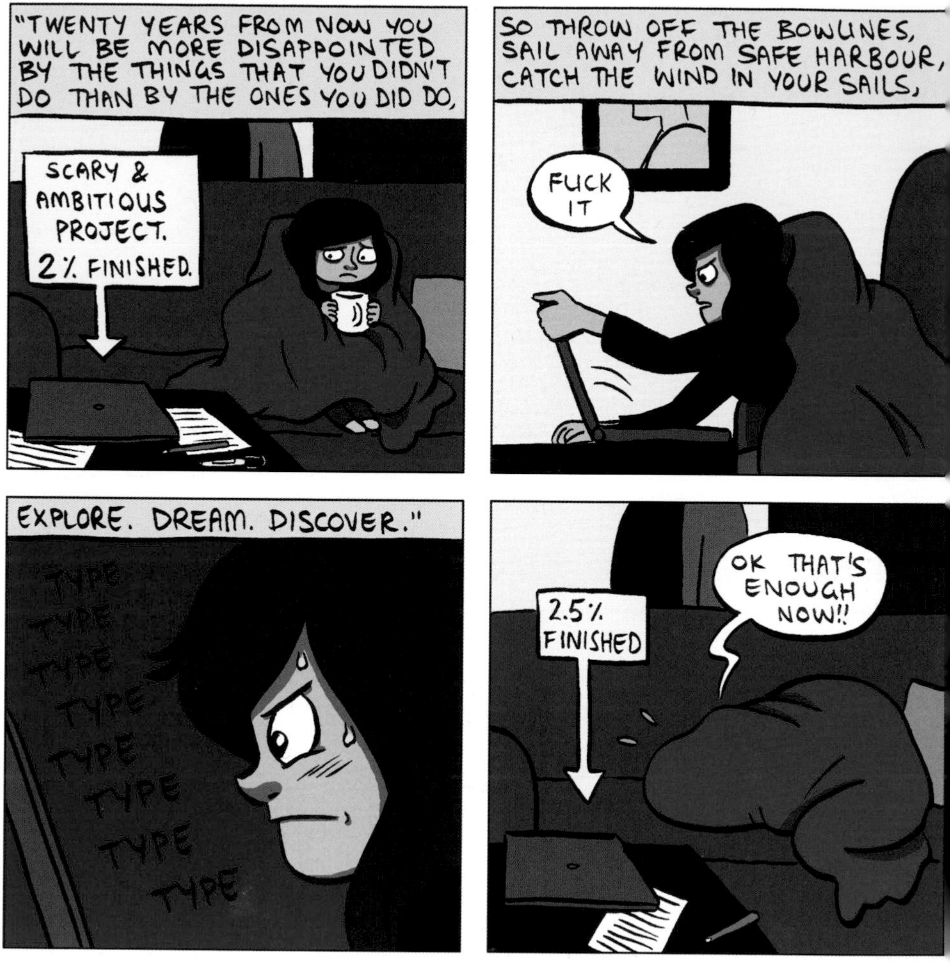
"TWENTY YEARS FROM NOW YOU WILL BE MORE DISAPPOINTED BY THE THINGS THAT YOU DIDN'T DO THAN BY THE ONES YOU DID DO,
SCARY & AMBITIOUS PROJECT. 2% FINISHED.
SO THROW OFF THE BOWLINES, SAIL AWAY FROM SAFE HARBOUR, CATCH THE WIND IN YOUR SAILS,
FUCK IT
EXPLORE. DREAM. DISCOVER."
TYPE TYPE TYPE TYPE TYPE TYPE TYPE TYPE
2.5% FINISHED
OK THAT'S ENOUGH NOW!!

– Mark Twain.

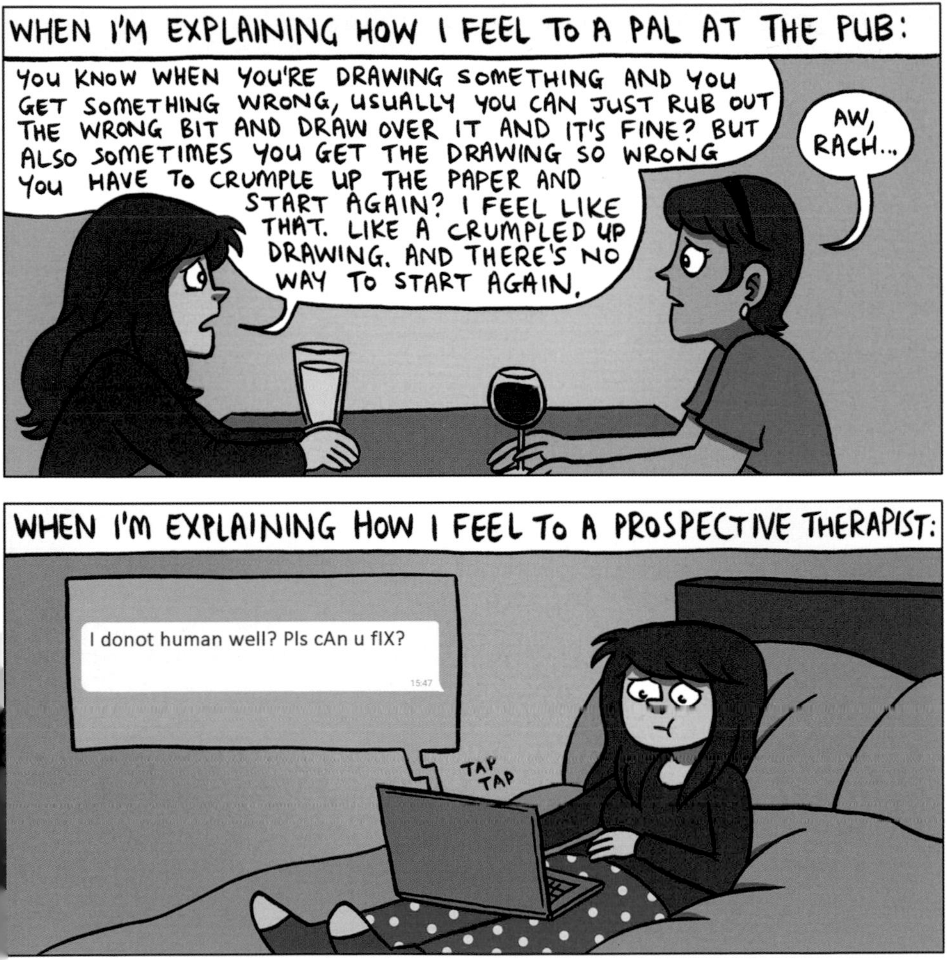
WHEN I'M EXPLAINING HOW I FEEL TO A PAL AT THE PUB:
YOU KNOW WHEN YOU'RE DRAWING SOMETHING AND YOU GET SOMETHING WRONG, USUALLY YOU CAN JUST RUB OUT THE WRONG BIT AND DRAW OVER IT AND IT'S FINE? BUT ALSO SOMETIMES YOU GET THE DRAWING SO WRONG YOU HAVE TO CRUMPLE UP THE PAPER AND START AGAIN? I FEEL LIKE THAT. LIKE A CRUMPLED UP DRAWING. AND THERE'S NO WAY TO START AGAIN.
AW, RACH...
WHEN I'M EXPLAINING HOW I FEEL TO A PROSPECTIVE THERAPIST:
I donot human well? Pls cAn u fIX?
15:47
TAP TAP

I am a natural writer right up until I actually need to be.

THERAPY APPOINTMENT #4

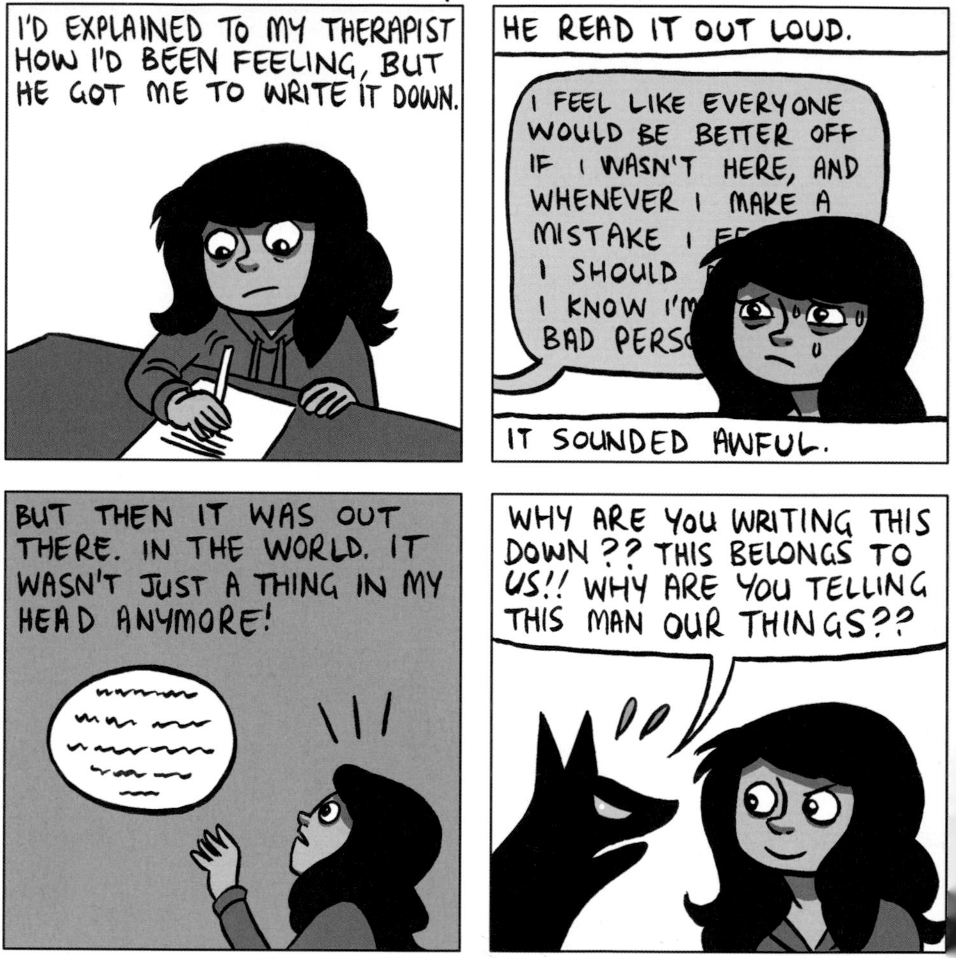
I'D EXPLAINED TO MY THERAPIST HOW I'D BEEN FEELING, BUT HE GOT ME TO WRITE IT DOWN.
HE READ IT OUT LOUD.
I FEEL LIKE EVERYONE WOULD BE BETTER OFF IF I WASN'T HERE, AND WHENEVER I MAKE A MISTAKE I
I SHOULD
I KNOW I'M
BAD
IT SOUNDED AWFUL.
BUT THEN IT WAS OUT THERE. IN THE WORLD. IT WASN'T JUST A THING IN MY HEAD ANYMORE!
WHY ARE YOU WRITING THIS DOWN?? THIS BELONGS TO US!! WHY ARE YOU TELLING THIS MAN OUR THINGS??

You can't fight something if you keep it in your head. Make that shit real and then BEAT THE CRAP out of it!! (I should be a therapist.)

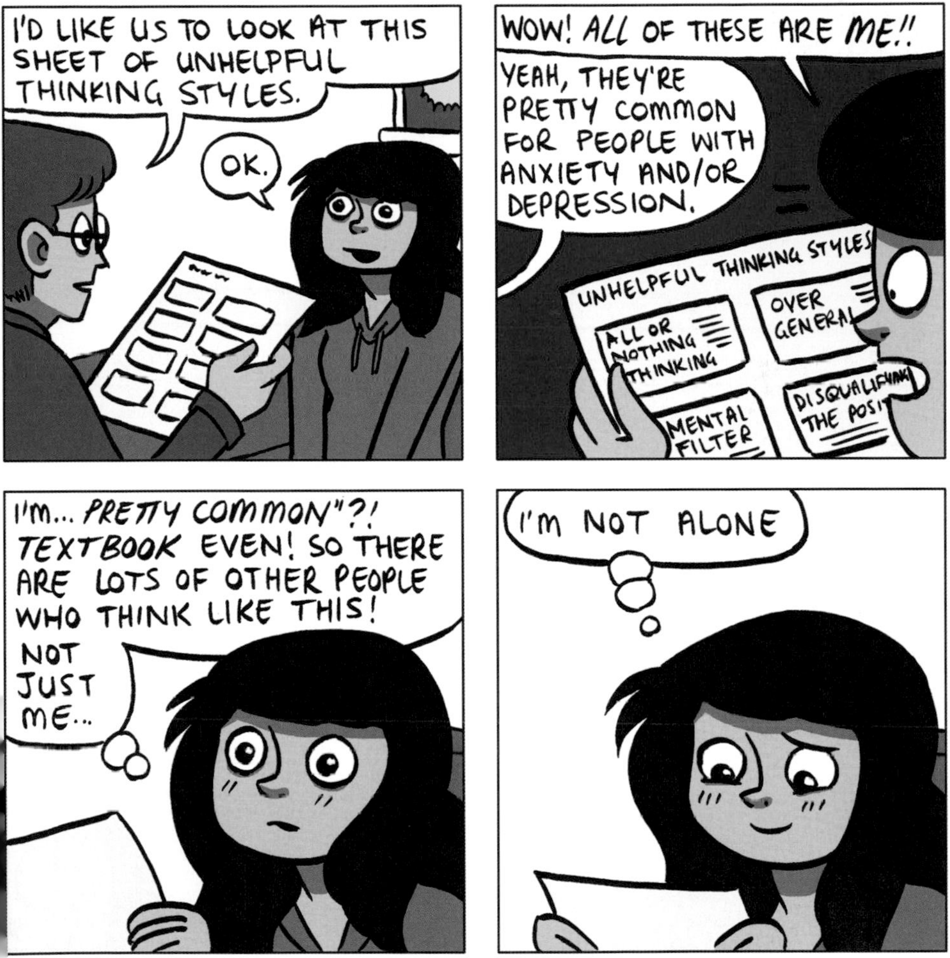
I'D LIKE US TO LOOK AT THIS SHEET OF UNHELPFUL THINKING STYLES.
OK.
WOW! *ALL* OF THESE ARE *ME!!*
YEAH, THEY'RE PRETTY COMMON FOR PEOPLE WITH ANXIETY AND/OR DEPRESSION.
UNHELPFUL THINKING STYLES
ALL OR NOTHING THINKING
OVER GENERAL
MENTAL FILTER
I'M... *PRETTY COMMON*"?! *TEXTBOOK* EVEN! SO THERE ARE LOTS OF OTHER PEOPLE WHO THINK LIKE THIS!
NOT JUST ME...
I'M NOT ALONE

You can download the sheet I'm looking at here at:
psychologytools.com/unhelpful-thinking-styles.html

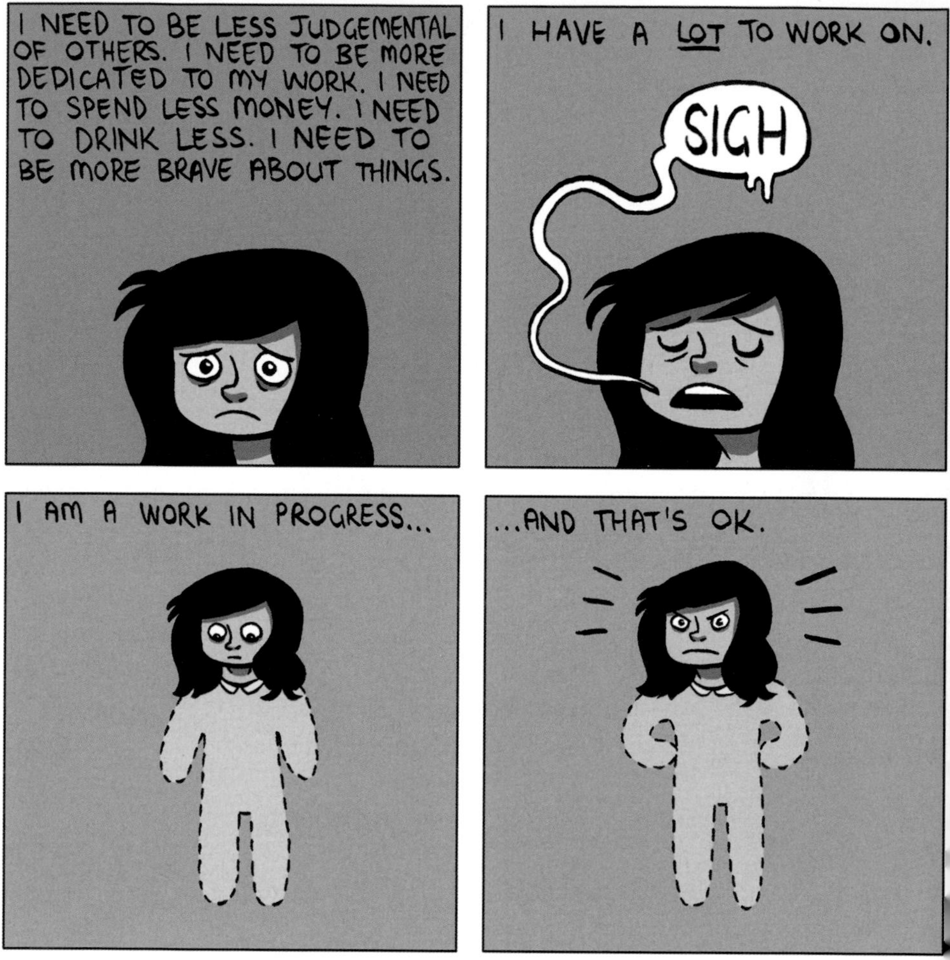
I NEED TO BE LESS JUDGEMENTAL OF OTHERS. I NEED TO BE MORE DEDICATED TO MY WORK. I NEED TO SPEND LESS MONEY. I NEED TO DRINK LESS. I NEED TO BE MORE BRAVE ABOUT THINGS.
I HAVE A LOT TO WORK ON.
SIGH
I AM A WORK IN PROGRESS...
...AND THAT'S OK.

I mean, I thought at 32 I'd feel a bit more ... finished.
But hey, progress is progress.

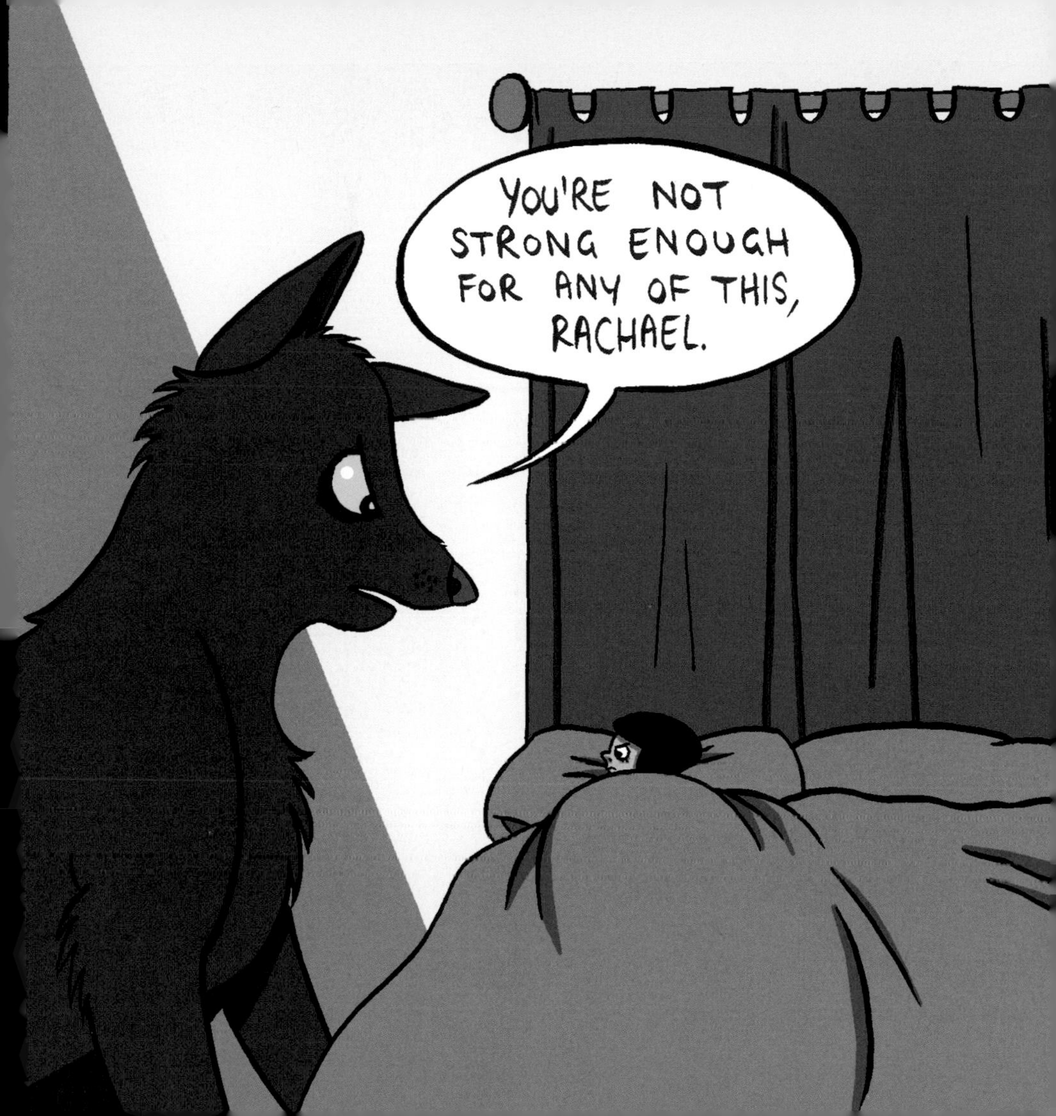
YOU'RE NOT STRONG ENOUGH FOR ANY OF THIS, RACHAEL.

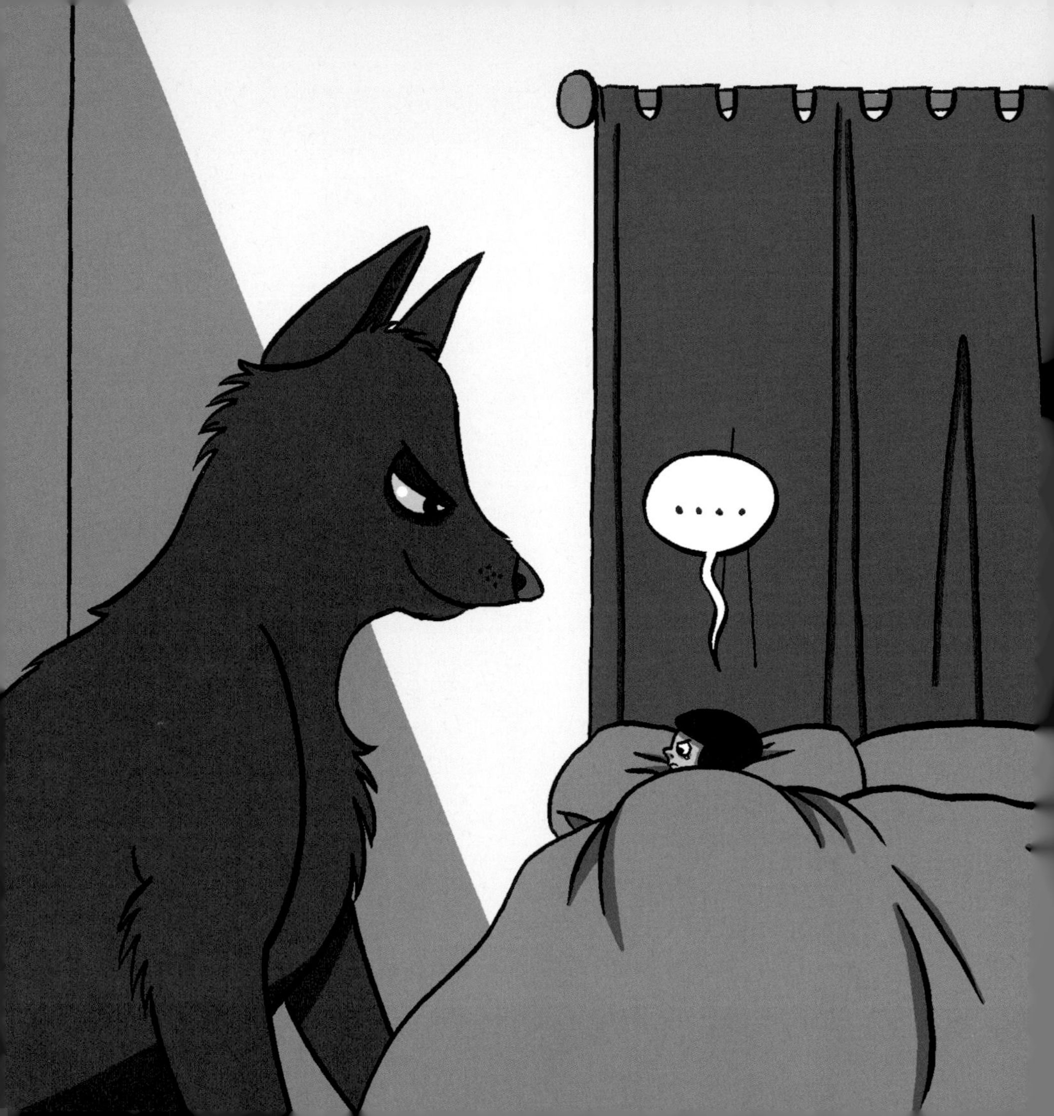
....

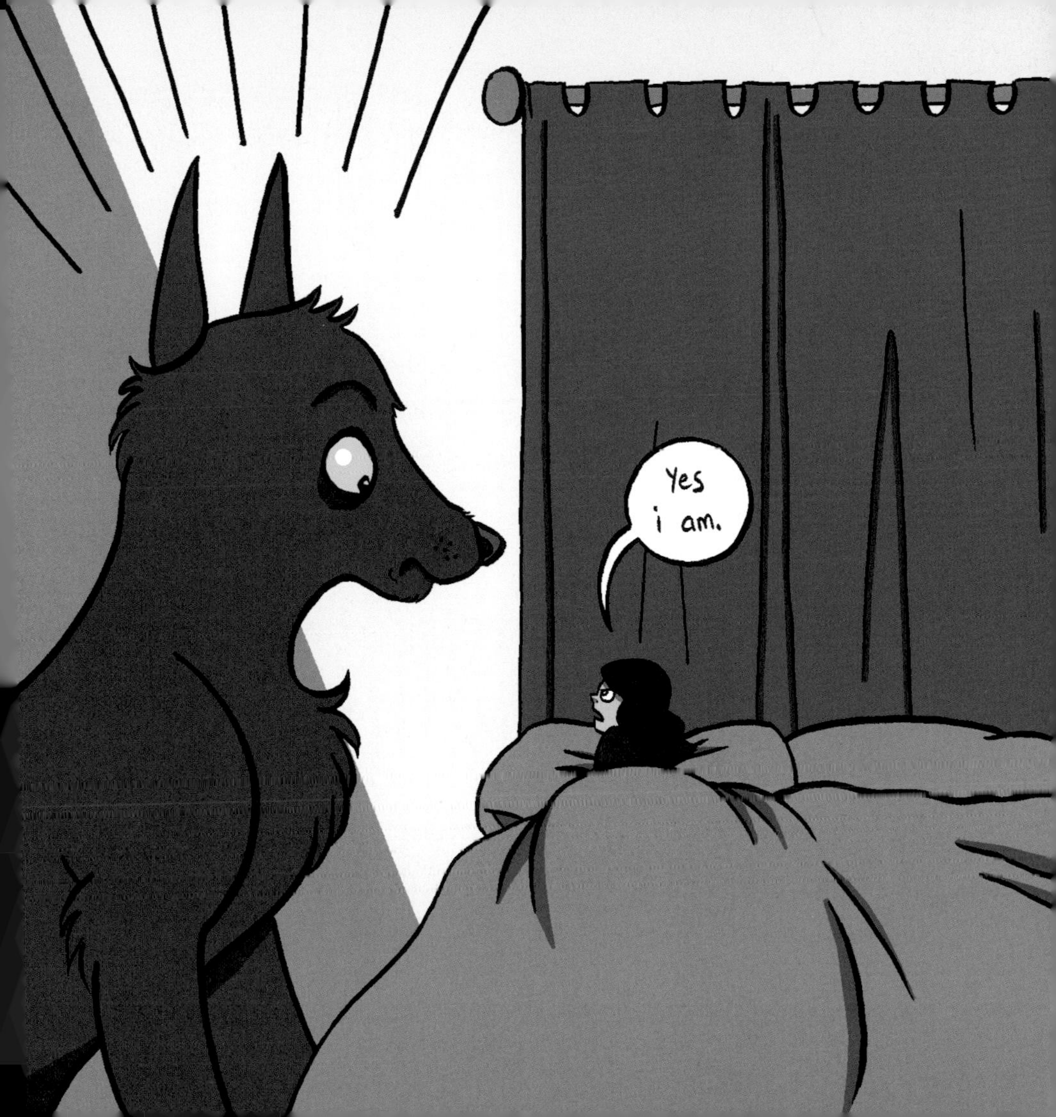
Yes i am.

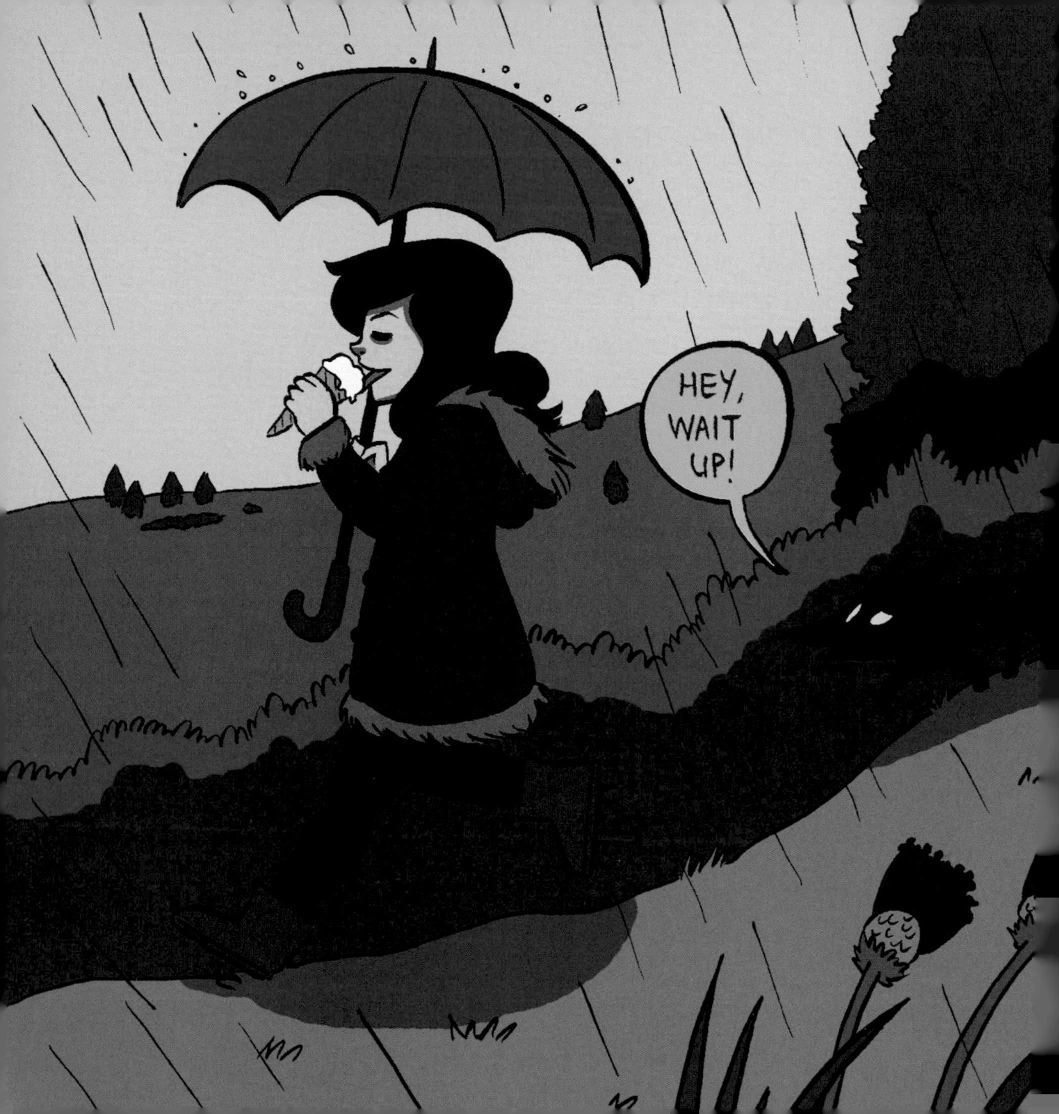
HEY, WAIT UP!

THANKS

This book wouldn't have been possible without the support and love from my Mum. I hope I grow up (ha!) to be even half the woman you are. xxx

Thank you also to my dear friends, those of you who appeared in this book, and those of you who will appear in future volumes. You keep me going.

Thank you to Rufus for the cuddles and head bumps. I'm sure you were doing that to encourage the writing of this book and totally not because you wanted food.

And thank **YOU** for reading! You are awesome.

Rachael xxx

RESOURCES

SAMARITANS:
www.samaritans.org
Tel.: 116 123
jo@samaritans.org

MIND
www.mind.org.uk
Text: 86463
info@mind.org.uk

NHS
www.nhs.uk/tools/pages/depression.aspx

ABOUT THE AUTHOR

RACHAEL ♥

Rachael Smith is a UK-based comics creator whose books include: **QUARANTINE COMIX**, **ARTIFICIAL FLOWERS** and **THE RABBIT**, which was nominated for Best Book in the 2015 British Comic Awards, following her nomination for Emerging Talent.

Website: rachaelsmith.org
Twitter: @rachael_
Instagram: flimsy_kitten

31192022404360